Question&Answer

ENGLISH LEGAL SYSTEM

Q&A LawExpress

Question&Answer

ENGLISH LEGAL SYSTEM

Gary Wilson
Liverpool John Moores University

Longman
is an imprint of

PEARSON

Harlow, England • London • New York • Boston • San Francisco • Toronto • Sydney • Singapore • Hong Kong
Tokyo • Seoul • Taipei • New Delhi • Cape Town • Madrid • Mexico City • Amsterdam • Munich • Paris • Milan

Pearson Education Limited
Edinburgh Gate
Harlow
Essex CM20 2JE
England

and Associated Companies throughout the world

Visit us on the World Wide Web at:
www.pearsoned.co.uk

First published 2012

ISBN: 978-1-4082-4112-7

British Library Cataloguing-in-Publication Data
A catalogue record for this book is available from the British Library

Library of Congress Cataloging-in-Publication Data
A catalog record for this book is available from the Library of Congress

10 9 8 7 6 5 4 3 2
15 14 13 12

Typeset in 10pt Helvetica Condensed by 30
Printed and bound in Great Britain by Henry Ling Limited, at the Dorset Press, Dorchester, DT1 1HD

Contents

Supporting resources

Visit the **LawExpress Question&Answer** series companion website at **www.pearsoned.co.uk/lawexpressqa** to find valuable learning material including:

- Additional **essay and problem questions** arranged by topic for each chapter give you more opportunity to practice and hone your exam skills
- **Diagram plans** for all additional questions assist you in structuring and writing your answers.
- **You be the marker** questions allow you to see through the eyes of the examiner by marking essay and problem questions on every topic covered in the book.
- Download and print all **Attack the question** diagrams and **Diagram plans** from the book.

Also: The companion website provides the following features:

- Search tool to help locate specific items of content.
- Online help and support to assist with website usage and troubleshooting.

For more information please contact your local Pearson sales representative or visit **www.pearsoned.co.uk/lawexpressqa**

Acknowledgements

I would like to thank Pearson for giving me the opportunity to write this book, my parents for their support since the very beginning of my academic career, and last, but certainly not least, Jenny, Becky and Katie for their love and patience throughout the time that I have been busy writing the book.

Gary Wilson

Publisher's acknowledgements

Our thanks go to all reviewers who contributed to the development of this text, including students who participated in research and focus groups which helped to shape the series format.

What you need to do for every question on the English Legal System

HOW TO USE THIS BOOK

Books in the *Question and Answer* series focus on the *why* of a good answer alongside the *what,* thereby helping you to build your question answering skills and technique.

This guide should not be used as a substitute for learning the material thoroughly, your lecture notes or your textbook. It *will* help you to make the most out of what you have already learned when answering an exam or coursework question. Remember that the answers given here are not the *only* correct way of answering the question but serve to show you some good examples of how you *could* approach the question set.

Make sure that you regularly refer to your course syllabus, check which issues are covered (as well as to what extent they are covered) and whether they are usually examined with other topics. Remember that what is required in a good answer could change significantly with only a slight change in the wording of a question. Therefore, do not try to memorise the answers given here, instead use the answers and the other features to understand what goes into a good answer and why.

English legal system (ELS) is a broad subject area which gives rise to possible questions covering a wide range of topics. However, there are some themes that are common across the subject as a whole and worth bearing in mind when preparing for examinations. Many of the issues covered in ELS are topical and you should ensure that you are abreast of new developments which may appear in the news and are relevant to your syllabus. Examiners will give credit where students draw upon contemporary events and effectively relate them to examination questions. The very nature of ELS syllabuses also presents students with much scope to present their discussion of relevant legal issues within a wider social, economic, and political context, which is not always so possible in some other more doctrinal legal subjects. Examiners are, again, likely to give credit to students who are able to demonstrate a clear awareness of the functioning of the legal system in its wider setting.

While ELS is taught under a number of topic headings, it is important that you do not 'pigeon-hole' topics. Sometimes you will be able to draw upon a point or example learnt as part of one topic when answering a question on another. Occasionally, examination questions will span more than one topic. For example, a question on judicial law-making will benefit from the understanding you have from having studied judicial precedent, statutory interpretation and the composition of the judiciary. Weaker students often fail to make these wider connections and, consequently, produce narrow answers to questions which do not gain the highest marks.

ELS is invariably assessed through the use of essay-type questions and problem questions are relatively rare. Therefore, when preparing for examinations you need to ensure that you are not simply able to apply legal principles to given scenarios, but are actually able to subject key principles, features and processes of the legal system to scrutiny. More so than many other subjects, where problem questions are often at least as common as essay questions, your ability to critically analyse and discuss legal issues will be crucial if you are to score well in assessment.

Guided tour

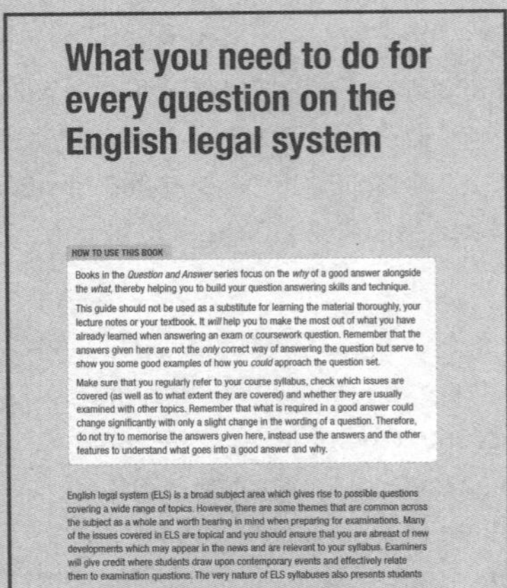

What you need to do for every question on the English legal system

HOW TO USE THIS BOOK

Books in the *Question and Answer* series focus on the *why* of a good answer alongside the *what*, thereby helping you to build your question answering skills and technique.

This guide should not be used as a substitute for learning the material thoroughly, your lecture notes or your textbook. It *will* help you to make the most out of what you have already learned when answering an exam or coursework question. Remember that the answers given here are not the *only* correct way of answering the question but serve to show you some good examples of how you *could* approach the question set.

Make sure that you regularly refer to your course syllabus, check which issues are covered (as well as to what extent they are covered) and whether they are usually examined with other topics. Remember that what is required in a good answer could change significantly with only a slight change in the wording of a question. Therefore, do not try to memorise the answers given here, instead use the answers and the other features to understand what goes into a good answer and why.

English legal system (ELS) is a broad subject area which gives rise to possible questions covering a wide range of topics. However, there are some themes that are common across the subject as a whole and worth bearing in mind when preparing for examinations. Many of the issues covered in ELS are topical and you should ensure that you are abreast of new developments which may appear in the news and are relevant to your syllabus. Examiners will give credit where students draw upon contemporary events and effectively relate them to examination questions. The very nature of ELS syllabuses also presents students

What to do for every question – Find out the key things you should do and look for in any question and answer on the subject in order to give one of your answers a great chance from the start.

1

Sources of law

How this topic may come up in exams

Examination questions on this topic may test understanding of any one or more of the various primary and secondary sources of law. You will need to be familiar with the operation specifically of common law, equity, statute, EU law, delegated legislation and custom. While examination questions may focus upon any one of these sources, requiring you to be able to demonstrate a critical understanding of that source, you may also be asked to contrast more than one source of law and/or explore the relationship between these sources. Thus, you should not 'pigeon-hole' the various sources of law as free-standing topics.

How this topic might come up in exams – Learn how to tackle and question on this topic by using the handy tips and advice relevant to both essay and problem questions. In-text symbols clearly identify each question type as it occurs.

Essay question **Problem question**

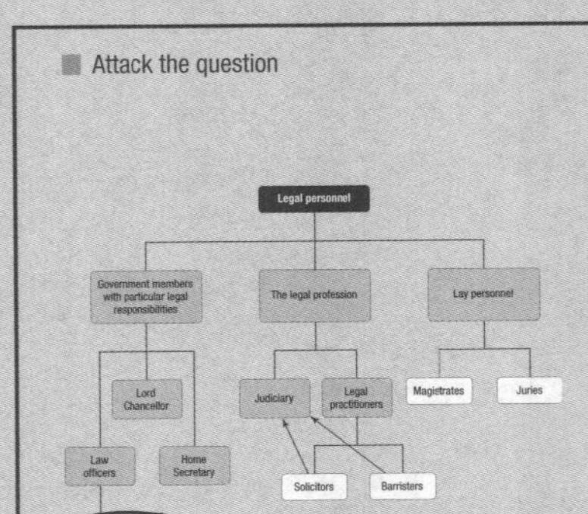

Attack the Question – Attack attack attack! Use these diagrams as a step by step guide to help you confidently identify the main points covered in any question asked.

Answer plans and Diagram plans – Clear and concise answer plans and diagram plans support the planning and structuring of your answers whatever your preferred learning style

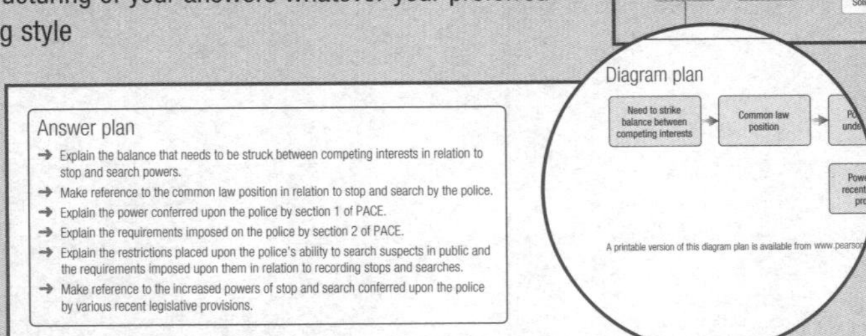

Answer plan

- Explain the balance that needs to be struck between competing interests in relation to stop and search powers.
- Make reference to the common law position in relation to stop and search by the police.
- Explain the power conferred upon the police by section 1 of PACE.
- Explain the requirements imposed on the police by section 2 of PACE.
- Explain the restrictions placed upon the police's ability to search suspects in public and the requirements imposed upon them in relation to recording stops and searches.
- Make reference to the increased powers of stop and search conferred upon the police by various recent legislative provisions.

Answer with accompanying guidance. – Make the most out of every question by using the guidance to recognise what makes a good answer and why. Answers are the length you could realistically hope to produce in an exam to show you how to gain marks quickly when under pressure.

1 SOURCES OF LAW

[1]The question asks you to consider the relative importance of these two sources of law. It will be helpful at the outset to explain that they are the two major domestic sources of law. You should also briefly explain what they are and how they differ from one another.

[2]In explaining the importance of statute, it is essential that you make reference to the doctrine of parliamentary sovereignty and explain its implications.

...tion asks you ...onsider the relative importance of these two sources of law. It will be helpful at the outset to explain that they are the two major domestic sources of law. You should also briefly explain what they are and how they differ from one another.

[2]In explaining the importance of statute, it is essential that you make reference to the doctrine of parliamentary sovereignty and explain its implications.

...ll receive credit for

Answer

Case law and statute are the two major domestic sources of English law.[1] Case law (or common law) constitutes the body of law contained in judicial decisions. It is an uncodified source of law and operates through the system of judicial precedent, whereby in reaching decisions judges have regard to decisions from earlier cases sharing similar material facts. Statute law refers to legislation made by Parliament in the form of Acts of Parliament. It is a formalised source of law, a bill passing through several potentially time consuming stages before finally adopted as a statute.

Historically, statute has been regarded as the supreme source of law due to the doctrine of parliamentary sovereignty.[2] In the words of Dicey,[3] this holds that Parliament has 'the right to make or unmake any law whatsoever', there being 'no person or body having the right to override or set aside the legislation of Parliament'. Outrageous or immoral legislation is not precluded, as Lord Reid emphasised in **Madzimbamuto v Lardner-Burke & George**

Case names clearly highlighted – Easy to spot bold text makes those all important case names stand out from the rest of the answer, ensuring they are much easier to remember in revision and in the exam.

[4]You are unlikely to have time to discuss further most of the case examples you cite in your answer. The main point is that you show that you are aware of actual scenarios when precedent has not been followed, and the grounds for this.

not follow its earlier decision in deference to the superior status of the Supreme Court. A case giving rise to this kind of situation was **Family Housing Association v Jones** [1990]. Finally, the Court of Appeal does not have to follow one of its own previous decisions when that decision had been made *per incuriam*, meaning the decision had been taken in ignorance of some relevant legal authority. An example of a case where such a situation arose is **Bonalumi v Secretary of State for the Home Department** [1985].[4]

In addition to the exceptions set out in **Young v Bristol Aeroplane**, as a consequence of the supremacy of EU law, when a previous Court of Appeal decision conflicts with a provision of EU law, the Court will not follow its own precedent. The Civil Division is not constrained by an earlier decision where the court assumed a proposition of law to exist which was not subject to consideration by the court, as a result of **R (Kadhim) v Brent Housing Benefit**

Make your answer stand out – Really impress your examiners by including these additional points and further reading to illustrate your deeper knowledge of the subject, fully maximising your marks.

✓ Make your answer stand out

- Make comparisons where appropriate with the police's treatment of Poppy and that of suspects in similar relevant cases, particularly where miscarriages of justice have resulted from police oppression to induce confessions.
- Indicate where appropriate what further information you may need in order to be able to provide a more definitive answer to certain questions.
- Be prepared to raise issues which are not expressly mentioned by the scenario, but may nonetheless be relevant, for example in this case the issue of tape recording of Poppy's interview or the standards applicable to her detention under Code of Practice C.

Don't be tempted to… – Avoid common mistakes and losing easy marks by understanding where students most often trip up in exams.

! Don't be tempted to . . .

- Provide detailed technical information on each of the institutions, such as their location;
- Explain the main functions of the institutions without commenting upon their roles within the legislative and law enforcement process;
- Confuse the EU institutions with the machinery of the European Convention on Human Rights.

Bibliography – Use this list of further reading to really explore areas in more depth, enabling you to excel in exams.

Bibliography

Abel, R.L., (1987) 'The Decline of Professionalism', *Arbitration*, v. 53, n. 3, pp. 187–208.
Allan, T.R.S. (1985) 'The Limits of Parliamentary Sovereignty', *Public Law*, p. 614.

Baldwin, J. and McConville, M (1979) *Jury Trials*. Oxford: Clarendon.
Benion, F.A.R. (1978) 'Statute Law: Obscurity and Drafting Parameters', *British Journal of Law and Society*, v. 5, n. 2, p. 235.

Guided tour of the companion website

Book resources are available to download. Print your own **Attack the question** and **Diagram plans**

Additional **Essay and Problem questions** with **diagram plans** arranged by topic for each chapter give you more opportunity to practise and hone your exam skills. Print and email your answers.

You be the marker gives you a chance to evaluate sample exam answers for different question types for each topic and understand how and why an examiner awards marks. Use the accompanying guidance to get the most out of every question and recognise what makes a good answer.

All of this and more can be found when you visit **www.pearsoned.co.uk/lawexpressqa**

Table of cases and statutes

Cases

Statutes

European Legislation

1 Sources of law

How this topic may come up in exams

Examination questions on this topic may test understanding of any one or more of the various primary and secondary sources of law. You will need to be familiar with the operation specifically of common law, equity, statute, EU law, delegated legislation and custom. While examination questions may focus upon any one of these sources, requiring you to be able to demonstrate a critical understanding of that source, you may also be asked to contrast more than one source of law and/or explore the relationship between these sources. Thus, you should not 'pigeon-hole' the various sources of law as free-standing topics.

Attack the question

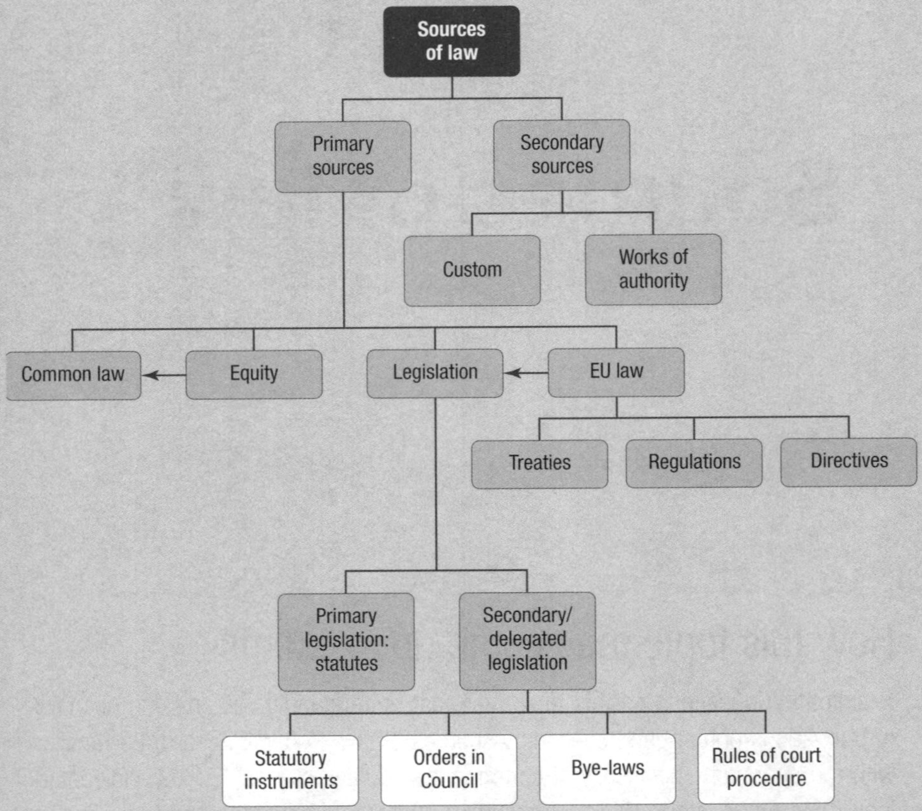

A printable version of this diagram plan is available from www.pearsoned.co.uk/lawexpressqa

Question 1

Explain the origins of the common law and how equity developed in response to its perceived shortcomings.

Answer plan

- → Explain how common law originated within England.
- → Explain the problems which came to be associated with the common law by the thirteenth century.
- → Explain how equity originated in response to problems with the common law.
- → Explain how the same courts came to administer both common law and equitable remedies.
- → Comment upon the role of equity today.

Diagram plan

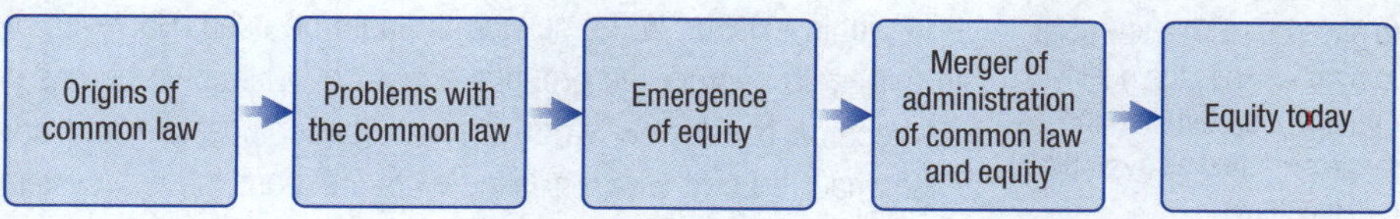

A printable version of this diagram plan is available from www.pearsoned.co.uk/lawexpressqa

Answer

Prior to the Norman Conquest of 1066, there was no unified system of law[1] common to England as a whole. Instead, customary laws applied which varied from one area of the country to another in accordance with local customs. Often these would bear the influence of the invading forces prominent in those regions,[2] so, for example, Dane law was particularly influential in the north of England, whereas in the south and west of the country Wessex law was a more dominant force. Thus, there was no effective central government and the King had little legal control over the country as a whole. The Norman Conquest represented a landmark in the eventual emergence of the English common law. William I initiated the process of standardising the laws applicable throughout the country. Representatives of the King, known as 'itinerant justices',

[1]It is important that you begin your answer by explaining what preceded the common law. You need to explain clearly that there was no system of law uniform to the country as a whole.

[2]Credit will be given for making a point like this. It shows a more detailed understanding of the system of law in force at the time and is likely to help make your answer stand out.

were despatched throughout the country to scrutinise local administration and adjudicate upon disputes in accordance with the customary law applicable in each region. As these itinerant justices returned to London and discussed their experiences from their visits to the regions, the principles of the common law began to emerge.[3] Over a period of time the justices would select the best local customs from which to develop uniform rules to be applied across the whole country. This process continued for about two centuries, and by the mid-thirteenth century there was an English common law. The principle of *stare decisis*, on which judicial precedent is founded, had been established, and common law courts of exchequer, common pleas and King's bench had been established.

[3]By asking you to explain the origins of the common law, the question is asking for a historical narrative of the factors which resulted in its emergence. It is particularly important that you be clear about the role of the itinerant justices in this process.

Litigants soon came to experience difficulties in using the common law due to both rigidity in the system by which actions could be lodged and the limited range of remedies available from the common law courts.[4] Civil actions had to be commenced by a writ which set out the cause of action. Initially, when an action could not be fit within existing writs, new writs could be used. However, by the thirteenth century the grounds on which writs could be based had become fixed. New writs were no longer possible and any actions had to be fit within existing writs. In short, the writ system had become rigid and deprived some litigants of the ability to commence an action within the common law courts. Furthermore, the only remedy granted by the common law was that of damages. In some disputes, for example those concerning the sale of land, this was hardly appropriate as monetary damages were often regarded as providing no substitute for a specific parcel of land.

[4]It is imperative that you connect the origins of the common law and the emergence of equity by explaining the problems which the common law came to give rise to. The key point to emphasise is the rigidity of the writ system and the range of remedies available at common law.

As a result of these shortcomings in the common law, aggrieved individuals began to petition the King for a fair outcome to their case in those situations where the common law had proven inadequate to give them just satisfaction. In practice, the King would pass these petitions over to his Chancellor for adjudication. The Chancellor was known as the 'keeper of the King's conscience' and he would attempt to resolve such cases in accordance with what he perceived to be principles of fairness, or equity. Eventually, individuals would begin to petition the Chancellor himself and by 1474 he had begun to hear petitions and make decisions in respect of them under his own authority. This marked the origins of the Court of Chancery. The Chancellor was not restricted by the more rigid rules of the common law. He enjoyed the power to question the parties to a case themselves, a power not enjoyed by the common law courts. Nor were damages the only possible remedy which could be granted. Instead, the Chancellor could grant whatever remedy best suited the case at hand. For example, in cases concerning land transactions, the remedy of specific performance could usefully be granted so as to compel that a particular piece of land be sold in accordance with a prior agreement reached by the parties, as opposed to the mere grant of damages which is all that could have been awarded by the common law courts. The principles developed by the Chancellor and Court of Chancery became known as equity, reflecting their prime concern with achieving fairness in individual cases.[5]

For a considerable period of time equity and common law operated as two separate systems, administered by different courts, and there was tension between the two bodies of rules. This tension was resolved by the landmark ruling of James I in the **Earl of Oxford's Case** [1615] 1 Rep Ch 1,[6] that whenever there was a conflict between common law and equity, equity was to prevail. This case thus established the supremacy of equity over common law. The administration of the two systems was finally brought together by the Judicature Acts 1873–5,[7] which merged the common law and equity courts and finally gave all courts the power to administer both common law and equitable remedies.

Equity continues to be a very important and influential source of law within this country.[8] It is especially important in the context of trusts law, but also impacts upon other areas such as land and contract. Unlike common law, equitable remedies are discretionary. There is a series of equitable maxims which are of great importance in cases where equitable remedies are sought. An important one of these is the principle that 'he who comes to equity must come with clean hands', essentially preventing those who have acted inequitably from reaping the benefits which equity might otherwise afford them. In **D & C Builders *v* Rees** [1966] 2 QB 617, no equitable remedy was available to a party who had taken unfair advantage of another's financial difficulties. Another important maxim is 'he who seeks equity must do equity,' meaning that strikers seeking an injunction to prevent their dismissal could not equitably continue to strike if the injunction were to be granted (**Chappell *v* Times Newspapers** [1975] 1 WLR 482). Another maxim is that equity cannot be invoked

[5]You need to explain the process by which equity came to emerge and the way in which it differed from the common law.

[6]It is essential for this case to be mentioned. It is a landmark case, asserting the superiority of equity over common law.

[7]This is another essential point. You must make clear that although equity and common law operated as rival systems, their administration was eventually brought together. However, ensure that you are clear that although their administration was merged, they continue to enjoy their own rules and principles.

[8]It is useful in your final paragraph to say something about the continuing important role of equity today. Relevant issues include its important role in particular areas of law, the discretionary nature of equitable remedies, important maxims equity lays down and the fact that most remedies are actually equitable in nature.

by those who delay their action. Thus, five years to eventually bring a case was held to be too long in **Leaf *v* International Galleries** [1950] 2 KB 86. Furthermore, it should also be noted that the most important remedies available from the courts today, apart from damages, are the product of equity. The remedies of injunction, specific performance, recission and rectification are all equitable in nature.

✓ Make your answer stand out

- Demonstrate that you have a clear understanding of the system of laws which preceded the emergence of the common law.
- Demonstrate that you are familiar with some of the key rules and remedies provided by equity, beyond simply being able to explain why it emerged.
- Make some comment upon the modern significance of equity.
- Read Burrows, A., 'We Do this at Common Law but that in Equity', *Oxford Journal of Legal Studies*, 2002, v. 22, n. 1, pp. 1–16, and cite his arguments to illustrate continuing inconsistencies between common law and equity today.

! Don't be tempted to . . .

- Simply explain what common law and equity are and the difference between them without any historical narrative of their origins;
- Explain the emergence of equity without firstly illustrating the problems in the common law which resulted in this.

Question 2

Critically assess the relative importance of case law and statute as sources of law, and their relationship with one another.

Answer plan

- → Explain the difference between case law and statute.
- → Illustrate the significance of statute as the supreme source of domestic law (subject to conflicting European law) with reference to the doctrine of parliamentary sovereignty.
- → Illustrate the continuing significance of case law with reference to the importance of judicial precedent and areas of law still covered predominantly by case law.
- → Explain the interaction that exists between case law and statute.
- → Conclude by commenting upon the relative significance of case law and statute as sources of law.

Diagram plan

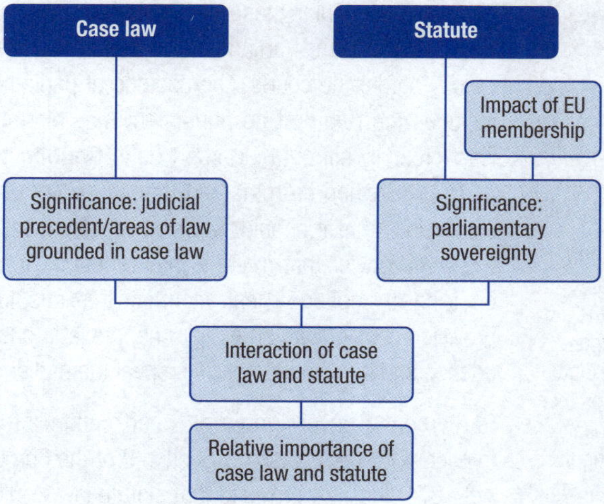

A printable version of this diagram plan is available from www.pearsoned.co.uk/lawexpressqa

Answer

Case law and statute are the two major domestic sources of English law.[1] Case law (or common law) constitutes the body of law contained in judicial decisions. It is an uncodified source of law and operates through the system of judicial precedent, whereby in reaching decisions judges have regard to decisions from earlier cases sharing similar material facts. Statute law refers to legislation made by Parliament in the form of Acts of Parliament. It is a formalised source of law, a bill passing through several potentially time consuming stages before finally adopted as a statute.

Historically, statute has been regarded as the supreme source of law due to the doctrine of parliamentary sovereignty.[2] In the words of Dicey,[3] this holds that Parliament has 'the right to make or unmake any law whatsoever', there being 'no person or body having the right to override or set aside the legislation of Parliament'. Outrageous or immoral legislation is not precluded, as Lord Reid emphasised in **Madzimbamuto *v* Lardner-Burke & George** [1969] AC 645,[4] when he noted that although the moral reasons against a particular piece of legislation may be very strong, this would not prevent Parliament from enacting it or affect its legal validity before the courts. The doctrine of parliamentary sovereignty includes the rule that no parliament may bind it successors. This was forcefully set out by Herbert CJ in **Godden *v* Hales** (1686) 11 St Tr 1165 when he remarked that, 'if an Act of Parliament had a clause in it that it should never be repealed, yet without question, the same power that made it may repeal it'. It also embraces the doctrine of implied repeal, meaning that should a later statutory provision conflict with an earlier one, the later one will receive precedence and be said to implicitly repeal the earlier one.

Parliament's sovereignty has been called into question by the impact of EU membership.[5] Section 2 of the European Communities Act 1972 implicitly provided that statute law would be overridden by contrary provisions of European law. The supremacy of EU law was finally firmly established in the case of **R *v* Secretary of State for Transport, *ex parte* Factortame (No. 1)** [1990] 2 AC 85,[6] where the European Court of Justice ruled that in any conflict between a provision of domestic law and a provision of European law, the latter would prevail. Parliamentary sovereignty is in practice therefore

[1]The question asks you to consider the relative importance of these two sources of law. It will be helpful at the outset to explain that they are the two major domestic sources of law. You should also briefly explain what they are and how they differ from one another.

[2]In explaining the importance of statute, it is essential that you make reference to the doctrine of parliamentary sovereignty and explain its implications.

[3]You will receive credit for being able to cite relevant quotations to illustrate the doctrine of parliamentary sovereignty. Dicey is especially worthy of mention because of his considerable writings in this area.

[4]Relevant reference to case law to illustrate the doctrine shows an awareness of the doctrine in practice, for which you will also receive credit.

[5]You cannot discuss the importance of statute without mentioning the restrictions placed upon parliamentary sovereignty by EU membership, as this goes directly to the heart of the question, reducing the relative significance of statute law when this clashes with European provisions.

[6]*Factortame* must be mentioned at this stage as it is the most significant case in terms of the impact of EU membership on parliamentary sovereignty.

limited, European law being effectively the supreme source of law for the English legal system.

Nonetheless, statute remains the most important of the domestic sources of law. Statute overrides all conflicting common law provisions. The validity of statutes may not be questioned by judges, unless a question of compatibility with European law is raised. The twentieth century witnessed a surge in the significance of statute law,[7] as the growth of the welfare state and government activity was accompanied by a wave of unprecedented legislative action on the part of Parliament. The increased need for legislation is evident in the huge amount of law-making left to be done through delegated legislation. Statute law enjoys the advantage of being democratic in nature. It is made by elected representatives of the people, who are theoretically held accountable at election time. A major problem with statute law, however, is the time-consuming process through which it is made.[8] Any parliamentary bill is likely to take several months, if not years, before it has exhausted all of the procedures to enter the statute book, sometimes meaning law reform can be long overdue.

[7]This is a relevant point, showing how statute has become more commonly used in law-making.

[8]It is relevant to refer to some of the drawbacks of statute, as this will lead nicely into the discussion of the importance of case law.

The supremacy of statute law should not detract from the continued significance of case law. Judicial precedent, through which it operates, is an important pillar of the English legal system and case law continues to fill many gaps and indeed still provides the main legal rules applicable in many important areas.[9] For example, the criminal law governing murder is still heavily based upon case law, as are many of the principles of tort law, perhaps most notably negligence, and the fundamental rules governing the making of contracts. Critics sometimes attack case law on the ground that it involves unaccountable judges effectively legislating on matters that are the proper province of Parliament, yet, at the same time an often extolled virtue of case law is its ability to be made instantaneously, responding to changing needs long before Parliament is able to do so.[10]

[9]In showing the importance of common law it is very useful to explain the extent to which some branches of law remain largely grounded in common law rules.

[10]Notwithstanding parliamentary sovereignty, you are showing here one of the key advantages of common law.

The relative importance of statute and case law cannot, however, be assessed simply by considering each as a separate source of law existing in isolation to the other.[11] The doctrine of the separation of powers emphasises the importance of the legislature and judiciary being separate and independent of one another, but they do not exist and work in isolation from one another. Parliament makes

[11]This goes to the heart of the question. You must not just consider the relative importance of these two sources of law, but also their relationship with one another. There are several relevant points that you can make here.

statutes and it is then the task of the judges to give effect to these. Through the tool of statutory interpretation[12] judges are given the means to shape the impact of legislation adopted by Parliament where its provisions are ambiguous, vague or not drafted with a particular scenario in mind. It is, thus, through case law that statute is given its practical meaning and effect. It has already been noted that statute law will be overridden by contrary provisions of European law. As a result of the **Factortame** decision, the courts are now empowered to set aside statutory provisions where there is such a conflict. Furthermore, in the human rights context the higher courts are able to declare statutory provisions to be incompatible with the Human Rights Act 1998,[13] although such declarations have no bearing on the legal validity or application of the relevant provisions. Clearly, there is a considerable degree of interaction between statute and case law. Regardless of the supremacy of the former, its application is significantly affected by case law through judicial decisions in a variety of circumstances. Case law also contributes to the creation of statute law. The slow pace of statutory reform sometimes leads case law to step in to respond to social change, as occurred for example in **R *v* R** [1991] 3 WLR 767[14] where for the first time it was held that a man could be guilty of raping his wife. Sometimes developments in case law lead to statutory reform or case law is codified in statutory form, as occurred for example with the Sale of Goods Act 1979.

It is naïve to treat statute and case law as mutually exclusive sources of law.[15] While statute remains theoretically the more important due to the doctrine of parliamentary sovereignty, this should not detract from the obvious importance of case law, especially in light of its close relationship with statute law in practice.

[12]This is one obvious example where case law and statute law feed into one another.

[13]Credit should be given for pointing out this relatively recent development.

[14]Again, one of the virtues of case law vis a vis statute is illustrated with an example. Wherever appropriate, try to cite examples in support of your arguments.

[15]The conclusion drawn is reasoned, rational and flows naturally from the discussion that has taken place of these two sources of law and their relationship with one another.

✓ Make your answer stand out

- Pay particular attention to the relationship that exists between case law and statute.
- Use practical examples to illustrate the importance of case law and statute, and their interaction with one another.
- Provide a clear explanation of the doctrine of parliamentary sovereignty and the manner in which this has been limited by EU membership.
- In explaining the importance of parliamentary sovereignty you might draw a distinction between legal and political concepts of parliamentary sovereignty, as exemplified by, for example, Allan, T.R.S., 'The Limits of Parliamentary Sovereignty', *Public Law*, 1985, p. 614.

! Don't be tempted to...

- Discuss case law and statute as two separate sources of law without considering their relationship with one another;
- List the advantages and disadvantages of case law and statute and weigh up their relative importance in light of these, as this is not what the question asks for;
- Omit any reference to Parliamentary Sovereignty or the impact of EU membership upon this.

Question 3

Explain the process by which an Act of Parliament is made, and discuss the relative importance of the House of Commons, House of Lords and Sovereign within this process.

Answer plan

→ Explain how parliamentary bills originate and the different kinds of bills that can be introduced.

→ Explain the different stages which a bill must go through in both Houses of Parliament.

→ Explain the impact of the Parliament Acts 1911 and 1949 upon the relative importance of the House of Lords within the legislative process.

→ Comment upon the extent to which royal assent is a mere formality within the legislative process.

Diagram plan

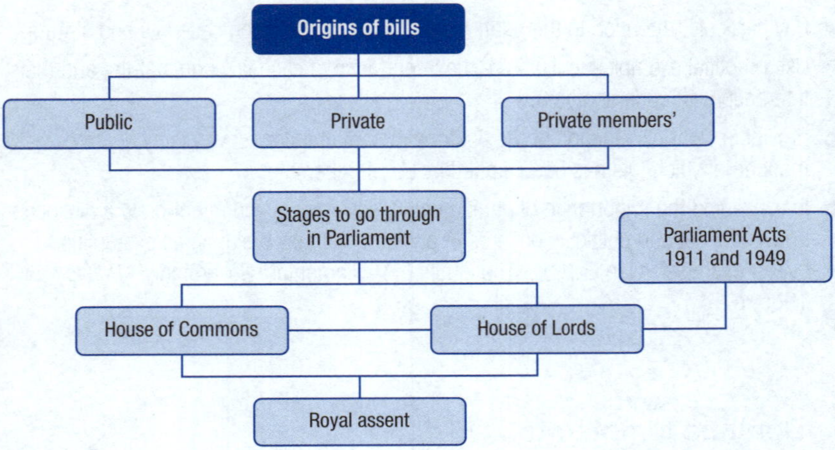

A printable version of this diagram plan is available from www.pearsoned.co.uk/lawexpressqa

Answer

[1]You should begin your answer by providing some explanation of the origins of bills before they begin the process of going through Parliament. It is useful to explain the different kinds of bills which exist, and also that the vast majority of Parliamentary legislation stems from government policy.

[2]It is worth mentioning private members' bills, although you should also point out that they are of very limited significance although some notable exceptions have been known.

[3]At this point your answer needs to focus upon explaining the various stages which a bill must go through in Parliament. This is explicitly asked of you by the question.

All Acts of Parliament begin life as bills.[1] The vast majority of bills are introduced by the government as part of its policy agenda. Government bills are usually preceded by white papers which set out the government's general proposals for new legislation. Sometimes green papers precede these, which set out more tentative policy options. Public bills apply to the country as a whole and affect everyone, for example by changing the criminal law. Private bills have limited application, for example to a specific corporation or local authority. Government bills are drafted by parliamentary counsel, skilled in the art of translating desired policy objectives into tight provisions that are understandable and enforceable.

Some bills, known as private members' bills,[2] are introduced by individual MPs. However, the lack of time set aside for these to be debated means that they rarely pass into law. There are some notable exceptions though, such as the Abortion Act 1967 sponsored by David Steel.

Bills must pass through several stages in both Houses of Parliament.[3] Ordinarily a bill will begin life in the House of Commons before moving to the House of Lords, but it may proceed the other way around. Indeed, private bills will usually proceed in the House of Lords first of all. At its first reading the title of the bill is simply read out. It is then printed and published. Before the bill receives its second reading, section 19 of the Human Rights Act 1998 requires that the responsible minister must make a statement to the effect that in his view the bill's provisions are compatible with the Convention rights incorporated into domestic law by the Human Rights Act.[4] If he is unable to make such a statement, he must state this but that the government wishes to proceed with the bill nonetheless. At its second reading there will be a main debate upon the bill where MPs or Peers will have a chance to ask questions of the government minister and argue over the merits of any particularly contentious provisions. Following the second reading the bill then goes to the committee stage. At this point a standing committee of MPs or Peers will scrutinise the provisions of the bill in much greater detail. Having done this, they may propose amendments to the bill which in their view will improve it as a whole. From the committee stage the bill is then sent back to the House as a whole. This is known as the report stage and MPs or Peers will engage in further debate upon the bill, and will also have the opportunity to vote to accept or reject any amendments made at the committee stage. The bill will come to its conclusion with a third and final reading, at which point there is a final debate on the contents of the bill followed by a vote. If the vote on the bill is positive, the bill is then sent to the other House of Parliament where it will go through all of the same stages once again in that house. If any amendments are made there, it must return to the other house for these amendments to be voted upon.

[4]This is an important point which can easily be overlooked. However, this provision clearly impacts upon the process by which a bill passes through parliament as it imposes a mandatory requirement upon the minister introducing a bill and so therefore, should, be mentioned.

Clearly, the parliamentary process is a lengthy one. There are several hurdles which a bill must overcome in both houses before the process has been completed and the bill is close to entering the statute book as a new piece of legislation. It is important to emphasise, however, that although bills must proceed through both Houses of Parliament, it is the House of Commons which is the preeminent body of the two.[5] The importance of the House of Lords to the legislative process has declined considerably in the twentieth century, largely as a result of the fact that whereas the Commons is a democratically elected, accountable and representative body, the Lords is an undemocratic, unaccountable and unrepresentative

[5]This relates back directly to the question which asks you to consider the relative importance of the Commons, Lords and Sovereign to the legislative process.

body. To restrict the ability of the House of Lords to block legislation, the Parliament Acts of 1911 and 1949 were adopted.[6] As a result of these two statutes, the House of Lords can only delay the passage of a bill into law as an Act of Parliament by one year. Thus, any bill which has been passed by the House of Commons need not necessarily receive a positive vote in the House of Lords to eventually become law. As far as 'money' bills are concerned, those which involve the raising of revenue, the House of Lords may only delay these by a period of one month. This reflects their fundamental importance to the effective functioning of government. In practice, it has not proven necessary for governments to make great use of the provisions of the Parliament Acts to force their legislative programme through the House of Lords. They have only actually been invoked on four occasions to ensure legislation could be passed in the face of a disagreeable House of Lords.[7] The first such occasion did not occur until 1991, when the War Crimes Act 1991 was passed into law. Since then, the provisions of the Parliament Acts have been utilised on a further three occasions to facilitate the passage of the European Parliamentary Elections Act 1999, the Sexual Offences (Amendment) Act 2000 and the Hunting Act 2004.

Government bills will usually pass smoothly into legislation as a consequence of the fact that governments ordinarily enjoy a majority in the House of Commons.[8] This is not always the case, however, and sometimes legislative proposals will have to be shelved where there is significant opposition including from the government's own backbenchers.

The final step in the making of an Act of Parliament is the granting of royal assent. This is a mere formality.[9] The monarch today enjoys no meaningful legal or political power and her consent is only required by constitutional convention. In practice, this is never refused. The last occasion on which this did happen was when Queen Anne refused to assent to the Scottish Militia Bill of 1707.[10] It is inconceivable that royal assent would be refused today, and if this did occur a constitutional crisis would be likely to ensue. The Royal Assent Act 1967 provides that royal assent is deemed to be given on the date on which this is informed to parliament. The Act of Parliament will come into force on this date unless the act itself provides otherwise, either by specifying an alternative date or leaving it to statutory instrument to bring the act into force.

[6] It is imperative that you refer to the impact of the Parliament Acts as it is these which are responsible for curbing the power of the House of Lords to block legislation, thus diminishing its relative importance in the legislative process.

[7] This is a convenient place to allude to some relevant examples to reinforce a point.

[8] This is an appropriate comment to make following discussion of the parliamentary process, evidencing awareness of the political context within which Acts of Parliament are made. You might wish to refer to the current political situation in which there is a coalition government and legislative proposals stem from compromises between the two parties.

[9] Do not forget to include coverage of this issue as the question specifically refers to it. You should demonstrate that the role of the sovereign in the parliamentary process is a mere formality.

[10] This reinforces the mere formality of royal assent. Making such a point also allows you to evidence wider knowledge of the subject area.

✓ Make your answer stand out

- Provide some context to the question by explaining the origins of parliamentary bills, in particular the extent to which they are largely driven by government policy.
- Use examples where appropriate, for example, cases in which the Parliament Acts have been invoked to pass a bill, or a private member's bill has been successful.
- Make reference to requirement imposed upon a minister introducing a bill into parliament by section 19 of the Human Rights Act 1998.
- Demonstrate a solid awareness of the impact of the Parliament Acts 1911 and 1949 and the norms applicable to the requirement of royal assent.

! Don't be tempted to . . .

- Explain only the main stages through which a bill must pass in Parliament without first providing an explanation of the origins of bills;
- Neglect to consider the role of the sovereign within the legislative process.

Question 4

Explain the main forms which delegated legislation takes and assess the extent to which its making is subject to adequate scrutiny.

Answer plan

→ Explain what delegated legislation is and why it is necessary.

→ Explain the main forms of delegated legislation that exist and illustrate the procedures which are followed for their implementation.

→ Comment upon the volume and importance of delegated legislation.

→ Comment upon the main methods through which the major forms of delegated legislation are scrutinised and their susceptibility to challenge in the courts.

Diagram plan

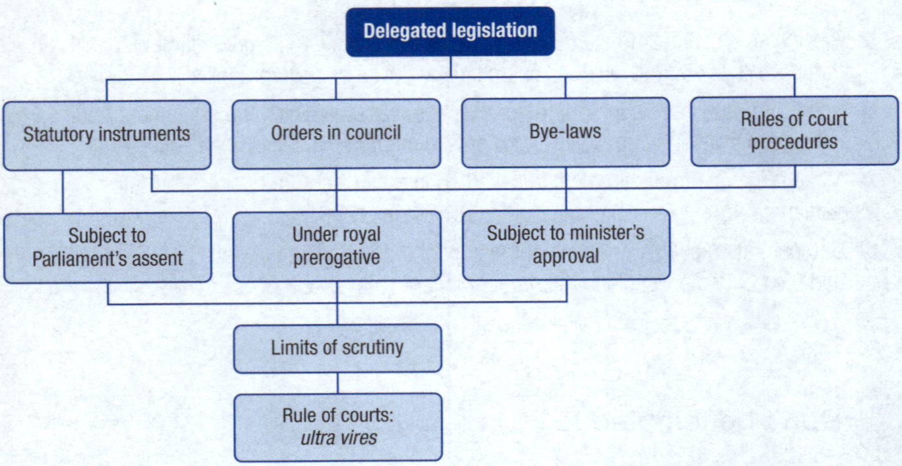

A printable version of this diagram plan is available from www.pearsoned.co.uk/lawexpressqa

Answer

Delegated legislation, also known as secondary legislation, is legislation made by persons or bodies other than Parliament,[1] under powers given to them by Parliament under statute or exercised under the royal prerogative. Statutes which confer the power to make delegated legislation are known as enabling Acts. The increase in the size of the state and its involvement in more areas of life from the mid-twentieth century onwards has been accompanied by a huge surge in the amount of delegated legislation. Its use is widely regarded as necessary[2] to save time within the legislative process, to enable legislation to be made with greater speed where necessary, and to provide the technical knowledge and expertise that are required for drawing up detailed rules on very specific subject matters.

[1]Before going on to explain the major forms of delegated legislation, you should, at the outset, briefly explain more generally what delegated legislation is.

[2]You can provide some useful context to your answer by briefly explaining the expansion in delegated legislation during the twentieth century and the main reasons why it is perceived as necessary.

Perhaps the most prominent form of delegated legislation are statutory instruments.[3] These are made by government ministers or civil servants within their departments and consist of rules, regulations and orders. Statutory instruments tend to cover lots of technical detailed matters which go beyond the general provisions set out in a statute. It is common for a statute to provide the general legal framework for a particular matter while empowering the relevant government minister to make regulations containing more detailed provisions.[4] The procedure by which a statutory instrument is made is usually laid down in the enabling act, although the Statutory Instruments Act 1946 also contains some rules in this respect. Before becoming law, statutory instruments require confirmation by Parliament. The enabling act will specify how this is to be obtained. Under the 'affirmative resolution' procedure,[5] the statutory instrument will only come into effect when Parliament passes a resolution approving it. More common, however, is the use of the 'negative resolution' procedure.[6] Under this, the statutory instrument will be laid before Parliament for a period of 40 days. Within this period, either House can move to annul it. If neither does so, at the end of the period it is taken to have been approved by Parliament.

Orders in Council are a form of delegated legislation made by the Privy Council, although, in practice, this is a forum through which the government often acts to make emergency resolutions or to implement international obligations.[7] UN Security Council resolutions are given effect through Orders in Council, as provided for by section 1 of the United Nations Act 1946. Economic sanctions against Southern Rhodesia were also imposed by way of Orders in Council pursuant to the Southern Rhodesia Act 1965. Provisions emanating from the European Union can also be effected through Orders in Council. Orders in Council may be made under the royal prerogative or under powers conferred by statute.[8] Orders made under the royal prerogative do not require Parliament's approval, but the second form of Order in Council is simply another form of statutory instrument and subject to the same procedures for parliamentary confirmation as other statutory instruments.

[3]You should begin your discussion of the main forms of delegated legislation with statutory instruments as these are arguably the most significant. Explain clearly who they are made by and the procedure which they go through in Parliament before coming into force.

[4]At this stage you may be able to provide examples of such legislation made by statutory instrument. There are many cases where a statute will lay down a general legislative framework while leaving many more detailed and technical matters to be legislated upon by the relevant minister. For example, in the area of social security law, statutes will often give effect to broader policy objectives of government, while leaving details concerning the procedures for benefit claims, or amounts claimants may be entitled to, to be provided in regulations drawn up by the relevant minister.

[5]It is [illegible]

[9]Don't forget to include coverage of bye-laws and focus only on measures adopted at the level of central government. They continue to be a prominent form of delegated legislation.

Bye-laws are a form of delegated legislation made by local authorities[9] in respect of matters of local interest or concern best tackled at a local level. The power to make bye-laws is invested in local authorities (and occasionally other corporations) through various statutes, such as the Local Government Act 1972. Generally speaking, bye-laws need the confirmation of the relevant government minister before they can come into force. This requirement can be found in section 235(2) of the Local Government Act 1972. However, this requirement has been relaxed and there are now some exceptions where the minister's confirmation is no longer necessary. Some such situations in which this is the case are set out by the Local Government and Public Involvement in Health Act 2007.

[10]This form of delegated legislation is often overlooked, but by mentioning it you show awareness of all forms of delegated legislation.

Finally, delegated legislation is made by the courts rules committees in the form of rules of court procedure.[10] These are made under powers conferred by various statutes, such as the Supreme Court Act 1981, the County Courts Act 1984 and the Magistrates' Court Act 1980, and are implemented by statutory instrument. The Supreme Court Act 1981 has now been renamed as the Senior Courts Act 1981 (see the Constitutional Reform Act 2005).

[11]This adds important context to your answer and sets up nicely the discussion to follow on the scrutiny of delegated legislation. That it accounts for so much legislation reinforces the need for effective scrutiny. Although examiners do not generally expect students to go into an examination armed with statistics, if you are able to remember some statistical information which you can use to reinforce arguments made in your answer, you should receive some credit.

The importance of delegated legislation becomes apparent when it is considered that it accounts for the vast majority of legislation that is made or in force today.[11] For example, in the year 2003 whereas 45 Acts of Parliament came into force, approximately 3,500 statutory instruments were made. The constraints of parliamentary time mean that most legislation is made by persons or bodies other than Parliament.

Given the fact that, unlike primary legislation, delegated legislation is not made by the democratically elected and accountable Parliament, much importance has been attached to the procedures by which scrutiny is exercised over measures of delegated legislation. Statutory instruments are technically subject to the approval of Parliament. Whether subject to the 'affirmative resolution' or the 'negative resolution' procedure, Parliament must effectively endorse the relevant instrument or will at least have the opportunity over a period of 40 days to challenge it, by either addressing issues of concern to the relevant ministers or moving to annul the instrument. However, in practice this is not a particularly effective method of control. Given the sheer number of statutory instruments enacted each year, there is simply insufficient time and inclination on the part of Parliament's membership to direct the necessary attention to these numerous measures. The Joint Committee on Statutory Instruments, established in 1973, is charged with examining statutory instruments laid before Parliament and bringing measures to Parliament's attention on various specified grounds, which include that the relevant measure imposes a charge on public revenues, appears to have retrospective effect contrary to the provisions of its parent act, or is poorly drafted. Notwithstanding its useful functions, constraints of time and the volume of delegated legislation, limit its ability to conduct effective scrutiny of statutory instruments. Orders in Council made under the royal prerogative require no further action before coming into force, meaning that they undergo no real scrutiny. Advance public notice of local authority bye-laws must be given, affording concerned local citizens the opportunity to make representations. As noted above, bye-laws must ordinarily be approved by the relevant minister, although these requirements have been relaxed in several circumstances. Whether there is adequate scrutiny of delegated legislation before its entry into force is, evidently, questionable.[12]

[12]This assertion flows naturally from the preceding discussion of scrutiny.

However, it is notable that unlike primary legislation, the validity of which cannot be questioned by the courts, delegated legislation may be struck down by the courts as *ultra vires*[13] when the person or body making it exceeds the powers conferred upon them by statute, rendering the relevant measure null and void. This occurred, for example, in the case of **Commissioners of Customs & Excise *v* Cure & Deeley Ltd** [1962] 1 QB 340.

[13]This is arguably the most robust form of challenging a piece of delegated legislation and should be mentioned.

✓ Make your answer stand out

- Provide examples, where appropriate, of the different forms of delegated legislation.
- Explain that the courts can strike down delegated legislation as *ultra vires*.

! Don't be tempted to . . .

- Simply explain what the main forms of delegated legislation are without considering how they are made or subject to any form of scrutiny;
- Discuss only statutory instruments and Orders in Council in your answer;
- Answer the question without any reference to relevant examples at appropriate stages.

Question 5

'While forceful criticisms can legitimately be levelled at the use of delegated legislation, its use is absolutely essential in modern society and it would be naïve to think it could simply be dispensed with.' Critically assess the validity of this statement.

Answer plan

- → Briefly explain what delegated legislation is and the major forms which it takes.
- → Discuss the perceived advantages of delegated legislation.
- → Discuss the perceived disadvantages of delegated legislation.
- → Conclude by commenting upon the extent to which you agree with the statement contained in the question.

Diagram plan

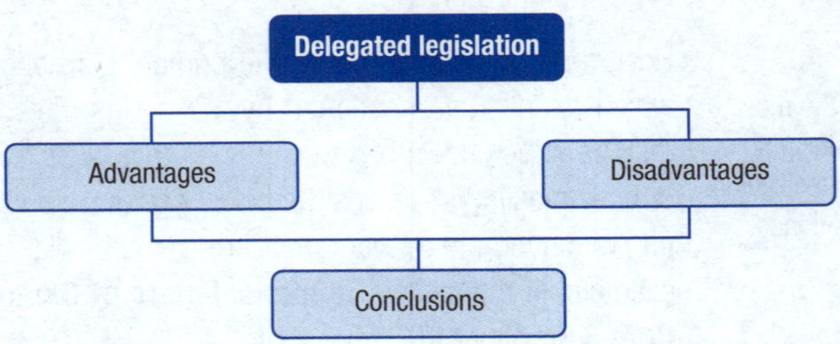

A printable version of this diagram plan is available from www.pearsoned.co.uk/lawexpressqa

Answer

Delegated legislation is legislation made by persons or bodies other than Parliament[1] under powers either conferred upon them by Parliament under statute or exercised under the royal prerogative. Statutory instruments are, arguably, the most prominent form of delegated legislation and consist of regulations, rules and orders made by government ministers or their civil servants under powers conferred by statute. Orders in Council are made by the Privy Council either under powers conferred by statute, in which case they are simply a form of statutory instrument, or under the royal prerogative. Rules of court procedure are made by the court rules

[1] Your introductory paragraph should briefly explain what delegated legislation is and the main forms which it takes. This should be brief however, as your main focus must be to consider the advantages and disadvantages of delegated legislation.

committees under powers conferred by statute, and local authorities and occasionally other corporations make bye-laws in respect of matters within their areas under powers conferred by statute.

Parliament simply has insufficient time to consider all matters requiring legislation and delegated legislation helpfully fills this gap.[2] The process by which an Act of Parliament is made is lengthy, consisting of several stages through which a bill must pass in both Houses of Parliament. These time constraints are evidenced by the fact that Parliament enacts very few statutes in comparison to the voluminous amount of delegated legislation that is made. For example, in 2003 only 45 statutes were adopted compared to approximately 3,500 statutory instruments.[3] It is simply impossible for Parliament to legislate itself on such an enormous amount of issues and delegated legislation fills this void.

[2]This is an absolutely essential point to make. It is the most often cited reason why delegated legislation is necessary.

[3]This is a useful statistic to cite as it reinforces the point that you have just made.

On a related point, delegated legislation can provide detailed rules going far beyond what could be contained in statute.[4] For example, the amount of detail required to effectively legislate in respect of matters such as taxation regulations or social security benefits is far greater than can be dealt with through the parliamentary process. Even when statute is used to advance government policy objectives, it is usually necessary to leave the finer points to be implemented through delegated legislation.

[4]Many of the arguments in support or criticism of delegated legislation are related to one another as opposed to being a series of mutually exclusive points. You should relate them to one another where appropriate. The argument made here builds upon from the previous one so make sure you show this connection.

Furthermore, members of Parliament lack not only time but the specialised knowledge necessary to oversee the implementation of much legislation of a technical nature. Leaving such matters to delegated legislation enables expertise in the relevant areas to be drawn upon during its drafting.[5] Heavily technical measures in particular can be drafted within a government department where there is a pool of expertise in this area. Taking the example of entitlement to social security benefits, the necessary detailed rules can be more effectively drafted by civil servants within the Department of Work and Pensions who deal with these issues on an ongoing basis. The same point can be made of taxation rules drafted by the Inland Revenue. Where bye-laws are made by local authorities, provision exists for relevant local knowledge to inform the law-making process, again illustrating the extent to which relevant expertise or specialist knowledge can be drawn upon. Clearly, in respect of matters of primarily local concern, the relevant local authority is in a much better position to make appropriate rules than is a parliament with little understanding of local needs and interests.

[5]This highly important advantage of delegated legislation must be mentioned. It is helpful to refer to some relevant examples to reinforce the point that it enables technical expertise to be drawn upon.

Delegated legislation can be used to change the law relatively quickly. As noted above, an Act of Parliament must go through several stages before becoming law. This will ordinarily take at least several months. By comparison, measures made through delegated legislation can be completed in a matter of weeks depending upon their relative complexity. A related final advantage of delegated legislation is that whereas statutes cannot always anticipate future needs or changes, delegated legislation can be used to respond quickly to these. To recall an earlier example, social security benefit entitlements are likely to need to change relatively regularly in light of other factors.[6] Parliament cannot envisage how often this need may arise, so the relevant minister will be empowered to make regulations where appropriate.

[6] If you have difficulty thinking of relevant examples, the same example can sometimes be used to reinforce more than one argument.

Undoubtedly, there are several very strong arguments that can be made in support of the role played by delegated legislation. In particular, it is necessary to tackle the many issues which Parliament is simply unable to and allows for relevant expertise on technical and specialist matters. However, its use has been subject to criticism on a number of grounds. It is argued that there is insufficient democratic involvement or accountability within the process by which delegated legislation is made,[7] as it is made by unelected persons and bodies who cannot effectively be held to account. This strengthens the need for proper scrutiny of delegated legislation, but it has often been contended that existing measures are inadequate. Delegated legislation is rarely debated in Parliament. Although statutory instruments theoretically require the assent of Parliament, many are approved through the 'negative resolution' procedure whereby they are laid before Parliament for 40 days at the end of which they are deemed approved in the absence of any objection being raised. It is rare for individual members to pay any real attention to a particular measure. Orders in Council made under the royal prerogative receive no further scrutiny and local authority bye-laws, although ordinarily subject to confirmation by the relevant minister, are now exempt from this requirement in an increasing number of cases as a result of measures such as those contained in the Local Government and Public Involvement in Health Act 2007. The courts may nullify measures that have been made ultra vires, but this is arguably a method of control applicable in more drastic circumstances and no real substitute for effective scrutiny of the law-making process.

[7] This is the most stinging criticism of delegated legislation. There is much that can be said in respect of the lack of proper scrutiny that takes place of measures of delegated legislation, and although you can only realistically give so much attention to it in a more general question on the advantages and disadvantages of delegated legislation, its inclusion is essential in your discussion of its disadvantages.

Another criticism of delegated legislation is that the sheer bulk in which it is produced makes it difficult to keep up to date with the introduction of new legal rules. This can be related to the constitutional principle of the rule of law, most models of which require that laws should be clear and intelligible.[8] It is understandable that keeping abreast of several thousand new pieces of legislation every year is far from easy. A related criticism is that although measures made under delegated legislation are published, they are not publicised either before or after their implementation as widely as Acts of Parliament are, which automatically tend to receive greater media attention. This adds to the difficulty of keeping up to date with new legislative measures.

[8]This is a very effective point which evidences the ability to understand the relationship between delegated legislation and broader legal principles.

Arguably, there is no question of the necessity of delegated legislation for the reasons set out earlier. Critics of delegated legislation rarely suggest that it should not exist. Their arguments are more concerned with the lack of meaningful scrutiny which it undergoes and, to a lesser extent, the limited publicity which is given to its introduction. Strengthening confidence in delegated legislation requires that steps be taken to respond to these concerns.[9]

[9]This is a reasoned and logical conclusion which flows naturally from the rest of the answer. A very strong case can be made for the necessity of delegated legislation, but there remain concerns over the lack of meaningful scrutiny which takes place of it.

✓ Make your answer stand out

- Draw upon examples from relevant areas of law to reinforce your arguments.
- Relate the various advantages or disadvantages of delegated legislation to one another where appropriate, as opposed to treating them as a series of mutually exclusive arguments.
- Demonstrate awareness of the main modes of scrutiny which take place of measures of delegated legislation and their limitations.
- You might usefully illustrate the danger of delegated legislation being used to circumvent Parliamentary scrutiny by reading and drawing upon some of the arguments made in relation to a specific example of a bill conferring wide delegated legislative powers in Burns, S., 'Tipping the Balance', *New Law Journal*, 2006, v. 156, p. 787.

Don't be tempted to . . .

- List the various advantages and disadvantages of delegated legislation with no real discussion;
- Discuss the various advantages and disadvantages of delegated legislation as mutually exclusive issues.

Question 6

Explain the major forms of EU law and the manner of their application within domestic law.

Answer plan

- → Explain that there are different forms of EU law and their manner of application within domestic law varies, briefly illustrating the concepts of direct applicability and direct effect.
- → Explain the application of treaties and that they are the most important source of EU law.
- → Explain the application of regulations, highlighting their generally automatic applicability within domestic law.
- → Explain the application of directives, highlighting the importance of direct effect for their enforceability.
- → Briefly explain the lesser importance of decisions, recommendations and opinions as sources of EU law.

Diagram plan

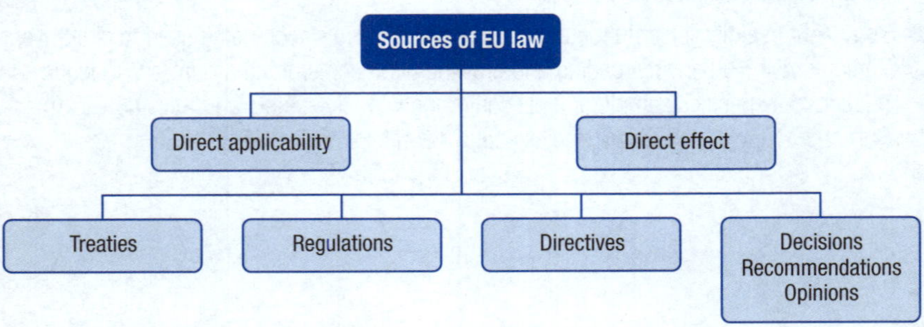

A printable version of this diagram plan is available from www.pearsoned.co.uk/lawexpressqa

Answer

[1]You cannot explain the manner of application of the different forms of EU law within domestic law without reference to the concepts of direct applicability and direct effect. As these are relevant to the discussion of all of the major sources of law, it will be helpful to briefly explain their meaning and relevance to the application of EU law at the outset of your answer.

[2]It is absolutely essential that you refer to *Van Gend en Loos* in explaining direct effect and the criteria which govern its application. It is a case of huge significance.

[3]This is a key point and emphasises the relative importance of treaties within the hierarchy of sources of EU law.

[4]You can evidence wider awareness of the development of EU law by briefly mentioning some of the key treaties to have been created.

There are three major sources of EU law: treaties, regulations and directives. The way in which these different forms of law apply in member states varies. Before explaining the sources in further detail, it will be useful first of all to briefly explain the concepts of direct applicability and direct effect as these are central to the enforceability of EU law within domestic law.[1] A provision of EU law which is directly applicable will have automatic application within the domestic law of member states without any need for implementing measures on their part. While treaty provisions and regulations are capable of direct applicability, directives are not. Direct effect refers to the ability of provisions of EU law to be relied upon within domestic law even where they are not directly applicable and have not been implemented within domestic law. The concept of direct effect was established in the case of **Van Gend en Loos v Nederlandse Tariefcommissie** [1963] ECR 3.[2] In this case the criteria which must be satisfied for a provision to be capable of direct effect were set out, these being that the relevant provision was clear, unconditional and required no further legislation on the part of the state.

Treaties comprise the highest source of law within the EU.[3] They set out its main aims and objectives and provide the institutional and normative framework within which EU institutions are to operate. The treaties also lay down the various rights and obligations of member states. There are several key treaties.[4] The Treaty of Rome (European Community Treaty) established the original European Economic Community in 1957. The Single European Act 1986 introduced measures as part of the process of creating a single economic market within Europe. The Treaty on European Union of 1991 created the European Union and in 1997 the Treaty of Amsterdam amended and re-numbered the European Community Treaty and Treaty on European Union. More recent treaties are the Treaty of Nice 2001 and the Lisbon Treaty 2007. **Van Gend en Loos** first established that treaty provisions are capable of enjoying direct effect if they are unconditional, clear and precise in terms of the rights and obligations which they give rise to and leave member states with no discretion as to their implementation. An example can be found with Article 139 of the European Community Treaty, which laid down the principle of equal pay for men and women. Article 139 was held to be directly effective in UK domestic law in **Macarthys Ltd *v* Smith** [1979] notwithstanding its absence in UK equal pay legislation.[5] Treaty provisions enjoy both vertical and horizontal direct effect,[6] that is to say that they can be enforced against both public (vertical direct effect) and private (horizontal direct effect) bodies. However, non-mandatory treaty provisions containing mere policy statements or objectives are not capable of enjoying direct effect.

[5]There is no better way of illustrating the direct effect of treaty articles than by providing an example of an occasion on which a treaty article has been held to be directly effective.

[6]At some point you need to distinguish vertical and horizontal direct effect.

It has been said that regulations are the European source of law that most closely resemble an Act of Parliament. Regulations apply throughout the EU as soon as they come into force. They are directly applicable. They do not need to be implemented in member states by domestic legislation, and must be applied even if they conflict with domestic legislation. Regulations must be published in the *Official Journal of the European Union*. Regulations are far more common than treaties as sources of EU law. Like treaty provisions, regulations are capable of enjoying direct effect provided that they meet the **Van Gend en Loos** criteria. There was some uncertainty as to whether regulations could enjoy both horizontal and vertical direct effect, but it was confirmed by the European Court of Justice in the case of **Munoz y Cia SA *v* Frumar Ltd** (2002) Unreported, 17 September that they could.[7]

[7]Credit ought to be given for making this point. The case is not particularly well known, yet is relevant to the question and evidences a wider awareness of EU legal developments.

Directives tend to be less precise in their content than do regulations. Generally speaking, they will establish broad policy objectives which member states are to implement through methods of their own choice. As such, directives are not directly applicable within member states but depend for their application on implementation through domestic legislation. Initially it was felt that directives would be unable to enjoy direct effect. However, in the case of **Van Duyn *v* Home Office** [1974] 1 WLR 1107 it was established that unimplemented directives may be relied upon in domestic law under the principle of direct effect where they impose clear and unconditional obligations on a government.[8] Directives will only have vertical direct effect though and cannot be enforced against non-state bodies. This is largely due to the perception that it would be inappropriate to bind a private body by a measure that has yet to be implemented into domestic law and the content which it may be unaware of. However, this could potentially mean that an aggrieved party suffering loss through the failure of a government to properly implement a directive may be left without an appropriate remedy.

[8]This case is central to the enforceability of directives in domestic law and ought to be included in your answer.

[9]The application of directives gives rise to more difficult issues than do treaty provisions and regulations. You would be expected to say more about their application in domestic law as a result. It is useful to explain some of the ways in which the European Court of Justice has sought to fill the gaps left by the more limited application of directives in domestic law. This evidences wide understanding of the subject area.

The European Court of Justice has attempted to plug this gap through a range of other initiatives.[9] Firstly, a broad approach has been taken to the definition of the state and public bodies so as to maximise the range of bodies against which directives can be enforced through the principle of vertical direct effect. For example, in the case of **Marshall *v* Southampton and South-West Hampshire Area Health Authority** [1986] QB 401, a health authority was considered to constitute a public body. In **Von Colson *v* Land Nordrhein-Westfalen** [1984] ECR 1891, the European Court of Justice developed the concept of indirect effect whereby domestic legislation is to be interpreted as far as possible in accordance with directives. As the ultimate sanction, states who fail to implement directives properly within the time frame provided can be held liable and required to provide compensation to those who suffer loss as a result, under the principle of state liability established in **Francovich *v* Italy** [1991] ECR I-5357.

[10]While the main focus of your answer should be on the major sources of EU law – treaties, regulations and directives – awareness of the complete range of sources is evidenced by brief reference to decisions, recommendations and opinions.

Treaties, regulations and directives are the most important sources of EU law. They are wide in their application and, in the right circumstances, can be enforced in domestic law courts. There are, however, also some less significant sources of law that ought to be briefly mentioned.[10] Decisions of EU institutions may be addressed to states or private individuals or bodies. They have the force of law under Article 249 of the European Community Treaty, but only bind their recipients. They have no general application beyond this. Recommendations and opinions of the Council and Commission, covered by Article 211 of the European Community Treaty, do not constitute binding law but may influence the conduct of member states.

✓ Make your answer stand out

- Explain clearly the concepts of direct applicability and direct effect and show how they are relevant to the application of the major sources of EU law within domestic law.
- Illustrate some of the measures taken by the European Court of Justice to fill gaps in situations where directives have not been capable of horizontal direct effect.

! Don't be tempted to . . .

- Simply explain what the different sources of EU law are without any explanation of the manner in which they are applied within domestic law;
- Treat directives as a less important source of law for the purpose of your answer as there is actually more to be said about issues relevant to the enforceability of directives than there is treaties or regulations;
- Confuse EU law with the European Convention on Human Rights, which is not relevant to this question.

Question 7

'Parliamentary sovereignty has been so significantly undermined by the impact of the UK's membership of the European Union to the extent that it has become meaningless.' Critically assess the validity of this statement.

Answer plan

→ Explain the doctrine of parliamentary sovereignty.

→ Briefly refer to the development of the concept of the supremacy of EU law through the jurisprudence of the European Court of Justice.

→ Explain the importance of Section 2 of the European Communities Act 1972.

→ Illustrate the recognition of the supremacy of EU law by domestic courts with particular reference to the *Factortame* case.

→ Conclude by commenting upon the constitutional significance of the UK's membership of the EU.

Diagram plan

A printable version of this diagram plan is available from www.pearsoned.co.uk/lawexpressqa

Answer

[1]The question asks you about the impact of EU law on parliamentary sovereignty, so you need to demonstrate that you understand what the doctrine of parliamentary sovereignty entails before you proceed to explore how it has been affected by the impact of EU law. Your first paragraph should explain the doctrine of parliamentary sovereignty.

[2]You will not usually need to recite the facts of a case. The main point is that you understand the legal principles which emanate from cases.

[3]Reference to *Costa* v *ENEL* is helpful as it illustrates that the notion that European law would take precedence over domestic law was rooted in the jurisprudence of the European Court of Justice prior to the UK's accession to the EEC. Although you cannot be expected to quote extensively from judgments in an examination setting, it is useful if you can incorporate some passages from particularly important cases, and when writing longer essays you should do so.

[4]It is absolutely essential that you consider the impact of the 1972 Act, as this gave effect to European law within the UK and hints at its supremacy over domestic legislation.

The doctrine of parliamentary sovereignty lies at the heart of the UK constitution. It holds that Parliament may make or unmake any law whatsoever. There are no restrictions upon its freedom to legislate.[1] The unlimited scope of this power was underlined in the case of **Madzimbamuto *v* Lardner-Burke & George** [1969] AC 645, where Lord Reid expressed the view that although 'the moral, political and other reasons against...doing [certain things] are so strong that most would regard it as highly improper...this does not mean it is beyond [Parliament's] power to'. There are two core strands to parliamentary sovereignty. Firstly, Parliament may not bind its successors. It may not enact provisions preventing later Parliaments doing certain things or requiring that a special procedure must be followed to change a particular law. Secondly, the doctrine of implied repeal holds that where later Acts of Parliament conflict with earlier ones, the later acts take effect and are said to implicitly repeal the earlier ones. Where an Act of Parliament conflicts with a provision of international law, it was established in **Mortensen *v* Peters** [1906] SLT 227 that the former prevails.[2] Prior to the accession of the UK to the then European Economic Community (EEC), European law was simply an alien form of international law with no binding effect on the UK. However, the UK's membership of the EU has forced a re-appraisal of the extent to which Parliament continues to enjoy sovereignty within the domestic legislative process.

The notion that European law would prevail over domestic legislation in the event of a clash between the two forms of law has deep roots in the jurisprudence of the European Court of Justice where the concept of the supremacy of European law developed. In the case of **Costa *v* ENEL** [1964] CMLR 425 it was suggested that in acceding to the EEC member states had 'limited their sovereign rights... and...created a body of law which binds both their nationals and themselves...the law stemming from the treaty...could not, because of its special and original nature, be overridden by domestic legal provisions...'[3] The European Communities Act 1972 gave effect to European law within the UK.[4] The two key provisions are sections 2(1) and 2(4). Section 2(1) provides that European legislation is to be given effect to in domestic law. Section 2(4) is potentially more controversial however, as it appears to provide that domestic legislation will be given effect subject to provisions of European law, implying the supremacy of the latter in the case of conflict. Although it would be two decades before the impact of European law upon parliamentary sovereignty was finally clarified, there were some early signs of recognition on the part of the UK courts of the monumental impact which European law would have upon the long established doctrine of parliamentary sovereignty.[5] Lord Denning, in particular, made prominent comments upon the subject. Not long after the passage of the European Communities Act, he prophesied in **HP Bulmer Ltd *v* J Bollinger SA (No. 2)** [1974] Ch 401, that the European Community Treaty was 'an incoming tide. It flows into the estuaries and up the rivers. It cannot be held back'. Later, in **Macarthys Ltd *v* Smith** [1979] 1 WLR 1189, he said, 'If...it should appear that our legislation is deficient or is inconsistent with Community law...then it is our bounden duty to give priority to Community law. Such is the result of s 2(1) and (4) of the European Communities Act 1972'.

[5]Reference to such decisions is useful as it builds up a picture of gradual recognition of the supremacy of European law on the part of the UK courts.

The impact of EU law on parliamentary sovereignty was finally confirmed in **R *v* Secretary of State for Transport, *ex parte* Factortame (No. 1)** [1990] 2 AC 85.[6] The case concerned a conflict between provisions of the UK Merchant Shipping Act 1988 and provisions of European law. The case was brought by the operators of fishing vessels who had been precluded by provisions of the 1988 Act from being able to register their vessels in the UK and where thus unable to fish in British waters. They claimed that the relevant provisions of the Merchant Shipping Act were in breach of European law and should therefore be disapplied by the courts. The case reached the House of Lords which ultimately ruled that the 1988 Act was in conflict with provisions of European law and consequently would be overridden. The House took the view that it had always been clear since the passage of the European Communities Act that in the case of a conflict a domestic court would be obliged to give precedence to European law. This was a landmark occasion in UK constitutional and legal history, representing the first occasion on which provisions of an Act of Parliament were set aside, and making clear that parliamentary sovereignty only exists to the extent that domestic legislation does not fall foul of European provisions.

[6]It is absolutely essential that you include coverage of the *Factortame* case in your answer. This is the most important case on the impact of European law on parliamentary sovereignty and goes to the very heart of the question, establishing firmly that European law will override conflicting provisions of domestic statutes. You need to stress very clearly the landmark status of the ruling in *Factortame*.

The impact of Factortame has been reinforced in subsequent cases.[7] For example, in **R *v* Secretary of State for Employment, *ex parte* Equal Opportunities Commission** [1994] 1 WLR 910 parts of the Employment Protection (Consolidation) Act 1978 were held to

[7]It is useful to follow up your discussion of *Factortame* by illustrating how it has been reinforced in later cases. Again, this evidences a wider understanding of the subject area.

be incompatible with European law. More recently, the constitutional significance of the European Communities Act 1972 was commented upon in **Thoburn *v* Sunderland City Council** [2002] EWHC 195 (Admin), where it was described by Lord Justice Laws as a 'constitutional Act' which could only be repealed by express provisions of an Act of Parliament.[8]

Parliamentary sovereignty has undoubtedly been radically affected as a result of the UK's membership of the EU. Although Parliament retains the ability to legislate on any matter of its choosing, should this conflict with a provision of European law it will be overridden by it. Parliamentary sovereignty appears to be thus heavily diminished. However, there is a strong argument to be made for the proposition that Parliament can reclaim its complete sovereignty anytime by simply repealing the European Communities Act 1972. It will be recalled that according to the doctrine of parliamentary sovereignty, no Parliament can bind its successor. It is the 1972 Act which has given European law effect within the domestic legal system, and if a later Parliament chooses to repeal that Act, it will cease to have effect and parliamentary sovereignty will be restored to its former state. This was evidently recognised by Lord Justice Laws in the case of **Thoburn**, where he re-stated the fundamental principle that no Parliament can bind its successors meant the 1972 Act could not become entrenched in domestic law to the point where it could not be repealed. Although political factors make this unlikely, it is nonetheless the case that parliamentary sovereignty can arguably be fully reasserted at any stage.[9]

[8]The *Thoburn* judgment is very interesting for its commentary on the constitutional significance of the 1972 Act as well as the modern relevance of the doctrine of parliamentary sovereignty. If you have time, you might embark on a lengthier discussion of this.

[9]Your conclusion should include comment upon the extent to which parliamentary sovereignty has been undermined by the impact of European law, and whether and how full parliamentary sovereignty might possibly be reclaimed. This relates directly back to the question which you have been asked to answer.

✓ Make your answer stand out

- Demonstrate a clear understanding of the meaning and scope of the doctrine of parliamentary sovereignty.
- Make reference to a range of relevant cases which touch upon the impact of European law on parliamentary sovereignty.
- Comment upon the constitutional significance of the European Communities Act 1972 and the UK's membership of the European Union.
- Refer to critical commentary upon the issues raised by the question by reading and drawing upon the discussion provided in Craig, P., 'Britain in the European Union'; and Bradley, A., 'The Sovereignty of Parliament'; both contained in Jowell, J. and Oliver, D. (eds), *The Changing Constitution* (6th edn). (Oxford: Oxford University Press, 2007).

! Don't be tempted to . . .

- Write an answer that is entirely or almost entirely focused upon the *Factortame* case and omits discussion of any other cases;
- Write about the application of EU law within domestic law more generally;
- Discuss the impact of the European Convention on Human Rights on domestic law.

Question 8

Critically evaluate the role played by the key EU institutions in the making and enforcement of EU law.

Answer plan

- → Explain the roles of the Council of Ministers and the European Council, highlighting their different roles and the role of the Council of Ministers within the legislative process.
- → Explain the role of the Commission, particularly in formulating legislative proposals and the enforcement of EU law.
- → Explain the limited role of the European Parliament within the legislative process.
- → Explain the major functions of the European Court of Justice, distinguishing its judicial and supervisory roles.
- → Conclude upon the relative importance of the major institutions as law-makers and enforcers.

Diagram plan

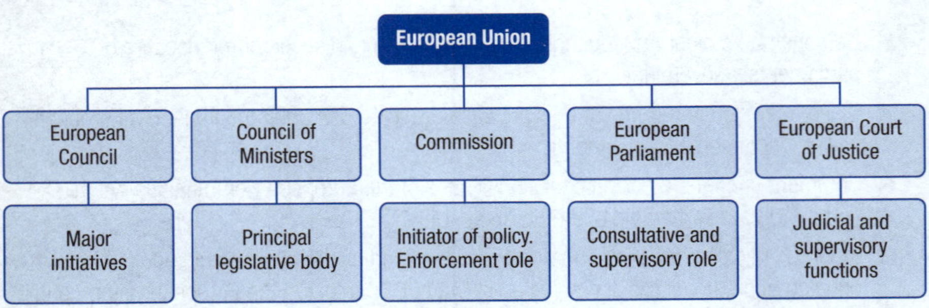

A printable version of this diagram plan is available from www.pearsoned.co.uk/lawexpressqa

Answer

[1]The question is rather straightforward, simply asking you to explain the main functions of the key EU institutions and to comment on their roles within the law-making and enforcement process. You need to ensure that you cover the five major institutions and do this for each of them.

[2]You should refer to the overlap in roles of the European Council and Council of Ministers. Although the former has no continuous presence, the latter performs the same functions on a more regular basis.

[3]It is imperative that you emphasise the role of the Council of Ministers as the supreme legislative power within the EU. This relates back directly to the question which asks you to comment upon the role of the institutions in law-making and enforcement.

[4]This is an important point to make, as although the Commission is not the supreme law-maker within the EU, it plays a highly influential role in the legislative process through the legislative proposals which it makes. In this sense it has a direct role in the shaping of EU law.

[5]Ensure that you do not overlook the enforcement role of the Commission. It is important that you explain its functions in the enforcement of EU law.

There are five major institutions involved in the making and enforcement of EU law.[1] The European Council comprises the heads of governments of member states and meets twice yearly. It has the same powers as the Council of Ministers which meets on a more regular ongoing basis and is discussed below.[2] The European Council's twice yearly meetings take the form of summits, at which decisions of a hugely significant nature will often be taken. Although the European Council does not meet very often, member state governments are represented on a regular basis through the Council of Ministers.

The Council of Ministers is the most powerful legislative body within the EU.[3] It comprises of ministers from all EU member states, although its exact membership varies with the subject matter which is under discussion at any given time. For example, if the Council was holding a meeting concerning financial matters, the finance ministers of member states would attend. If environmental issues were on the table, it would be environment ministers. The member states take it in turn to hold the presidency of the Council which rotates every six months. As already stated, the Council of Ministers is the most powerful legislative body within the EU. Legislation on all important matters will be made within this forum. The Council has three methods of taking decisions depending on the particular issue under discussion. Some decisions must be taken unanimously, others by a simple majority and some require a qualified majority.

The European Commission is the key protagonist in the development of EU policy proposals. Each member state nominates one commissioner, although commissioners do not represent the interests of their home states but rather the interests of the EU as a whole. To some extent the Commission might be described as the closest thing to an executive body within the EU. Each commissioner is assigned an area of responsibility, for example agriculture or trade. It draws up the EU budget, negotiates external agreements and the accession of new states, and is the principal initiator of new legislative proposals, which all begin with the Commission. Although the Council of Ministers is the principal legislative body, the proposals upon which it votes are heavily shaped by the Commission from which they originate.[4] Aside from its role in the formulation of policy, the Commission is endowed with important responsibilities for enforcing EU law.[5] It investigates alleged breaches of the law by member states and is empowered to take enforcement actions against them to the European Court of Justice if it deems them to have not complied with their obligations under EU law. This power has been exercised by the Commission on a considerable number of occasions.

The European Parliament is the only democratically elected of the EU institutions with elections being held in all member states every five years. Unlike the situation in respect of domestic parliaments, the European Parliament has very limited legislative powers. It cannot accurately be called a legislative body, but rather a consultative and supervisory body within the EU law-making process.[6] Over time the Parliament has been afforded greater input within the legislative process, but its role within this process remains largely consultative. The Parliament must be consulted on legislative proposals. The Single European Act enhanced its role in this respect. However, it is not afforded a direct say in respect of the adoption of new legal measures. The Parliament can make amendments to legislative proposals and is able to delay the passage of new measures, but it is not capable of blocking the introduction of new legislation *per se*. This is far removed from the situation in domestic law where parliaments can in theory block legislative proposals with ease. Despite its restricted role within the legislative process, the European Parliament performs a vital supervisory function. It has important powers over the EU budget, retaining the final say on non-obligatory expenditure. It also appoints an ombudsman who investigates cases of maladministration by EU institutions and reports to the Parliament. Perhaps the most critical power enjoyed by the Parliament is its ability to remove the Commission. This theoretically very important power, however, is undermined by the fact that the Parliament may only remove the Commission as a whole, not individual commissioners. Although never exercised, it was arguably indirectly influential in 1999 when the Commission resigned en masse in the midst of a series of scandals.

[6]This is the key point to make about the functions of the European Parliament. You need to explain that it only has a limited role within the law-making process, but at the same time it does enjoy key supervisory powers over the Commission and EU budget.

No discussion of the major EU institutions would be complete without coverage of the European Court of Justice (ECJ). This is the principal court of the EU, although it has been assisted by a court of First Instance since 1986 to ease its heavy workload. The European Court of Justice performs both a judicial and supervisory role in the interpretation and application of EU law.[7] In its judicial role the European Court of Justice hears disputes between member states or between member states and the Commission and adjudicates upon their compliance with their obligations under European law. An example of a contentious case heard by the ECJ can be found in the dispute between the UK and France over France's ban on the sale of British beef in the aftermath of the outbreak of BSE.[8] In **Commission of the European Communities *v* France** (2001) (Unreported), the ECJ ruled that the French ban contravened EU law. The ECJ also performs a supervisory role by making preliminary rulings under Article 234 of the European Community Treaty on matters referred to it by member state courts. This occurs when a national court is uncertain as to the appropriate scope or application of EU law in a given situation. The national court may refer the matter to the European Court of Justice for a preliminary ruling in response to the national court's request. Preliminary rulings were obtained by UK courts in cases such as **HP Bulmer Ltd *v* J Bollinger SA (No. 2)** [1974] Ch 401, and **Marshall *v* Southampton and South West Hampshire Area Health Authority** [1986] QB 401.

[7]You need to distinguish these two functions of the European Court of Justice: it is easy to forget that it performs a supervisory function in relation to Article 234 references as well as the more traditional judicial role which it exercises.

[8]You can effectively reinforce your point by citing examples of both contentious cases and Article 234 references to have been heard by the court, while at the same point showing off clear awareness of legal developments under EU law.

All of the major institutions play an important role within either the law-making or enforcement process, although clearly some are more significant than others.[9] The Council of Ministers undoubtedly plays the most important role within the legislative process, although the Commission is responsible for the initiation of legislative proposals, the Parliament has a consultative function in this process and the European Council is directly involved in major legislative initiatives. The Commission plays a key role within the enforcement of EU law through its power to take member states to the European Court of Justice, which is the ultimate arbiter on their compliance with, and the correct application of, EU law.

[9]The conclusion should relate back to the question by summarising the relative importance of the key institutions within the law-making and enforcement process.

✓ Make your answer stand out

- Ensure that you highlight what you consider to be the key functions(s) of each of the key institutions.
- Provide relevant examples of both contentious cases and Article 234 (now Article 267) references to have been heard by the European Court of Justice.

! Don't be tempted to . . .

- Provide detailed technical information on each of the institutions, such as their location;
- Explain the main functions of the institutions without commenting upon their roles within the legislative and law enforcement process;
- Confuse the EU institutions with the machinery of the European Convention on Human Rights.

2 Judicial precedent

How this topic may come up in exams

There are relatively few ways in which understanding of judicial precedent is assessed. You might be asked to generally explain how the system of binding judicial precedent operates. You may be asked to demonstrate an understanding of the ways in which judges are able to avoid the application of precedent, or the particular position of the Supreme Court or the Court of Appeal with respect to the extent to which they are bound by precedent and the circumstances in which they may depart from it. Questions which ask you to evaluate the relative merits of binding judicial precedent are also popular.

Attack the question

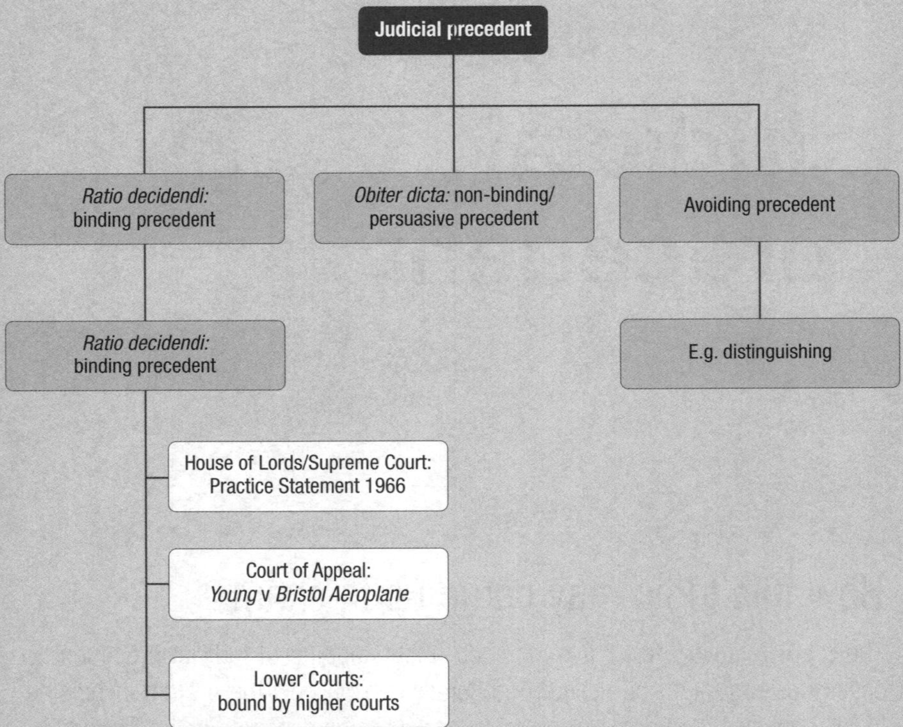

A printable version of this diagram plan is available from www.pearsoned.co.uk/lawexpressqa

Question 1

Discuss the extent to which the Court of Appeal is able to depart from its own previous decisions and comment upon whether it should enjoy the same position as the Supreme Court.

Answer plan

- ➜ Explain briefly the system of binding precedent.
- ➜ Explain briefly the importance of the court hierarchy, and the place of the Court of Appeal within this hierarchy.
- ➜ Illustrate the circumstances in which the Court of Appeal is able to depart from its own previous decisions.
- ➜ Contrast the position of the Court of Appeal to that of the Supreme Court and assess whether the Court of Appeal should be similarly unbound by any of its previous decisions.

Diagram plan

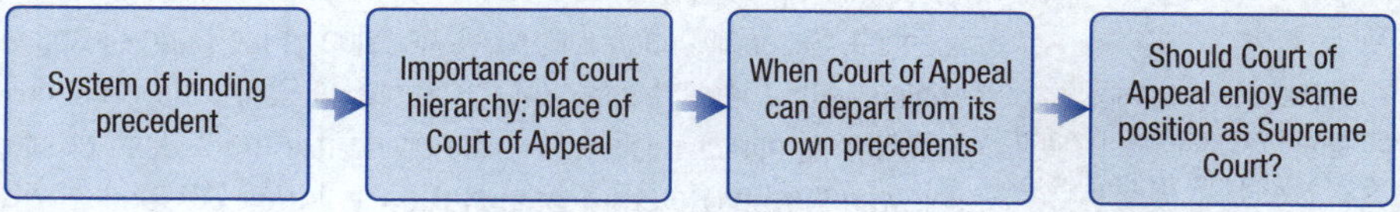

A printable version of this diagram plan is available from www.pearsoned.co.uk/lawexpressqa

Answer

The system of judicial precedent requires courts to follow decisions reached in previous cases sharing the same material facts – those facts of central importance to the decision reached – to the cases before them. It is based on the maxim of '*stare decisis*', meaning 'let the decision stand' and its rationale lies essentially in treating like cases alike.[1] It is important to distinguish between *ratio decidendi* and *obiter dicta*. The *ratio decidendi* is that part of a judgment containing the legal principle underlying the decision reached in a case; the reason for the decision. This part of the judgment forms binding precedent for future cases. The term *obiter dicta* refers to any part of a judgment not forming the *ratio decidendi*, including dissenting judgments and hypothetical scenarios. While non-binding, *obiter dicta* may form persuasive precedent in later cases.

[1]Although the question asks specifically about the ability of the Court of Appeal to depart from its own previous decisions, it is useful to explain briefly what judicial precedent is by way of your introduction. You should distinguish *ratio decidendi* and *obiter dicta* as only the former provide binding precedent.

The court hierarchy is central to the operation of binding precedent. Decisions of higher courts are binding upon those below them in the hierarchy. Thus, decisions of the Supreme Court are binding upon the Court of Appeal. The Court of Appeal's decisions bind those courts below it. However, whereas the Supreme Court need not follow its own previous decisions since Lord Gardiner's 1966 Practice Statement, generally the Court of Appeal is obliged to follow its own previous decisions.[2]

The general rule that the Court of Appeal's previous decisions bind it was re-stated in the case of **Young *v* Bristol Aeroplane** [1944] KB 718.[3] However, Lord Greene MR set out three exceptions where the Court of Appeal (CA) could depart from its own previous decisions. Firstly, when two previous conflicting decisions of the CA existed, it could choose which to follow and disregard the other. Such a situation arose in *Tiverton Estates Ltd* v *Wearwell Ltd [1974]*, a case concerning the interpretation of a provision of the Law of Property Act 1925. This exception is uncontroversial as clearly it is impossible to follow two conflicting decisions, and cannot be regarded as a meaningful exception. Secondly, when a previous decision of the Court of Appeal conflicts with a later decision of the Supreme Court, the CA should not follow its earlier decision. A case giving rise to this kind of situation was **Family Housing Association *v* Jones** [1990] 1 All ER, where an earlier Court of Appeal decision concerning the distinction between a licence and tenancy had been superseded by more recent House of Lords (now Supreme Court) decisions. Likewise, this cannot be regarded as a notable exception to the general rule as decisions of the Court of Appeal are inferior to those of the Supreme Court anyway. Finally, the Court of Appeal does not have to follow its own previous decisions which have been made *per incuriam*, meaning 'through want of care', for example when taken in ignorance of some relevant legal authority. An example of a case where such a situation arose is **Bonalumi *v* Home Secretary** [1985] QB 675.[4]

There are now arguably additional situations in which the Court of Appeal is not bound by its own previous decisions.[5] The European Court of Justice is now firmly ensconced at the top of the court hierarchy when matters of European law are involved and when a previous decision conflicts with a provision of EU law, the CA must ignore its earlier decision in deference to the European provision. Section 2 of the Human Rights Act 1998 requires domestic courts

[2]Before launching into discussion of the circumstances in which the Court of Appeal is not required to follow its own previous decisions, it is worthwhile briefly stating the importance of the court hierarchy to the operation of binding precedent and the position of the Court of Appeal within that hierarchy, and particularly that whereas the Court of Appeal is generally bound to follow its own previous decisions, the Supreme Court is not.

[3]It is absolutely essential that you refer to *Young* v *Bristol Aeroplane* as this is the major case.

[4]You should avoid simply listing the exceptions. Try and provide case law examples in which they have been applied. The question asks you to 'discuss' the circumstances in which the Court of Appeal may depart from its own previous decisions, so you should try and comment on their significance or the extent to which they increase the flexibility afforded the Court of Appeal.

[5]You should make sure your answer takes account of post-*Bristol Aeroplane* developments by referring to the obvious impact of European law and possible influence of the Human Rights Act on the ability of the Court of Appeal to depart from its own previous decisions.

to take account of the jurisprudence of the European Court of Human Rights. It does not make decisions of the Strasbourg institutions binding upon domestic courts, but they are likely over time to impact upon domestic judicial decision-making on matters which give rise to issues under the Human Rights Act. It was also held in **R (Kadhim) *v* Brent Housing Benefit Review Board** [2001] QB 955 that the Civil Division is not bound by its own previous decisions where an earlier Court of Appeal assumed a proposition of law to exist which was not subject to consideration by that court.

Although the exceptions set out in **Young *v* Bristol Aeroplane** [1944] KB 718, apply to both Civil and Criminal Divisions of the Court of Appeal, a more flexible approach is taken to the application of its own previous precedents by the Criminal Division, due to the fact that individual liberty is often at stake in criminal cases.[6] The Criminal Division stated clearly in **R *v* Spencer** [1985] 1 All ER 673, that it need not adhere to past precedent as rigidly as the Civil Division and would depart from its own decisions when an individual's liberty is at stake. This more flexible approach is likely to be strengthened as a result of the incorporation of the ECHR into domestic law, which enshrines the right to liberty in Article 5. At the same time, it has increased uncertainty in the criminal law.

[6]The Criminal Division of the Court of Appeal enjoys greater flexibility to depart from its past decisions than the Civil Division. You should demonstrate that you are aware of this.

Although there is some scope for the Court of Appeal to depart from its own previous decisions, this is relatively limited when its position is contrasted to that of the Supreme Court. The result of the **1966 Practice Statement** is that the Supreme Court is free to depart from its own previous decisions when it considers it appropriate to do so. There have been strong suggestions that the Court of Appeal should enjoy similar flexibility. Lord Denning, in particular, led a campaign to assert the same power for the CA, but the then House of Lords maintained in cases such as **Davis *v* Johnson** [1978] 2 WLR 553, that the Court of Appeal remained generally bound by its own previous decisions.[7] An objection to conceding such power to the Court of Appeal is that it may place it on a par with the Supreme Court, undermining the latter's status as the superior court in the country, or weaken the system of binding precedent. However, a strong argument for extending the same freedom to the Court of Appeal lies in the fact that in most cases, the CA is the final appeal court, with very few cases reaching the Supreme Court. Given that a major reason put forward in the **1966 Practice Statement** for allowing the then House

[7]The question also asks you to consider whether the Court of Appeal should enjoy the same freedom to avoid past precedent as the Supreme Court. You should provide some context to this debate.

[8]Conclude by evaluating the arguments concerning whether the Court of Appeal should have the same freedom as the Supreme Court and answering the question directly: should it? Why/why not?

of Lords to depart from its own precedent was that too rigid adherence to precedent could lead to injustice, it is arguably sensible to apply the same logic in extending this flexibility to the Court of Appeal given that few cases heard by it will have an opportunity to be heard in the Supreme Court. Furthermore, the Supreme Court's status within the court hierarchy would remain unaffected as its decisions would remain binding on the Court of Appeal and an ultimate right of appeal would lie to the Supreme Court.[8]

✓ Make your answer stand out

- Use case law examples where appropriate of situations in which the Court of Appeal has applied the exceptions to the rule obliging it to follow its own previous decisions.
- Point out the greater flexibility exercised by the Criminal Division of the Court of Appeal when considering whether to follow its own decisions.
- Put forward clear arguments as to whether the Court of Appeal should have the same freedom to depart from its previous decisions as the Supreme Court.

! Don't be tempted to . . .

- Simply explain the exceptions set out in *Young* v *Bristol Aeroplane*;
- Write an essay which is largely concerned with the court hierarchy and the Court of Appeal's place within this.

Question 2

Assess the extent to which judges are able to avoid applying precedent to cases before them.

Answer plan

- Briefly explain the doctrine of judicial precedent and the importance of the court hierarchy to its operation.
- Explain when the Supreme Court and the Court of Appeal may depart from their own previous decisions.
- Explain the concept of distinguishing and how it empowers judges to avoid precedents.
- Explain other judicial techniques for avoiding unwelcome precedents.
- Comment upon the extent to which the system of judicial precedent operates flexibly.

Diagram plan

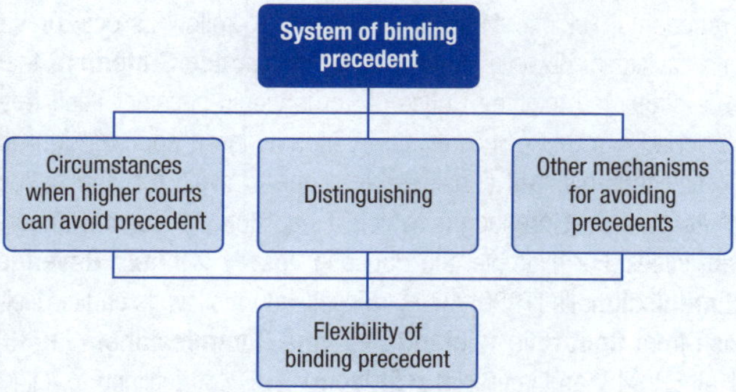

A printable version of this diagram plan is available from www.pearsoned.co.uk/lawexpressqa

Answer

Under the system of judicial precedent, courts are ordinarily obliged to follow the decisions reached in previous cases sharing the same material facts to those of the cases before them. The hierarchy of the courts is central to its operation. Courts are bound by previous decisions of higher courts within the court hierarchy, but not lower courts. While the Supreme Court is not obliged to follow its own previous decisions, the Court of Appeal and High Court are theoretically bound by their own previous decisions subject to a number of recognised exceptions. The lower courts, while not bound by their own decisions, are bound by the decisions of the higher courts. Although a common criticism of the doctrine of judicial precedent is that it is rigid, there are various circumstances in which courts are able to avoid giving effect to precedent.[1]

[1]The introductory paragraph of the answer should briefly show that you understand what judicial precedent is, and how the court hierarchy is fundamental to its operation. This will lead nicely into the discussion to follow of the ability of the higher courts to avoid the application of precedent.

The higher courts enjoy special powers to avoid applying their own previous precedents.[2] The highest domestic court, the Supreme Court, enjoys the strongest powers to avoid being bound by past precedents. Prior to **1966**, it was bound to follow its own previous decisions. However, Lord Gardiner's **Practice Statement** that year stipulated that the House of Lords would consider itself free to depart from its own previous rulings 'when it appears right to do so', thus giving it considerable scope to avoid the application of its own past precedent, which it has done in several important cases. For example, the House in **Vestey *v* Inland Revenue Commissioners** [1980] AC 1148 declined to follow its earlier decision from **Congreve *v* Inland Revenue Commissioners** [1948] 1 All ER 948, and later in **R *v* Shivpuri** [1987] it declined to follow a previous decision on a matter of criminal law for the first time. In another prominent case, **Murphy *v* Brentwood DC** [1990] 3 WLR 414, the House departed from its earlier ruling on the liability of local authorities for the inspection of building foundations, **Anns *v* Merton LBC** [1978] AC 728.[3]

[2]A significant part of the answer should be focused upon the higher courts because of the special position which they enjoy in terms of their ability to avoid the application of precedent.

[3]There are several examples of cases which could be cited as examples of the House of Lords (now the Supreme Court) departing from its own previous decisions. Those included here are just some possible examples that might be used.

Although in theory the Court of Appeal is generally bound to follow its own previous decisions, there are such significant exceptions to this rule as to give it considerable ability to avoid having to apply them. In **Young *v* Bristol Aeroplane** [1944] KB 718, Lord Greene set out three situations where the court would be entitled to depart from its own previous decisions. Firstly, when there are two previous conflicting decisions of the Court of Appeal, the court can choose which of these decisions to follow and disregard the other. The court found itself in this position in **Tiverton Estates Ltd *v* Wearwell Ltd** [1974] 2 WLR 176. Secondly, when a previous decision of the Court of Appeal conflicts with a later decision of the Supreme Court, the CA should not follow its earlier decision in deference to the superior status of the Supreme Court. A case giving rise to this kind of situation was **Family Housing Association *v* Jones** [1990] 1 All ER 385. Finally, the Court of Appeal does not have to follow one of its own previous decisions when that decision had been made *per incuriam*, meaning the decision had been taken in ignorance of some relevant legal authority. An example of a case where such a situation arose is **Bonalumi *v* Secretary of State for the Home Department** [1985] QB 675.[4]

[4]You are unlikely to have time to discuss further most of the case examples you cite in your answer. The main point is that you show that you are aware of actual scenarios when precedent has not been followed, and the grounds for this.

In addition to the exceptions set out in **Young *v* Bristol Aeroplane**, as a consequence of the supremacy of EU law, when a previous Court of Appeal decision conflicts with a provision of EU law, the Court will not follow its own precedent. The Civil Division is not constrained by an earlier decision where the court assumed a proposition of law to exist which was not subject to consideration by the court, as a result of **R (Kadhim) *v* Brent Housing Benefit Review Board** [2001] QB 955. Furthermore, it is important to note that the Criminal Division of the Court of Appeal takes a more flexible approach to the application of past precedents due to the fact that individual liberty is often at stake in criminal cases. As a result, it feels less restrained by its own precedents than the Civil Division. A clear statement to this effect was given in the case of **R *v* Spencer** [1985]. The divisional courts enjoy the freedom to depart from their own previous decisions in the same circumstances as the Court of Appeal (**Police Authority for Huddersfield *v* Watson** [1947] 1 KB 842).

To avoid the application of precedent more generally, courts can make use of the concept of distinguishing. Distinguishing is a useful concept which potentially enables any court within the hierarchy to avoid the application of an unwelcome precedent. It usually involves a court finding that the material facts of a past decision and the present case are not sufficiently alike for the earlier decision to serve as a precedent in the present case. Any court can theoretically distinguish a decision of any other court, even if that court is higher in the hierarchy, if it can find such a distinction. For example, in **R *v* Secretary of State for the Environment, *ex parte* Ostler** [1977] QB 122, the Court of Appeal distinguished the earlier House of Lords decision from **Anisminic Ltd *v* The Foreign Compensation Commission** [1969] 2 AC 147. In this sense, it is the most useful tool open to the courts in general to avoid the application of precedent.[5] A court may also avoid a precedent by distinguishing an earlier decision on either a point of law or the issue to be addressed by the court, effectively proclaiming that these are not sufficiently alike in the earlier and present cases.

[5]This is a crucial point. Whereas the higher courts enjoy specific rules enabling them to avoid precedent, the concept of distinguishing is one that can be invoked by any court to avoid a decision of any court.

There are also other methods which can be employed by the courts to avoid applying precedent.[6] A court may interpret a past decision in such a way as to give it a narrow *ratio decidendi* that cannot be applied to the case before it. It may also determine that there is no clear *ratio decidendi* in the earlier case, which will be a sustainable argument in a substantial number of cases given that decisions are based upon judgments given by a number of judges who invariably place emphasis on different points in their reasoning. A court can also avoid applying an unwelcome precedent if it considers it to have been superseded by more recent precedents, to have been decided *per incuriam*, or is inconsistent with a more recent deicison of a higher court which can be regarded as having implicitly overruled it.

[6]You are unlikely to have sufficient time to discuss these in any detail, but should be aware of their relevance. If you are able to provide examples of any of these mechanisms being utilised by the courts you will receive credit.

Judicial precedent is not rigid. There are various circumstances in which particular courts may avoid binding precedent and more generally there exist tools which can be utilised by courts in general to depart from precedent when they deem it appropriate to do so.[7]

[7]This conclusion flows logically from the preceding explanation of the circumstances in which courts can avoid the application of precedent. It shows an understanding of the implications of the various matters discussed in the essay as opposed to a simplified awareness of the rules governing the application of precedent lacking in any critical insight.

✓ Make your answer stand out

- Provide relevant examples from case law of situations in which courts have departed from precedent to reinforce the points you make in your answer.
- Emphasise the extent to which the various means which can be employed by courts to avoid the application of precedent make it a flexible doctrine.
- Explain clearly that the concept of distinguishing gives all courts considerable ability to avoid precedent.
- For a more sophisticated understanding of the application and avoidance of judicial precedent, read Duxbury, N., *The Nature and Authority of Precedent* (Cambridge: Cambridge University Press, 2008) and make reference to some of his arguments.

! Don't be tempted to . . .

- Focus your answer only on general tools such as distinguishing as means of avoiding precedents, omitting consideration of the privileged position of the higher courts with respect to their ability to depart from previous precedent;
- Focus only on the position of the Supreme Court and Court of Appeal in avoiding precedent, as lower courts are able to avoid precedent also as discussion of distinguishing will demonstrate.

Question 3

Evaluate the relative merits and drawbacks of the system of binding precedent.

Answer plan

→ Briefly explain the doctrine of binding precedent.

→ Outline and discuss, with examples, the purported advantages of the system of binding precedent.

→ Outline and discuss, with examples, the purported disadvantages of the system of binding precedent.

→ Explain whether you consider the system of binding precedent to be desirable or not.

Diagram plan

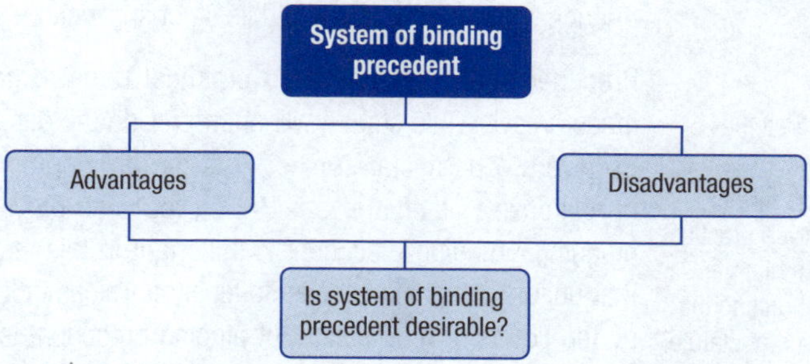

A printable version of this diagram plan is available from www.pearsoned.co.uk/lawexpressqa

Answer

The system of binding precedent is a cornerstone of the English legal system. Courts are required to follow previous decisions sharing the same material facts. The hierarchy of the courts is central to the operation of judicial precedent, courts being bound by decisions of higher courts.[1] Although the doctrine of binding precedent is fundamental to the English legal system, it is not common to all legal systems. While operating in jurisdictions with a common law tradition – such as the US and former British colonies – it is alien to civil law jurisdictions, such as those comprising continental Europe where previous judicial decisions enjoy merely persuasive authority.[2]

Binding precedent is said to produce consistency. As courts are required to follow previous decisions from cases sharing similar material facts, there ought to be consistent outcomes in such cases. This promotes a sense of formal and substantive justice, similar cases resulting in similar outcomes. Binding precedent is also said to create certainty in judicial decisions. As past decisions are followed, potential parties can anticipate the likely outcome of their own cases. This produces another advantage, of time-saving. Time is saved for would be parties, lawyers and judges. Greater predictability of decisions means that there is less likelihood of actions being pursued by parties which past precedent indicates will probably be unsuccessful. Judicial decision-making in individual cases is also theoretically quickened by the need to simply follow past precedent.[3] However, as will be seen, critics of binding precedent would dispute the extent to which it delivers consistency and certainty in practice as a consequence of the various means through which judges can avoid its strict application.

Precedent generates detailed practical rules to govern specific areas of law. While statute will often provide the general framework to govern a particular subject, it is the development of case law in response to factual events that gives such provisions practical meaning.[4] Binding precedent is important in this respect, ensuring that uniform meaning is given to legal provisions in their application by the courts. A final benefit of binding precedent is said to be its flexibility. The higher courts can quickly change the law in response to social changes whereas Parliament must go through lengthy procedures to enact new legislation. A new precedent can be

[1] The question asks you specifically to evaluate the advantages and disadvantages of binding precedent so a detailed explanation of what it entails is not necessary. You will not have the time for this if you are to answer the question asked well.

[2] Here a little context is provided to the answer, which shows wider understanding of the subject area. Binding precedent is not universally recognised within legal systems – in fact, far from it – and this strengthens the case for probing its value.

[3] The most compelling arguments advanced in favour of binding precedent are considered in this paragraph. It makes sense to take them together here as they all relate to one another; consistency and certainty ought to lead to the efficiency of time-saving.

[4] This point concerns the relationship between statute and case law. The former is developed and given practical meaning through the latter. Precedent contributes to the uniform application of statute.

established which has the effect of changing the law immediately, instead of having to wait for Parliament to have the opportunity to do so. There are several mechanisms which courts can use to avoid precedent when it is felt that this is desirable either in the interests of justice or to remedy bad law. The Supreme Court may depart from its own precedent when it is felt right to do so, the Court of Appeal and Divisional Courts are able to depart from their own past precedents in certain specified circumstances, and courts in general are able to use the devices of reversing, overruling and distinguishing to avoid precedents. Thus, rigid adherence to the doctrine can be avoided when it may produce an undesirable outcome, although it may also call into question binding precedent's perceived advantages of certainty and consistency.[5]

[5]A great deal can be said about the flexibility with which binding precedent operates. For example, there are various means which can be employed by judges to avoid the application of precedent. However, to discuss this in any detail would constitute a separate essay in itself.

Several criticisms have been made of the system of binding precedent. Some are reverse arguments of some of its alleged benefits. Its certainty and consistency are disputed. Critics argue that the sheer complexity and volume of case law mean that certainty and consistency cannot be guaranteed. Judges cannot be expected to be aware of all relevant past decisions. Furthermore, the mechanisms by which judges are able to avoid the application of precedent also undermine its certainty. Through the process of distinguishing cases, judges may avoid precedents by making illogical distinctions between cases actually sharing very similar material facts. Critics of binding precedent therefore assert that rather than being time-saving, it is actually a time-consuming device which requires judges to spend lengthy periods of time consulting previous judicial decisions, without necessarily resulting in predictable results.[6]

[6]This paragraph effectively relates back to the first paragraph on the purported advantages of binding precedent. It shows how some of its benefits can also serve as some of its drawbacks and evidences an ability to relate these arguments to one another.

It is often maintained that binding precedent is a rigid system which allows decisions that are either unjust or bad law to perpetuate judicial decision-making for lengthy periods of time. While any claim of rigidity may seem to purport to contradict the apparent flexibility of the system of binding precedent, the two arguments are not mutually exclusive. Although courts may avoid precedent in certain circumstances, sometimes a bad precedent will endure for a long period if an opportunity does not present itself for a higher court to overrule it or it becomes so firmly entrenched in the law. An example can be found with the law on rape within marriage, which only became regarded as unlawful in 1991.[7]

[7]*R* v *R* [1991]. More could be said about this, but there is not really time when answering a question of this nature in an examination setting to do more than allude to such examples. However, simple references to legal developments such as this evidence that you are aware of some of the problems experienced as a result of the operation of binding precedent in practice.

Other criticisms of binding precedent are that it represents judicial law-making, that it results in the law being changed retrospectively, and that it does not involve any judicial consideration of the wider societal effects of particular decisions. The question of whether judges 'make law' is beyond the scope of this essay, although it is arguably preferable that if judges are to 'make law' there is consistency in the rulings which they hand down. The creation of a new precedent applying to events which occurred before it was laid down may appear unjust. Theoretically, however, the new decision has the effect of rendering old precedents invalid, meaning that they never truly represented correct law. Admittedly, this is of little comfort to the individual who has channelled his conduct based on the law as established in previous decisions. Critics of binding precedent would argue that judges are not best suited to consider the wider effects of their ruling, which is a role that properly lies with the democratically elected and accountable Parliament.

Evaluating whether the system of binding precedent is desirable is not simply a case of counting its advantages and disadvantages.[8] The logic for a system of binding precedent is irrefutable. Like cases should be treated alike and predictability of outcomes ought to promote efficiency within the legal system. The flexibility of the system protects against over rigid adherence to precedent. For these reasons, binding precedent can be seen as a desirable practice. At the same time, it is not a perfect doctrine. Some of its advantages can also be its drawbacks. The ability of judges to avoid precedent mean that consistency and certainty cannot always be assured. Bad precedents may also perpetuate themselves for lengthy periods if courts do not have the opportunity to correct them. However, these problems are unavoidable and should not detract from what is essentially a useful feature of the legal system.[9]

[8] You are likely to find in some textbooks that there is an extensive list of purported disadvantages to binding precedent. To answer the question effectively you will need to focus on what you consider to be the most persuasive arguments. These criticisms of binding precedent are, arguably, not as persuasive as some of those considered earlier and are summarised towards the end of the answer for the sake of thoroughness.

[9] This is a balanced conclusion which reflects the arguments considered within the answer. Your conclusion needs to naturally follow from the content of the essay. As binding precedent is shown to enjoy logical benefits while potentially suffering from certain drawbacks, this would be an appropriate conclusion to draw.

✓ Make your answer stand out

- Provide some context to your answer by explaining that binding precedent is a practice restricted to common law systems, thus showing that it is not an unquestioned feature of legal systems in general.
- Show how some of the various advantages or disadvantages of binding precedent are related to another and not a series of mutually exclusive merits or drawbacks.
- Explain that some of the strengths of binding precedent also have the potential to operate as its weaknesses.

! Don't be tempted to . . .

- Simply note the advantages and disadvantages of binding precedent without any further explanation;
- Refer to the various advantages and disadvantages of binding precedent as issues independent of each other as they are very often related.

3

Statutory interpretation

How this topic may come up in exams

Examination questions on statutory interpretation will invariably require you to demonstrate an understanding of the methods employed by judges to interpret statutes. You should be able to evaluate the merits of the main rules of interpretation used by judges, the intrinsic and extrinsic aids which they may use, and rules of language and presumptions applicable to the process of statutory interpretation. Narrower popular questions might ask you to consider the growth of purposive approaches to interpretation or the value of *Hansard* as an extrinsic aid to interpretation. Be prepared also for questions which require you to consider the role of judges in law-making more generally, combining issues of statutory interpretation and judicial precedent.

Attack the question

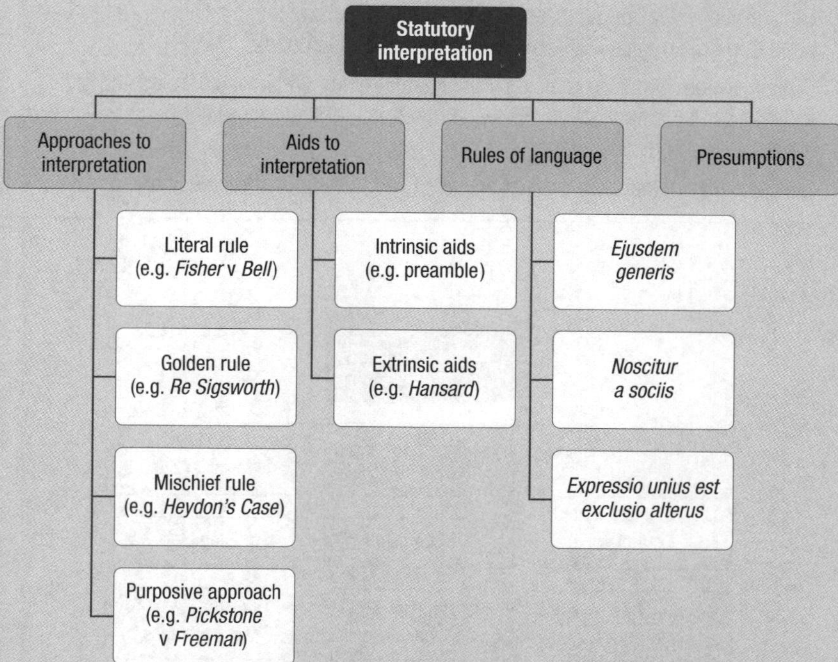

A printable version of this diagram plan is available from www.pearsoned.co.uk/lawexpressqa

Question 1

Discuss the three traditional rules of statutory interpretation used by the courts and their relative merits.

Answer plan

- Explain briefly why judges need to interpret statutes and that traditionally there have been three main rules of interpretation applied by the courts.
- Explain, in turn, what is entailed by the literal, golden and mischief rules and give examples of their application. For each rule briefly discuss its major perceived advantages and disadvantages.
- Conclude on whether you consider any one rule to be superior to the others, and if so, why.

Diagram plan

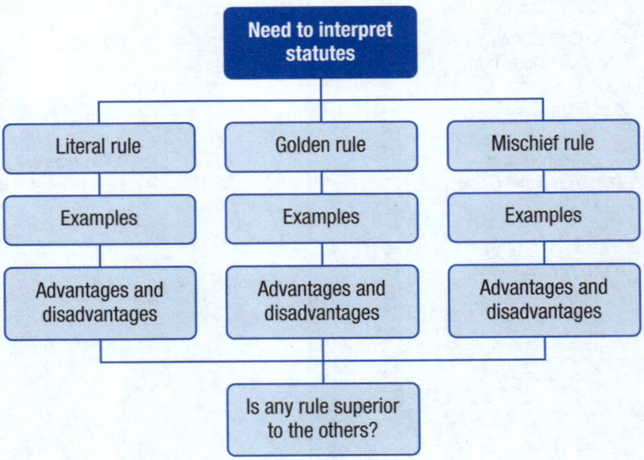

A printable version of this diagram plan is available from www.pearsoned.co.uk/lawexpressqa

Answer

[1]It is useful to begin by explaining why judges are required to interpret statutes. This provides context to the discussion of the traditional rules of statutory interpretation.

[2]The question asks you to explain the traditional rules of statutory interpretation used by the courts. This requires that you discuss the three traditional rules of interpretation – literal, golden and mischief – and this should form the focus of your answer. You are not asked about the newer, purposive approach or rules of language and aids to interpretation, so you do not need to enter into discussion of these.

[3]Use case law examples throughout to illustrate the rules in operation. This demonstrates a sound understanding of what the rules entail and how they are applied in practice, and the citation of examples can also help to illustrate the weaknesses or strengths of the different rules.

[4]The question asks that you explain the relative advantages and disadvantages of the rules, so ensure that you are able to highlight at least one advantage and disadvantage of each rule.

The judiciary's role is to apply laws made by Parliament. However, this is not always a straightforward task. Poor drafting of statutes may create ambiguity which the courts will need to resolve. Furthermore, language is naturally imprecise on occasion. Words may have more than one meaning and a court may need to impose one. It is not always possible to have every future eventuality in mind when drafting a statute. Sometimes draftsmen deliberately leave ambiguity in provisions in order to enable courts to tailor them to future situations that cannot yet be anticipated.[1]

Traditionally, the courts have relied on three main approaches to interpret statutes: the literal, golden and mischief rules.[2] A court may follow any approach and will not necessarily explain which it is using or why.

The literal rule requires that words are given their ordinary, grammatical meaning, even if this produces an absurd outcome. An example of the literal rule in operation is found in the case of **Fisher *v* Bell** [1960] 3 All ER 731. A shopkeeper was charged under the Restriction of Offensive Weapons Act 1959 with offering for sale a prohibited knife. He was acquitted as under contract law the display of an item did not constitute an offer for sale but an invitation to treat, even though the Act had been created to restrict the sale of such items. Similarly, in **Whiteley *v* Chappell** (1868) LR 4 QB 147, a person charged with 'impersonating any person entitled to vote' at an election was acquitted because the person impersonated was deceased, and thus not entitled to vote. These cases illustrate the major criticism of the literal rule, that its emphasis on adherence to the literal interpretation of statutes results in absurd outcomes not intended by Parliament.[3] Furthermore, words cannot be understood literally, but only in the wider context within which they are used as they often carry multiple meanings. Defenders of the literal rule argue that it respects parliamentary sovereignty by focusing upon the words used by Parliament rather than attempting to second guess its intentions in enacting the relevant provision. Furthermore, by focusing upon the literal meaning of words, the courts have less ability to interfere with the application of legislation. However, words are imprecise tools and courts will continue to need to ascertain the meaning of particular words used by parliament.[4]

The literal interpretation of just one word can yield several different outcomes, giving courts considerable discretion even using this theoretically narrow approach to statutory interpretation.

[5]It is useful to recall that the golden rule is taken as having both a narrow and wider meaning. This evidences understanding.

The golden rule is an extension of the literal rule and was set out by Lord Wensleydale in **Grey *v* Pearson** (1857) 6 HL Cas 61. Essentially the literal meaning of a provision should be applied unless producing absurdity or repugnance. The golden rule is often divided into narrow and wider meanings.[5] The former occurs when two alternative meanings can be applied to a provision, one of which will result in absurdity or repugnance. The court is to apply the meaning which will not have this effect. An example is **Adler *v* George** [1964] 1 All ER 628, where it was an offence to obstruct a member of the armed forces in the vicinity of designated locations. The defendant was actually caught within such a location. A literal interpretation of the provision would acquit the defendant, as he was actually in the place in question rather than its vicinity. This would be absurd given the rationale for the legislative provision. The term 'vicinity', therefore, was taken to extend to the specified place itself. The wider meaning applies when there is only one meaning to the provision which will result in absurdity or repugnance. The court may then substitute an alternative meaning. This occurred in **Re Sigsworth** [1935] Ch 89 where intestacy rules entitled the defendant to inherit the estate of his mother who he had murdered, obviously regarded as a repugnant outcome. An alternative meaning to the relevant provision was substituted so that he could not inherit. The golden rule has the benefit over the literal rule of avoiding absurd results which cannot have been intended by Parliament, by looking at the actual effect of particular interpretations. However, critics of the golden rule argue that there is no agreement on what constitutes absurdity. This may be so to some extent, but it would be difficult to argue with decisions in cases such as **Adler *v* George** and **Re Sigsworth**, where the application of the literal rule would clearly have produced undesirable outcomes.

The mischief rule originates from **Heydon's Case** (1584) 3 Co Rep 7a. The court is directed to ask four questions to ascertain the state of the common law before the enactment of the statutory provision, the mischief in the common law which the statute sought to remedy, the remedy for this mischief provided by Parliament and the true purpose of this remedy. The core aim is to give effect to the purpose underlying the provision. The mischief rule was applied in **Smith *v* Hughes** [1960] 2 All ER 859 where prostitutes were convicted of soliciting in the street under the Sexual Offences Act 1959. Although the statute made it an offence to solicit 'in the street', the prostitutes actually solicited men who were in the street from a window overlooking the street. The court looked towards the 'mischief' the act was intended to remedy – solicitation by prostitutes – and convicted the defendants. The Law Commission in 1969 commented that the mischief rule was a 'rather more satisfactory approach' than the other two established rules.[6] It is arguably more likely to affect the legislative purpose of a statute and, therefore, avoid absurdity. However, it has been suggested that at the time of **Heydon's Case** it was much easier to ascertain the previous law and the statute's purpose due to the much minor role which statute law played. Identifying the purpose of legislation today may not always be so straightforward.

[6]It is often difficult to remember quotations that may be appropriate for citation in an examination answer, but credit is normally given when you are able to do so. The Law Commission's view of the mischief rule is worth remembering and quoting if you are asked to comment on its merits.

Each of the rules of statutory interpretation has its merits and drawbacks. A court may use any of the rules.[7] The literal rule may suit many non-controversial cases, but is arguably badly suited to those where it produces absurd outcomes contrary to the purpose of the statutory provision in question. The golden rule may remedy the shortcomings of the literal rule, but does not really consider the legislative purpose underlying the statute. The mischief rule is perhaps the most satisfactory approach, as it attempts to understand the purpose underlying the provision in question. Indeed, largely as a result of European influences, the courts are increasingly utilising a purposive approach to statutory interpretation which emphasises a provision's legislative purpose when interpreting it. This increasingly important approach is more closely connected to the mischief rule of the traditional approaches to statutory interpretation.[8]

[7]In your conclusion attempt to briefly summarise the relative merits of the different rules and, if you have a view on what is the preferred rule, give it.

[8]The question does not ask you to give consideration to the newer, purposive approach to statutory interpretation. However, it is worth briefly mentioning its increased importance in your conclusion, as it would suggest that of the traditional rules the mischief rule comes closest to this increasingly significant approach to statutory interpretation.

✓ Make your answer stand out

- Use case law examples to illustrate the rules in operation and their relative merits.
- Provide a reasoned opinion on what rule of statutory interpretation is to be preferred.
- Show that you understand the connection between the mischief rule and the purposive approach.
- In considering the reasons why statutory interpretation can be problematic, particularly in an extended essay, you may find it useful to read and refer to Bennion, F.A.R., 'Statute Law: Obscurity and Drafting Parameters', *British Journal of Law and Society*, 1978, v. 5, n. 2, p. 235.

! Don't be tempted to . . .

- Simply state the rules of statutory interpretation without any consideration of their merits;
- Try and cover all of the tools which make up the courts approach to statutory interpretation – rules of language, intrinsic and extrinsic aids to interpretation, presumptions, etc.

Question 2

Explain the intrinsic and extrinsic aids which are available to assist judges to interpret statutes and consider how helpful these are.

Answer plan

→ Briefly explain what intrinsic and extrinsic aids are, and what the difference is between them.

→ Explain the main intrinsic aids available to judges and the extent to which these assist judges to interpret statutes.

→ Explain the main extrinsic aids available to judges and the extent to which these aid judges to interpret statutes, with particular comment upon the usefulness of Hansard in helping judges to ascertain parliament's intention.

→ Conclude by commenting upon the relative importance of intrinsic and extrinsic aids.

Diagram plan

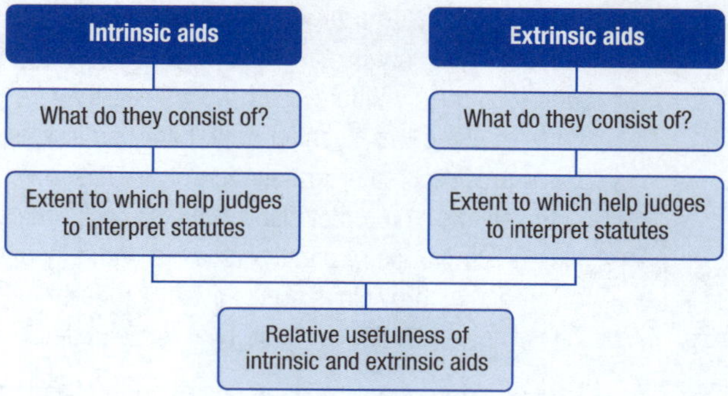

A printable version of this diagram plan is available from www.pearsoned.co.uk/lawexpressqa

Answer

Interpreting statutes can be problematic due to ambiguously worded provisions or the failure of draftsmen to take into account all possible eventualities when drafting them.[1] To assist in interpreting statutes, judges are able to use intrinsic and extrinsic aids. Intrinsic aids are those parts of a statute which might assist in understanding the purpose of its particular provisions. Extrinsic aids are things external to a statute which may assist in understanding its aims.[2]

Some parts of a statute are generally more useful than others in aiding understanding of its provisions. A statute's short title is seldom useful as it is usually simply descriptive. By contrast, its long title may be more useful and may be considered where there is ambiguity within the body of the act. In cases such as **Royal College of Nursing *v* DHSS** [1981] 2 WLR 279 and **R (Quintaville) *v* Secretary of State for Health** [2003] 2 WLR 692, a majority of the House of Lords specifically referred to the relevant statute's long title in seeking to understand the objectives of the legislative provision in question.[3] Other enacting words within the statute may help to resolve ambiguity. Older statutes commonly contained a preamble setting out the general legislative purpose of the act. Preambles can assist in understanding the meaning of a provision where there is ambiguity. However, they tend not to be found in recent statutes and so are therefore only of limited value in understanding the underlying purpose of legislative provisions.[4]

[1]It is helpful to provide a little context to the question at the beginning of your answer. Here you briefly explain why statutory interpretation can be problematic without becoming diverted from the main focus of the question.

[2]It is useful to briefly draw the distinction between intrinsic and extrinsic aids to interpretation.

[3]Here you show the utility of an intrinsic aid to interpretation with the citation of relevant examples from some significant cases. You are also showing awareness of the use of aids in practice.

[4]In this first substantive paragraph you have already shown how some aids to interpretation are likely to be of wider relevance than others, for example long titles in contrast to short titles.

Explanatory notes, headings and side notes are of limited assistance in aiding understanding of statutory provisions.[5] While they may indicate a provision's purpose, they are not debated in Parliament, cannot be used to change the meaning of clear enacted words, and are seldom used. Schedules may be of some use in understanding the meaning of statutory provisions, as they sometimes provide greater explanation of matters covered more briefly in the statute's core provisions. Statutes occasionally provide examples which can carry great persuasive authority as to the meaning of particular provisions. The Law of Property Act 1925 and the Consumer Credit Act 1974 are two such statutes.[6]

Various extrinsic aids may be consulted to ascertain the underlying purpose of legislative provisions. Dictionaries and textbooks may be consulted as a starting point to provide guidance on the meaning of particular words or perceptions of the current legal position on a given issue, but their wider value is limited.[7] Despite its title, the Interpretation Act 1978 provides only limited assistance with statutory interpretation.[8] It provides meanings for words commonly used within statutes, for example providing that references to the masculine gender should be construed to include the feminine gender.

Reference to the historical setting within which a statute has been enacted may shed some light upon the underlying reasons for a particular provision, thus providing guidance upon its most appropriate interpretation. Certain extrinsic materials may assist the courts specifically to attempt to identify the objective behind a statutory provision, in order that they might apply it in the manner intended by Parliament.[9] Reports preceding a piece of legislation – for example, government white papers – may help to identify why a particular provision was felt necessary, although some commentators have expressed concern that the same reasons may not have provided the basis for Parliament's passage of the ultimate statute. Reference to treaties to which the UK is a party may be useful when a statute raises issues relating to international law, as there is a presumption that Parliament does not intend to legislate in breach of the UK's obligations under international law.

[5] It is worth taking explanatory notes, headings and side notes together as very similar observations can be made in respect of them.

[6] Again, practical examples are usefully cited to show the use of aids in practice.

[7] Although there are several aids to interpretation, you cannot be expected to enter into lengthy discussion of them all within the constraints of an examination. For what you consider to be the least interesting or significant aids, brief explanation will suffice.

[8] While the Interpretation Act 1978 should be mentioned, do not make the mistake of thinking it merits lengthy consideration. Its utility is very limited.

[9] It makes sense to consider these extrinsic aids in the same paragraph as they all relate to understanding the factors which led to the adoption of a particular provision.

Other statutes and statutory instruments may be useful aids to interpretation. Related statutes may form part of the context to an area of law and help resolve ambiguity in a particular provision. Statutory instruments adopted under a particular statute may build upon some of its provisions further, and enhance understanding of their meaning. In **Hanlon *v* The Law Society** [1981] AC 124, Lord Lowry formulated six propositions applicable to their use as an extrinsic aid to interpretation. Courts may also on occasion find it beneficial to look at the legislative antecedents to a particular provision in order to better understand its purpose. For example, in **Beswick *v* Beswick** [1968] AC 58, the court spent some time looking at the origins of section 56 of the Law of Property Act 1925.[10]

[10]Once again, useful practical examples are cited of aids to interpretation being used by the courts. This reinforces their utility, and relates directly back to the second part of the question which asks how useful the various aids are to judges.

Arguably, the most significant development in the use of extrinsic aids to interpretation came with the landmark decision of the House of Lords in **Pepper *v* Hart** [1993], that judges may use *Hansard* as an aid to interpretation.[11] The House ruled that *Hansard* may be consulted when legislation is ambiguous or obscure, or its literal meaning leads to an absurdity; the material relied on consists of statements by a minister or other promoter of the bill; and the statements relied on are clear. The use of *Hansard* may assist judges in understanding Parliament's intention in enacting statutory provisions the meaning of which is not clear. The major rationale for permitting courts to consult *Hansard* is that as the official record of Parliamentary debates, it may provide explanation from government ministers or the promoters of a bill as to its purpose, which can be helpful where there is doubt over the meaning of a provision. Furthermore, in an age of constant media reporting it would be nonsensical to expect judges to turn a blind eye to Parliamentary debates which they are readily exposed to. Those opposed to judges having recourse to *Hansard* were concerned that it would add to time and expense incurred in judicial proceedings, and that while *Hansard* may record the statements of some politicians, these do not equate to the intention of parliament as a whole in voting for the passage of the relevant legislation. Since **Wilson *v* Secretary of State for Trade and Industry** [2003] UK HL 40, the use of *Hansard* has been restricted to cover only comments of the relevant minister or promoter of the bill, in order to ascertain the statute's purpose.

[11]The use of *Hansard* as an aid to interpretation deserves greater detail than the other aids due to the relatively recent landmark nature of the decision to permit its use by judges and its value as a means of ascertaining Parliament's intention in adopting legislation. Although you will not have time to enter into a lengthy discussion of the background to *Pepper v Hart* and the debate over the use of *Hansard*, it will be appropriate to make some comment upon the value of using *Hansard* and the rationale for this.

Clearly judges are able to consult various intrinsic and extrinsic aids to assist them when interpreting statutes. As has been shown, some are likely to be of greater general value than others in enabling judges to identify the underlying legislative purpose. Which aids are likely to be of the greatest use to judges will depend very much on the circumstances of each individual case. Since judges have been able to consult *Hansard* as an aid to statutory interpretation, it is arguable that they have been given the widest range of tools possible to facilitate their ability to effectively ascertain the meaning of statutory provisions and give effect to their intended purposes.[12]

[12]The conclusion relates back to the question. The main body of the essay has explained what intrinsic and extrinsic aids are available for judges to use, and has commented on their respective utility. The conclusion reinforces these points that have been made.

✓ Make your answer stand out

- Comment especially on the significance of the decision in *Pepper* v *Hart* to allow judges to use *Hansard* as an aid to interpretation.
- Try to provide examples of some of the aids to interpretation having been used in practice.

! Don't be tempted to . . .

- Simply list the various intrinsic and extrinsic aids to interpretation;
- Engage in lengthy discussion of the use of *Hansard* at the expense of providing necessary coverage of the other aids to interpretation.

Question 3

Discuss, with examples, the rules of language and presumptions applicable to statutory interpretation.

Answer plan

- ➜ Explain that three main rules of language and a series of presumptions are used by judges in interpreting statutes.
- ➜ Explain the main rules of language and provide examples of their use from relevant case law to illustrate how useful they are in practice.
- ➜ Explain some of the main presumptions applied by the courts when interpreting statutes and provide examples of some of these being applied from relevant case law to show their significance.
- ➜ Conclude on the significance of the rules of language and presumptions in aiding statutory interpretation.

Diagram plan

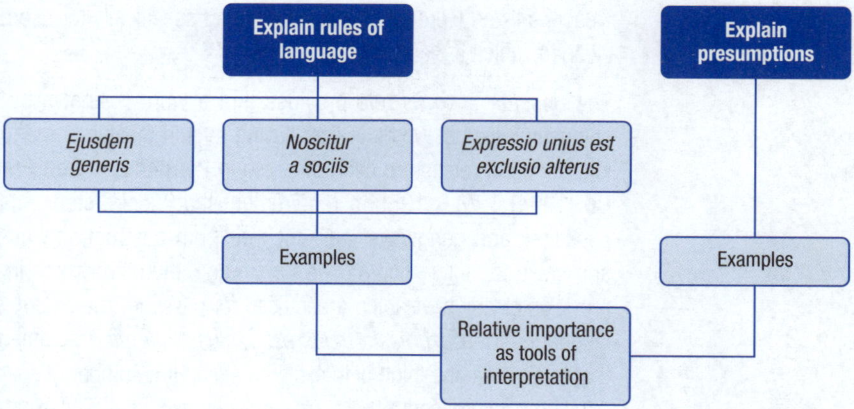

A printable version of this diagram plan is available from www.pearsoned.co.uk/lawexpressqa

Answer

Judges use various mechanisms in order to ascertain the appropriate meaning to be given to uncertain statutory provisions. In addition to intrinsic and extrinsic aids to interpretation, judges employ three main rules of language and a series of presumptions in interpreting statutes.[1]

The first rule of language used by judges is the *ejusdem generis* rule, meaning that when words with a general meaning follow a list of specific words within a statute, those general words are to be construed to apply only to things of the same type as the specific words used. Examples illustrate the rule well.[2] In **Powell *v* Kemptown Park Racecourse** [1899] AC 143, the phrase 'house, office, room or other place' could not extend to an outdoor betting ring. The specific words listed were all indoor, so 'other places' was to be construed to encompass only indoor places. Similarly, in **Wood *v* Commissioner of the Police of the Metropolis** [1986] 2 All ER 570, a weapon was defined as 'any gun, pistol, hangar, cutlass, bludgeon or other offensive weapon'. A piece of glass could not be regarded as an 'other offensive weapon', as the specific weapons listed were all of a type designed specifically for use as a weapon, which a piece of glass was not.

The *noscitur a sociis* rule provides that a word is known by the company it keeps. Words in lists having related meanings are to be interpreted in relation to each other, so in **Pengelley *v* Bell Punch Co** [1964] 1 WLR 1055, a requirement that 'floors, steps, stairs, passages and gangways' be kept free from obstruction was not applicable to factory floors used for storage, the other words in the provision clearly envisaging areas used for passage. The final rule of language is the *expressio unius est exclusio alterus* rule, meaning that to express one thing is to exclude others. If a number of specific things are expressed, others are implicitly excluded. For example, in **Tempest *v* Kilner** (1846) 3 CB 249, a provision relating to contracts for the sale of 'goods, wares and merchandise' was taken to exclude contracts for the sale of stocks and shares by implication. Similarly, in **R *v* Inhabitants of Sedgley** (1831) B & Ald 65, it was held that a poor rate levied on owners of 'lands, houses, tithes and coal mines' did not apply to owners of limestone mines. The express inclusion of coal mines explicitly excluded limestone mines.[3]

[1] In the introduction, the wider context to statutory interpretation – to which rules of language and presumptions are a part – is alluded to. Like intrinsic and extrinsic aids, these are also effectively means of assisting judges to understand the appropriate meaning to give to statutory provisions.

[2] By providing examples you show clearly how the rules of language apply in practice, and also evidence that you are aware of the operation of these rules. Citation of relevant cases evidences both knowledge and understanding.

[3] Most of the cases concerning the rules of language being applied are not particularly widely known. You will need to ensure you have some relevant examples in mind beforehand. Knowledge of a good range of cases on this area is very impressive.

A series of presumptions is made by judges when interpreting statutes. In the absence of clear evidence to the contrary, these apply. It is presumed that Parliament does not intend to alter the common law. In **Beswick *v* Beswick** [1968] AC 58, the House of Lords refused to interpret section 56 of the Law of Property Act 1925 to overturn the long established common law doctrine of privity of contract in the absence of any express intention by the statute to do so. There is also a related presumption that statutes do not intend to exclude the jurisdiction of the courts.[4] The courts have proven willing to construe provisions as far as they can to preserve their jurisdiction. Even where ouster clauses have been used, they have endeavoured to construe statutory provisions to allow judicial review, as for example in **Anisminic Ltd *v* Foreign Compensation Commission** [1969] 2 AC 147.

[4]As there are several presumptions worth discussing, it is worthwhile to group them together. In this paragraph you explain two related presumptions. For each, again you are showing knowledge and understanding through the choice of examples provided.

There is a series of presumptions particularly relevant to criminal law and individual rights.[5] It is presumed that a mental element (*mens rea*) is required for criminal liability. This can be rebutted by express words or implication in offences of strict liability, and the courts will consider all relevant factors. The presumption is strongest in cases of a truly criminal character. For example, in **Sweet *v* Parsley** [1970] AC 132 it was held that a landlord was not criminally liable for the use of cannabis by tenants in her property in the absence of any knowledge of the commission of the offence on her part. The courts will also presume that statutes do not intend to interfere with private rights or deprive individuals of their property. Wherever possible, statutes will be interpreted to respect these rights. It is presumed that statutes do not intend to deprive individuals of their liberty. If a statute is designed to deprive individuals of their liberty, clear words must be used to this effect. It is significant that even when statutes evidence an intention to interfere with individual liberty, the courts have sought to construe the statute's provisions as narrowly as possible so as to permit only the least possible interference. This has happened in a number of cases brought under mental health legislation.

[5]Again, related presumptions are tackled together with relevant examples being cited. This flows on nicely from the preceding paragraphs and the essay is being developed naturally and within a logical structure.

There are three further notable presumptions made by the courts. It is presumed that statutes are not intended to have retrospective effect. This reflects the ideal of the rule of law, a key principle of which is that law should only apply prospectively. However, this presumption may be rebutted by the inclusion of express words.

For example, the War Crimes Act 1991 made criminally punishable acts committed a half century earlier. Statutes are not presumed to apply to the Crown unless they are expressly stated to do so or necessary implication requires this. The Crown is expressly bound by the terms of statutes such as the Occupiers Liability Acts 1957 and 1984, the Equal Pay Act 1970 and the Sex Discrimination Act 1975 amongst others. Finally, it is presumed that Parliament does not intend to legislate in breach of the UK's obligations in international law. However, as established in **Mortensen *v* Peters** (1906) SLT 227, the effect of parliamentary sovereignty is that a clear statutory provision which clashes with a provision of international law will be afforded precedence.[6]

The rules of language used by judges are clearly helpful in clarifying the meaning of particular provisions, as the examples cited illustrate. To some extent they represent a commonsense approach to interpreting statutes where the correct scope of particular words or phrases can be understood by reference to the broader provision of which they are a part. However, their value is likely to be limited to those scenarios where it is possible to understand a word or phrase by reference to the context within which they appear. This will not always be possible, for example where the meaning of an entire provision is ambiguous, and judges may need to have recourse to other aids in order to interpret it appropriately.[7] The presumptions made by judges are not absolute. They serve as a useful starting point to guard against statutes having a more radical impact than may have been intended, while still being rebuttable when the underlying aim of a statute was clearly to override a particular presumption.[8]

[6]The discussion of presumptions is concluded in the same vein as it has been tackled in the preceding two paragraphs. Throughout, the discussion has also shown how presumptions are relative concepts which can be dispensed with when there is clear statutory intention to override them. This will lead nicely into the overall conclusion to the answer.

[7]The conclusion follows naturally from the main body of the answer. The earlier discussion of rules of language illustrated through the case examples cited that these are mainly a means of understanding particular words in statutory provisions and the conclusion here reinforces that.

[8]Likewise, this concluding comment on the use of presumptions flows naturally from their discussion within the main body of the answer. They serve a valuable function without impinging upon parliamentary sovereignty.

✓ Make your answer stand out

- Cite a good range of relevant examples from case law and/or statute to illustrate the rules of language and presumptions being utilised in practice and to support any points that you make.
- Emphasise the balance which the relativity of presumptions made by the courts when interpreting statutes allows to be struck between preventing against unintended radical effects of statutes, and respecting Parliament's ability to make any law it wishes when this is its clear intention.
- Demonstrate that rules of language have limited value, being applicable to words or phrases that can be interpreted by reference to the wider provision of which they are part.

! Don't be tempted to . . .

- Simply list the rules of language and presumptions;
- Confuse the rules of language with the well-known rules of interpretation (the literal rule, golden rule and mischief rule).

Question 4

'Although it is now clear that *Hansard* can be referred to in order to find evidence of parliamentary intention, there is still much debate as to how useful it is', Elliott & Quinn, *English Legal System* (11th edition), p. 68. discuss.

Answer plan

→ Briefly explain what *Hansard* is and that until the decision in *Pepper* v *Hart*, courts were not permitted to use it as an aid to statutory interpretation.

→ Discuss the main arguments in favour of and against the use of *Hansard* as an aid to interpretation.

→ Explain the decision in *Pepper* v *Hart.*

→ Consider how the courts have refined the decision in *Pepper* v *Hart* in subsequent cases.

→ Conclude upon the extent to which the courts make appropriate use of *Hansard* as an aid to interpretation.

Diagram plan

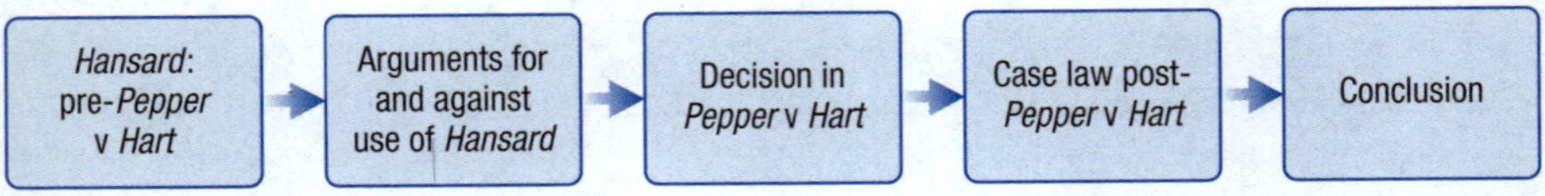

A printable version of this diagram plan is available from www.pearsoned.co.uk/lawexpressqa

Answer

[1]It is useful by way of introduction to briefly explain what *Hansard* is and the traditional position in respect of its use as an aid to statutory interpretation.

Hansard is the official daily report of parliamentary debates. Prior to the decision in **Pepper *v* Hart** [1993] 1 All ER 42, the courts were not permitted to refer to Hansard in order to obtain any assistance with the interpretation of statutory provisions.[1] However, as courts began to adopt a more purposive approach to statutory interpretation, in which they increasingly sought to ascertain the intention of Parliament when enacting a particular statutory provision, calls grew for the prohibition on the use of *Hansard* as an aid to interpretation to be relaxed. Lord Denning especially argued strongly for the use of *Hansard* as an aid to interpretation, and indeed made use of it in **Davis *v* Johnson** [1978] 2 WLR 553, although he was heavily criticised for doing so by the House of Lords.

[2]The quotation which you are asked to discuss is rather general and essentially raises the issue of the extent to which *Hansard* is useful in enabling judges to ascertain the Parliamentary intention underlying statutory provisions. You can begin your answer by considering the main arguments advanced as part of this debate, beginning with the case for *Hansard's* use. You may draw upon the views of judges like Lord Denning to reinforce the reasons why judges should be able to consult *Hansard*.

The principal reason advanced for the use of *Hansard* rests upon the assumption that allowing judges to consult debates from the time when a provision was approved by Parliament may be helpful in assisting them to clarify its intended meaning.[2] Lord Denning adopted such reasoning in **Davis *v* Johnson** [1978], where he commented that to ignore things said in Parliament would be to 'grope in the dark for the meaning of an Act without switching on the light'. As Lord Griffiths acknowledged in **Pepper *v* Hart** [1993], the courts now adopt a purposive approach when interpreting statutes. Thus, it would appear nonsensical to deprive them of the use of a key source of information to assist in understanding the purpose underlying particular legislative provisions, especially when they may consult other extrinsic aids such as government white papers and other law reform proposals. Reference to legislative debates have long been an established source for consultation by the judiciary in other jurisdictions. Furthermore, proceedings in Parliament are widely reported in the media, to which the judiciary is as exposed as anyone else. To ignore *Hansard* essentially would involve the judiciary turning a blind eye to the obvious.

However, although a prima facie case can be made for the utility of *Hansard* to judges, there are grounds to be cautious about the extent to which it assists in ascertaining the purpose underlying a particular provision.[3] Hansard only reveals the views of a small minority of MPs on any one issue, and the statement of any one member can never be definitive of the views of Parliament as a whole. Even looking to the views expressed by a minister introducing a bill in Parliament has its difficulties, as it cannot be assumed that these are shared by other MPs. Furthermore, statements in Parliament do not always provide a clear perspective of the intended objective of legislative provisions, a point commented on by Lord Scarman in **Davis *v* Johnson** [1978], where he noted that anything said in the cut and thrust of public debate was not 'conducive to a clear and unbiased explanation of the meaning of statutory language'. A further objection to the use of *Hansard* is that it increases the time and expense spent on litigation. This was mentioned by Lord Steyn in a 2001 article, where he suggested that much of appellate courts' work is now more concerned with the interpretation of documents than examining precedents.

[3]You must clearly articulate the reasons why reference to *Hansard* may not provide a reliable means of ascertaining parliamentary intention. Again, cite relevant judicial/academic opinions in considering these points.

The House of Lords, in ruling that judges could use *Hansard* as an aid to interpretation in **Pepper *v* Hart** [1993], seems to have recognised that whereas it may prove useful in some circumstances, its unrestricted use would be undesirable for the reasons discussed above. The House ruled that for *Hansard* to be consulted, the provision in question must be ambiguous, obscure or result in an absurdity if given its literal meaning, the material relied upon must only consist of statements of the minister or promoter sponsoring the legislation, and that such statements must be clear. Thus, it could only be consulted in a limited range of circumstances, in which a clear ministerial statement would shed light on the appropriate application of an unclear provision.[4] The use of *Hansard* in this case was particularly useful as the kind of situation raised by the case had been specifically mentioned by the relevant minister at the time of the statute's passage. *Hansard* was referred to in several subsequent cases, beginning with **Warwickshire County Council *v* Johnson** [1993] 1 All ER 299. Its use was extended in **Three Rivers DC *v* Bank of England** [1996] 2 All ER 363 to cover situations where legislation itself is not ambiguous but might be ineffective in its intention to give effect to EC directives, and reference to *Hansard* may assist in determining the provision's actual purpose.

[4]While you need to explain the decision in *Pepper* v *Hart*, it is very important that you emphasise that the House of Lords did not permit unrestricted reference to *Hansard*. This is central to the issue raised by the question, and shows that even at this stage the courts entertained reservations over the extent to which *Hansard* provided a reliable means of identifying Parliament's intention in enacting statutory provisions.

That the courts entertain doubts over the utility of *Hansard* in deciphering the intention of parliament has become more apparent in subsequent cases where they have restricted its usage.[5] For example, in **Melluish (Inspector of Taxes) *v* BMI (No. 3)** [1995] 4 All ER 453, it was held that only ministerial statements at the time of the statute's passage can be considered, and not anything said subsequently about the purpose of the Act, and in **R *v* Secretary of State for the Environment, Transport and the Regions, *ex parte* Spath Holme** [2001] 2 AC 349, it was ruled that only statements pertaining to the meaning of a statutory provision could be consulted, and not those relating to matters of policy. The clear implication of recent case law is that use of *Hansard* as an aid to interpretation should be the exception rather than the rule. This was reinforced in **Wilson *v* Secretary of State for Trade and Industry** [2003] UKHL 40, where the House of Lords stressed that courts must be careful not to regard ministers or sponsors' statements as being indicative of the objective intention of Parliament, and that *Hansard* could only be used to interpret the meaning of words in legislation, and not the reasons for the legislation.

[5]By considering some of the post-*Pepper* v *Hart* case law you are able to make connections between theory and practice in relation to the use of *Hansard*. You can illustrate effectively that the courts' restrictive approach to the extent to which judges may consult it, demonstrates that the question of its utility as a means of identifying parliamentary intention continues to influence judicial thinking.

In conclusion, the quotation bears much truth.[6] Whilst *Hansard* may prove very useful to courts in certain circumstances, in assisting them to interpret the underlying intention behind specific statutory provisions, there are limitations to the extent to which it can provide them with reliable means of ascertaining the purpose of a provision, and thus should not be regarded as foolproof. The problems associated with the use of *Hansard* appear to have been recognised in the approach of the courts since **Pepper *v* Hart**, as they have attached much caution to *Hansard's* use by restricting the circumstances in which recourse may be had to it as an aid to statutory interpretation. While it can be useful to the courts, it should not be assumed that this will always be so, hence the restrictive approach of the courts which consider its use as being exceptional rather than the norm.

[6]Your conclusion should refer back to the original quotation and draw together the arguments made throughout the answer in summarising whether you agree with it or not.

✓ Make your answer stand out

- Make the connections between the theoretical debate over the merits of allowing judges to use *Hansard* to ascertain the intention of Parliament and the courts' approach to its usage in practice.
- Refer, where appropriate, to the opinions of judges and/or academics upon the utility of *Hansard* in helping judges to discover the intention underlying a particular statutory provision, for example, Steyn, J., '*Pepper* v *Hart*: A Re-examination', *Oxford Journal of Legal Studies*, 2001, v. 21, n. 1, p. 59.

! Don't be tempted to . . .

- Focus too heavily on *Pepper* v *Hart* without considering how later cases have contributed to the development of the debate over *Hansard's* utility;
- Discuss only the relative merits of Hansard as an aid to statutory interpretation in abstract form, without making reference to the relevant case law on the issue.

Question 5

'The role of the judiciary may theoretically be to apply the law, but the reality is that judges in fact do also make law.'

Answer plan

→ Briefly explain the doctrine of separation of powers whereby Parliament makes the law and the role of judges is simply to apply it.

→ Discuss the role played by the judges in the development of the common law.

→ Discuss the ability of the judges to determine the meaning of statutes.

→ Refer to some of the most significant cases where judicial decisions have had the effect of changing the law.

→ Conclude by commenting upon whether judges make law.

Diagram plan

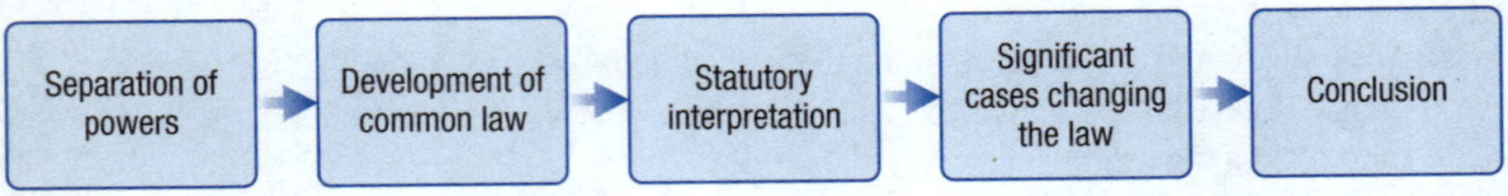

A printable version of this diagram plan is available from www.pearsoned.co.uk/lawexpressqa

Answer

According to the doctrine of the separation of powers, Parliament makes the law and the role of the judiciary is simply to apply the law to the cases which come before them. Unelected judges do not, and should not, become involved in law-making which is the constitutional preserve of the democratically elected Parliament. However, notwithstanding conventional theory, the fact is that judges play a significant role in the development of the law which goes beyond simply applying an objectively definable set of legal rules to the cases before them.[1]

[1]In your introduction you should make brief reference to the traditional notion that judges merely apply the law, before stating that in practice their role is much more significant than this. This sets the scene nicely for the arguments to follow.

Much law is not actually found in statute, but rather is contained in the common law, the legal principles which have emerged from judicial decisions.[2] Considerable branches of law, for example contract and tort, consist predominantly of principles developed within the common law. Murder is also a crime found in common law. It is difficult to claim that judges play no part in law-making given the huge volume of common law which exists. The actual content of the law here is the product of judicial decisions. Through the system of judicial precedent, higher courts are theoretically able to establish legal principles which are to be followed by lower courts in similar cases, thus theoretically creating a degree of certainty within the common law and restricting the ability of judges to depart from established legal principles. In practice, however, judges have considerable flexibility to avoid being bound by precedent, in particular through the process of distinguishing cases from earlier ones. This can create much uncertainty in the common law. Often there will be no clear precedent to govern a particular issue, and a court's ruling will have the practical effect of declaring the relevant legal position for the first time. This occurred in **Airedale NHS Trust *v* Bland** [1993] AC 789,[3] where the House of Lords had to determine whether it was lawful to stop artificially feeding a patient in a

[2]This is an essential point to make. The common law is the most obvious example of judges making law and you can provide examples of huge areas of law which are governed by principles developed by judges.

[3]This reinforces the significance of judicial decisions. Where there is no clear legal position, judicial rulings on the matter are tremendously important.

coma. That many Supreme Court or Court of Appeal decisions are settled by narrow margins demonstrates that there is much judicial disagreement as to the correct state of the law. Often the question of 'what is the law?' on a matter will only be answered following a lengthy court process. While judges may argue that rather than 'making' law they are actually 'declaring' or 'finding' the law, the fact that much judicial disagreement exists upon the correct state of the law demonstrates that judicial decisions can have the practical effect of creating new legal rules.[4]

[4]This builds upon the points made above. By referring to the considerable uncertainty in the law, you show that in making their rulings on unsettled issues, judges are effectively determining what the relevant legal position will be.

Even where Parliament has legislated upon a particular matter, it is naive to say that the judiciary are simply tasked with giving effect to its enactments. Statutory provisions are sometimes ambiguous or unclear in their meaning. In such cases the judiciary have to interpret their meaning. While it is often said that this process involves the judiciary attempting to discover the intention of Parliament, which would imply that the judiciary seeks to avoid playing the role of 'law-maker' when interpreting statutes, the reality is that there is a series of different approaches to statutory interpretation which a court might take with radically different outcomes in terms of a statutory provision's practical application.[5] For example, whereas literally interpreting statutory provisions may be appropriate in many cases, applying a literal approach to some statutory provisions may result in the court giving a provision an absurd meaning which Parliament clearly did not intend it to have. For example, in **Fisher *v* Bell** [1960] 3 All ER 731, the display of flick knives in a shop window was held not to amount to the offence of offering such weapons for sale contrary to the Restriction of Offensive Weapons Act 1959 as under principles of contract law such a display was regarded as an invitation to treat. This outcome clearly ran counter to the objectives of the relevant legislation. Although the court could argue it simply interpreted the law, the fact is that its interpretation determined how the provision in question would be applied, effectively giving it a practical application of its choosing. The courts have moved increasingly towards the adoption of a purposive approach to statutory interpretation, in which their main objective is to identify the purpose behind a particular provision. The decision in **Pepper *v* Hart** [1993] 1 All ER 42, to allow judges to consult *Hansard* when interpreting statutes, reinforced this. While a more purposive approach to statutory interpretation might be felt

[5]Be careful not to enter into a discussion of the various rules of statutory interpretation. The main point to make is that judges have some input into the practical application of statutory provisions, which may vary depending upon the particular approach which they utilise.

to minimise the danger of judges giving meanings to provisions at odds with their intended objectives, there remain difficulties in ascertaining the intention of Parliament and judges nonetheless retain the discretion to use any approach to statutory interpretation which they wish. Although they may simply be interpreting the law, the approach which they choose to take will in practice determine what the law is understood to be.

[6]If you have time, you could make more of this point through the provision of a greater range of examples. These highlight the landmark effects of judicial rulings upon the state of the law.

Case law is replete with examples of situations in which the judiciary have effectively re-written the law through their development of common law principles, particularly in order to accommodate societal changes.[6] For example, the landmark case of **R *v* R** [1991] 3 WLR 767 overturned a century of acknowledged precedents to establish that a man could commit the offence of rape against his wife. More recently, in **R *v* Dica** [2004] QB 1257, the Court of Appeal determined that a person could be criminally liable for recklessly infecting someone with HIV. In both cases a legal position is declared by the court which had not previously been assumed to exist, without any legislation having been enacted by Parliament to change the law. The conclusion that judges had effectively made new law here would appear difficult to rebut.

[7]This is a balanced conclusion which relates back to the quotation and reinforces the main points made in the answer.

While some would argue that judges clearly make law, others would prefer to say that judges simply 'discover' the law, they ascertain its correct meaning and apply it to the cases before them. Arguably, it is not so important which of these summations of the role performed by the judiciary is accepted.[7] There is no real disagreement that judges play a significant part in the development of the law. They develop the principles contained in the common law and give practical meaning to statutes. The actual content of the law is not a clear cut matter, as the amount of non-unanimous decisions reached by the higher courts should make apparent. The decisions reached by judges ultimately tell us what the law is, and whether those judges have made or simply interpreted the law is irrelevant to those who are disadvantaged by their rulings. The reality is that judges have a huge bearing upon the law's content and practical application.

✓ Make your answer stand out

- Use practical examples to reinforce your points.
- Emphasise the importance of the practical application of the law, which takes effect through judicial decisions.

! Don't be tempted to . . .

- Describe in detail the main principles of judicial precedent and statutory interpretation;
- Engage in more general discussion upon the appropriate constitutional role of the judiciary.

4

Human rights and the constitution

How this topic may come up in exams

Examination questions pertaining to human rights are likely to test your understanding of the main features of the Human Rights Act, its manner of operation, the remedies which are available for infringements of human rights, or more specifically the impact of the Act on human rights protection in the UK. More general constitutional questions may test your understanding of the doctrine of separation of powers in relation to the role of the judiciary, executive and legislature in law-making, or may seek to assess your awareness of events of topical interest, such as changes introduced by the Constitutional Reform Act 2005.

Attack the question

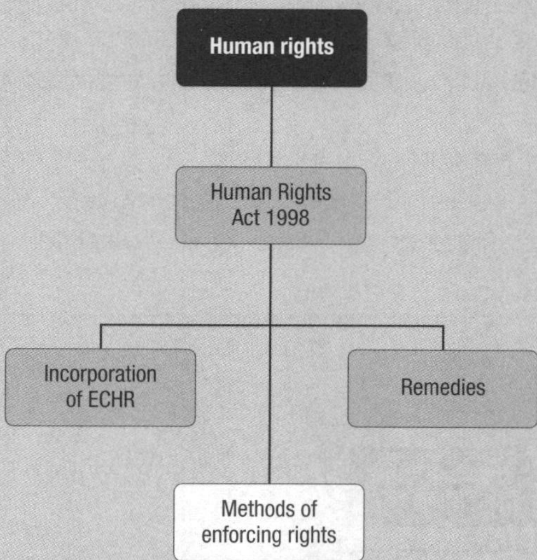

A printable version of this diagram plan is available from www.pearsoned.co.uk/lawexpressqa

Question 1

Discuss the extent to which the provisions of the Human Rights Act 1998 strengthen the protection afforded to the rights contained in the European Convention on Human Rights in domestic law.

Answer plan

- → Explain the status of the European Convention on Human Rights in domestic law prior to the Human Rights Act.
- → Explain that the Human Rights Act incorporates the Convention rights into domestic law, but that although public authorities are bound to respect these, Parliament is not.
- → Discuss the extent to which the duty of interpretation placed upon the courts empowers them to protect Convention rights.
- → Discuss the use of declarations of incompatibility by the courts.
- → Comment upon the availability of remedies for breaches of Convention rights.
- → Comment upon whether the Human Rights Act has strengthened the protection of individual rights in the UK.

Diagram plan

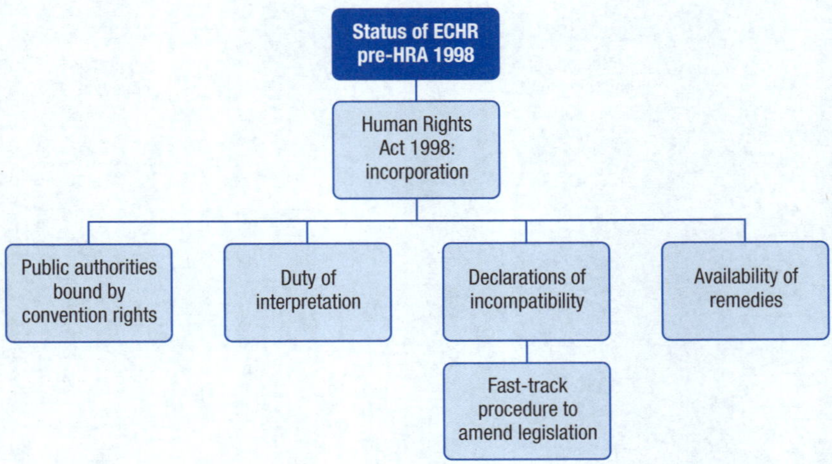

A printable version of this diagram plan is available from www.pearsoned.co.uk/lawexpressqa

Answer

Although the UK was the first state to ratify the European Convention on Human Fights in 1951, for five decades it could not be directly enforced in comestic courts due to its non-incorporation in domestic law.[1] Indiv duals enjoyed no positive rights as such, but rather a series of liberties: they were free to do anything not prohibited by law. This was illustrated in **Malone v Metropolitan Police Commissioner (No. 2)** [1979] 2 All ER 620, where surveillance of a suspect's telephone calls was not deemed illegal in the absence of any legislation prohibiting it. In **Malone v UK** (1984) 7 EHRR 17, the European Court of Human Rights would later rule that such activity breached the right to privacy. The Convention occasionally aided statutory interpretation in light of the presumption that Parliament does not intend to legislate in breach of the UK's international obligations. However, individuals seeking to enforce the Convention against the state would ordinarily have to take their action to the European Court of Human Rights in Strasbourg, a lengthy and costly process.

[1]The question asks for a discussion of the extent to which the provisions of the HRA 1998 have strengthened the protection afforded to Convention rights in domestic law. It is important, therefore, to explain the domestic status of the Convention rights prior to the HRA.

The Human Rights Act 1998 incorporates into domestic law the rights contained in the Convention, but they are not entrenched with any special status.[2] The Act enjoys the force of ordinary law and can be repealed like any other statute. This is reinforced by the fact that although it is unlawful for a public authority to act incompatibly with a Convention right (section 6(1)), Parliament is expressly stated not to be a public authority. This essentially preserves the doctrine of parliamentary sovereignty, leaving Parliament free to legislate in breach of Convention rights should it so choose.[3] However, political pressure upon Parliament to conform to Convention rights is indirectly brought about by section 19's requirement that the relevant minister must make a statement to the effect that in his view the bill's provisions are compatible with the Convention rights prior to a bill's second reading. If such a statement cannot be given, the minister must say so but that the government wishes to proceed with the bill anyway. To date, no minister has failed to make this statement of compatibility.[4] It is unlikely that any government would want to acknowledge a possible intention to infringe human rights and to do so would arguably put Parliament, and the public, on alert and possibly lead to the emergence of opposition to the proposed bill.

[2]It is essential that you make the point that the HRA does not confer any special status upon the Convention rights in domestic law as this goes to the very heart of the question.

[3]This relates back to the previous comment. You must ensure that you explain clearly that the provisions of the HRA do not mean that legislation cannot be enacted which infringes upon the Convention rights.

[4]A key theme which can be developed in your answer is the role which political factors play in the strength of the HRA as an instrument for the protection of human rights. The importance of the statement of compatibility required of a government minister responsible for a bill should be emphasised in this context.

[5]It is essential that you explain the limited but important role of the duty of interpretation in giving effect to Convention rights. You should try and provide an example or two of situations in which the courts have effectively exercised their duty of interpretation to uphold Convention rights.

Proceedings may be brought against public authorities for a violation of the Convention rights or alternatively they may be relied upon in any court proceedings (section 7). The main mechanism for the courts to give effect to the Convention rights is their duty of interpretation (section 3).[5] This requires them to give effect to legislation in a way compatible with the Convention rights as far as possible. The duty of interpretation can obviously only be taken so far, being of no help where provisions clearly infringe Convention rights and cannot be read any other way. However, it has proven useful to the courts on a number of occasions. In **R *v* A** [2001] 2 WLR 1546, the House of Lords read the provisions of the Youth Justice and Criminal Evidence Act 1999 so as to allow evidence to be admitted where considered necessary by the trial judge to make the trial fair. In applying Convention rights, courts are to take into account any relevant jurisprudence of the European Court and Commission of Human Rights, which should ensure that there is some consistency in the protection of human rights between the national and European level.

[6]The declaration of incompatibility is the most important power which the courts have in relation to legislation which violates Convention rights. You must point out that such a declaration has no effect on the validity of legislation. Provide some examples of situations when the courts have made declarations of incompatibility.

Where legislation cannot be interpreted to uphold Convention rights, higher courts may issue a declaration of incompatibility (section 4).[6] This does not invalidate the Act or provision in question (although secondary legislation may be invalidated as ultra vires if it violates Convention rights), but simply states that it is incompatible with the Convention rights. The declaration has no direct legal impact, but the resulting political embarrassment will often result in political pressure for a change to the law. The courts have now issued several declarations of incompatibility. For example, in **Wilson *v* First County Trust (No. 2)** [2003] EWCA Civ 633, a provision of the Consumer Credit Act 1974 was declared to be incompatible with Article 6 of the Convention and Article 1 of the first protocol to the Convention. In **R (on the application of H) *v* Mental Health Review Tribunal for North and East London Region** [2001] EWCA Civ 415, section 73 of the Mental Health Act 1983 was declared to be incompatible with Article 5 of the Convention.

A court may award an individual who has been the victim of a human rights infringement any remedy deemed by the court to be 'just and appropriate' in the circumstances (section 8). Previously, no remedies had been available to victims of infringements of Convention rights under domestic law. Effectively, a victim may now receive any remedy that is most suited to his situation. For the wider society, the most effective remedy to tackle legislative provisions which violates Convention rights is a change in the law. Although the courts cannot invalidate provisions of primary legislation, section 10 provides a fast-track procedure by which legislation declared incompatible with Convention rights can be amended quickly by the relevant minister without the need to go through the ordinary time-consuming legislative process. The political embarrassment which accompanies a declaration of incompatibility means the section 10 procedure is likely to be utilised in most cases such a declaration has been issued by the courts and underlines the political force of the Act's provisions.[7] For example, following the House of Lords declaration that Part 4 of the Anti-Terrorism, Crime and Security Act 2001 was incompatible with certain Convention rights **(A and Others v Secretary of State for the Home Department** [2004] UKHL 56, the government quickly moved to replace offending provisions with the Prevention of Terrorism Act 2005.

[7]This builds upon earlier references to the political factors which are likely to influence the impact of the HRA in practice. Here you are able to point to the fact that although legislation does not become invalid if it infringes Convention rights, in practice such legislation is likely to be rectified following a declaration of incompatibility. You can cite relevant examples to support this point.

In one sense, the Human Rights Act could be said to fall considerably short of providing adequate human rights protection. It does not entrench any rights in domestic law, Parliament may legislate in breach of them, and the courts cannot invalidate offending legislative provisions. However, a case can be made for the positive contribution of the Act. Individuals can finally invoke Convention rights in domestic courts, public authorities must abide by them, and although offending provisions of statutes cannot be overturned by the courts, political factors mean that a declaration of incompatibility is likely to result in a change in the law to remove any offending provisions. In this sense, the Human Rights Act has brought about a marked improvement in the domestic protection of the rights contained in the European Convention on Human Rights.[8]

[8]This is a balanced conclusion which flows naturally from the discussion that has taken place in the answer. From a legal perspective, the HRA does not guarantee respect for the Convention rights but, in practice, its provisions are likely to operate in a way which enhances their protection.

✓ Make your answer stand out

- Explain the domestic status of the European Convention on Human Rights prior to the entry into force of the Human Rights Act 1998 and the extent to which this supported the case for incorporation, by making reference to academic commentary, such as Bingham, T.H., 'The European Convention on Human Rights: Time to Incorporate', *Law Quarterly Review*, 1993, v. 109, p. 390.
- Make clear that the strength of the Human Rights Act lies not so much in the legal nature of its provisions but their acceptance and operation within the UK political culture.
- Refer to relevant examples of cases where courts have exercised the duty of interpretation and issued a declaration of incompatibility, as well as where the law has been changed following a declaration of incompatibility.

! Don't be tempted to . . .

- Confuse the Convention rights with provisions of EU law;
- Engage in detailed discussion of specific Convention rights or to list them all.

Question 2

Discuss the range of remedies available to an individual whose human rights have been infringed by a public authority.

Answer plan

→ Briefly explain that an individual may bring an action against a public authority alleging a violation of his Convention rights, or rely upon the Convention rights in any legal proceedings.

→ Briefly explain the nature of the courts' power to award remedies under section 8 of the Human Rights Act 1998.

→ Explain the major private law remedies which might be awarded to a victim of a human rights violation.

→ Explain the major public law remedies which might be awarded to a victim of a human rights violation.

→ Explain that non-judicial remedies may also be available in cases of human rights violations.

Diagram plan

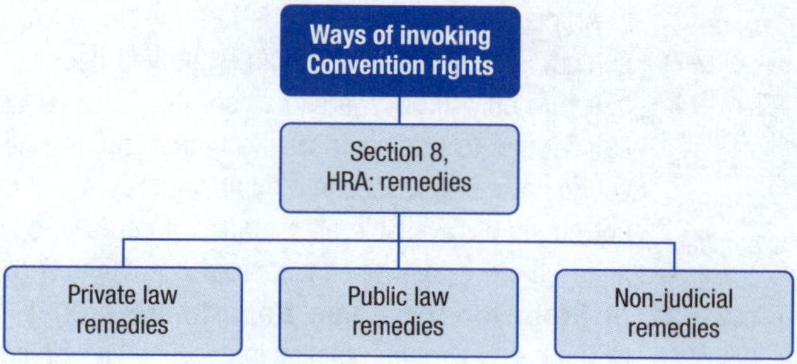

A printable version of this diagram plan is available from www.pearsoned.co.uk/lawexpressqa

Answer

Although Parliament is not obliged to legislate in accordance with the Convention rights incorporated into domestic law by the Human Rights Act 1998, an obligation is placed upon public authorities to act in accordance with these rights by section 6 of the Act. An individual who feels that his Convention rights have been infringed may initiate legal proceedings against a public authority alleging that such an infringement has taken place, or may alternatively rely upon these rights in any proceedings (section 7). Section 8 of the Act governs remedies in cases where a violation of a convention right is found to have occurred and provides that a court may award any remedy within its powers which it considers to be just and appropriate. Thus, a wide range of remedies is available in cases of human rights infringements. Whether a particular remedy is just and appropriate in a given case will hinge upon the powers of the court hearing the case, the route through which the case has come to court and the circumstances relevant to the individual case itself.[1]

There is a series of private law remedies open to the courts to award in cases where a public authority violates a Convention right. The most relevant to human rights cases will often be the common law remedy of damages,[2] which can be awarded in any case where a civil wrong has been committed. Many actions which amount to an infringement of a Convention right will also constitute a civil wrong.[3] To give just two examples, an action constituting the tort of false imprisonment may at the same time amount to the denial

[1] Your introductory paragraph should refer to the key provisions of the Human Rights Act relating to remedies against public authorities. You should explain clearly that section 8 empowers the courts to award any remedy 'just and appropriate' to the victim of a human rights infringement, thus illustrating the wide range of remedies available in such cases.

[2] You must ensure that you give some attention to the remedy of damages as it is arguably the most significant private law remedy available for human rights violations.

[3] This is a useful point to make as it illustrates the wide range of situations in which an action constituting a human rights violation will also give rise to liability, and thus a remedy, under the civil law.

of the right to liberty under Article 5 of the convention, whereas an act which amounts to inhuman or degrading treatment contrary to Article 3 might also take the form of the tort of trespass to the person. Section 8 of the Human Rights Act does provide that damages are only to be awarded where this is necessary to afford just satisfaction to the victim of the human rights violation,[4] and the courts have emphasised in a number of cases that damages should not be simply available as a matter of course. For example, damages were not considered just or appropriate in **R (IH) *v* Secretary of State for the Home Department** [2003] *The Times*, 14 November, where the violation in question had already been publicly acknowledged and put an end to. By contrast, in **R (Bernard) *v* Enfield LBC** [2003] HRLR 4, damages were awarded for a violation of Article 8 of the convention when the claimants had been left in unsuitable accommodation for 20 years.

[4]To illustrate the relevance of damages it is important that you are able to explain that they are not simply available as a matter of course, but must be just and appropriate in the circumstances. Your explanation of damages as a remedy will benefit from the inclusion of examples from the case law of occasions upon which courts have awarded them or declined to do so.

Several equitable remedies are available in private law proceedings, of which arguably the most useful to victims of human rights infringements is that of injunction.[5] An injunction is essentially a court order to refrain from doing something and will be useful where a public authority intends to take an action which might amount to the infringement of a convention right. For example, in **Doherty *v* Birmingham City Council** [2009] 1 AC 367, caravan dwellers sought an injunction to prevent the local authority from evicting them, alleging that to do so would violate their right to respect for privacy and family life under Article 8 of the convention. Injunctions will be particularly relevant in situations where a particular infringement is taking place on a persistent basis and the most suitable means for responding to it is to prevent its continuation. Other equitable remedies are generally of less significance in the human rights context, although specific performance might be awarded where a public authority's failure to fulfil an obligation will result in the infringement of an individual's convention rights. An award of specific performance would require the authority to fulfil its obligations, thus remedying any infringement.

[5]There is no need to enter into any detailed discussion of most equitable remedies as most are of only minimal relevance in the context of human rights violations. Injunctions are worth mentioning, however, as they have a clear relevance which you may be able to illustrate with examples from case law.

Where an action against a public authority is brought by way of an application for judicial review, an additional series of public law remedies – known as prerogative orders – are available if the authority is found to have acted unlawfully.[6] A quashing order has the effect of quashing the decision of a public authority where that decision is found to be invalid. A quashing order is potentially

[6]Credit should be given for your ability to mention that prerogative orders are available when a case has been brought through the route of judicial review. You are unlikely in an examination setting to have time to enter into a lengthy discussion of their utility, but if you do have time could do so with reference to cases in which they have been awarded for violations of convention rights.

available in any judicial review action where a public authority has made a decision which is incompatible with any convention rights, given the obligation placed upon public authorities by section 6 of the Human Rights Act. A prohibiting order prohibits public authorities from taking decisions or actions which will amount to them exceeding their jurisdiction. It will be relevant in the human rights context where a public authority plans action which will result in it infringing upon convention rights. By prohibiting planned action it prevents the infringement occurring in the first place. A mandatory order directs public authorities to perform legal duties. In the human rights context a mandatory order can be used to ensure that a public authority performs a duty which, if it failed to perform, would result in the infringement of a convention right.

Although the full range of judicial remedies may be made available in cases where a public authority has violated convention rights, it is important to note that some significant non-judicial remedies are also available in certain circumstances.[7] In the context of the criminal law, statutory compensations schemes exist for both the victims of violent crime and miscarriages of justice. Where a human rights violation takes the form of a violent criminal action which causes injury to the victim, for example severe mistreatment at the hands of the police, compensation may be available under the Criminal Injuries Compensation Scheme. Where the violation of an individual's convention rights results in him being wrongly convicted of a criminal offence, most commonly because the Article 6 right to a fair trial has been compromised, he may be eligible for compensation under section 133 of the Criminal Justice Act 1988 which makes compensation available to victims of miscarriages of justice. Some public authorities' functions are also subject to the jurisdiction of an ombudsman, to whom complaints of maladministration against such authorities can be referred. This is a limited form of remedy, however, as the ombudsman's powers are declaratory and recommendatory only, and do not include the power to award compensation.

[7]The question does not restrict itself to judicial remedies. Therefore, it is highly relevant to explain that some important non-judicial remedies may be of value to victims of human rights infringements in certain circumstances.

Victims of human rights violations potentially can avail themselves of the full range of judicial remedies under the law, as well as a series of non-judicial means of redress. While the remedy suited to each case will vary with its circumstances, there are several means through which a just and appropriate form of redress can be afforded to the victim of a human rights infringement.[8]

[8]The conclusion flows naturally from the discussion within the answer. It was explained at the outset that potentially a victim of a human rights infringement can avail themselves of the full range of remedies under the law, and the answer has highlighted the most relevant of these.

✓ Make your answer stand out

- Demonstrate that victims of human rights infringements can potentially benefit from both private and public law remedies.
- Refer to some of the non-judicial remedies which may be of potential relevance to victims of human rights infringements.
- Read Leigh, I. and Lustgarten, L., 'Making Rights Real: The Courts, Remedies and the Human Rights Act', *Cambridge Law Journal*, 1999, v. 58, n. 3, pp. 509–45, and draw upon some of the critical insights provided into the remedies provided for by the Act.

! Don't be tempted to . . .

- Explain or refer to every judicial remedy available under the general law, as not all will be as relevant in the human rights context;
- Explain the various forms of legal action through which individuals may allege a violation of their convention rights.

Question 3

'The creation of the Human Rights Act 1998 has resulted in greater conflict between the executive and legislature with the judiciary.' Assess the validity of this statement.

Answer plan

→ Explain the limited ability of the judiciary to pronounce upon the conformity of government actions or legislative provisions with recognised human rights norms prior to the introduction of the Human Rights Act.

→ Explain the main mechanism which the Human Rights Act affords courts to rule upon the conformity of government actions or legislative provisions with the European Convention on Human Rights.

→ Discuss examples of cases where the courts have issued declarations of incompatibility, or interpreted provisions in a way which conforms to the ECHR.

→ Assess the extent to which the Human Rights Act has brought government and the judiciary into greater conflict.

Diagram plan

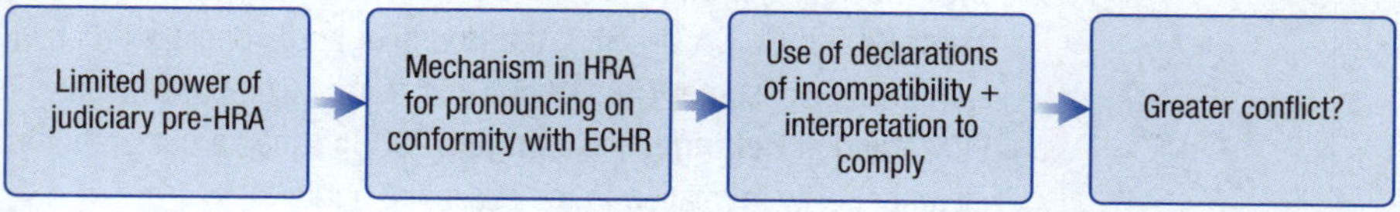

A printable version of this diagram plan is available from www.pearsoned.co.uk/lawexpressqa

Answer

Prior to the entry into force of the Human Rights Act 1998 (HRA), the UK was only bound by the European Convention on Human Rights (ECHR) in international law, it not forming part of the law which could be invoked in domestic courts. As a consequence, the judiciary had only very limited means with which to pronounce upon the protection of human rights in domestic law.[1] They could have some recourse to the ECHR as an aid to statutory interpretation in light of the presumption that Parliament is presumed not to want to legislate in breach of the UK's international obligations. However, in general if government acted or Parliament legislated in a manner contrary to an ECHR provision, there was very little the courts could do.

[1]At the outset it is useful if you briefly explain the limited means available to judges prior to the HRA to rule on human rights issues. This will then reinforce the significance of the powers entrusted to the judiciary under the terms of the HRA.

The HRA, while incorporating the ECHR into domestic law, does not empower courts to strike down legislative provisions. It does, however, enhance the authority of the courts in human rights matters in some important respects.[2] Most significantly, while courts should try to interpret domestic legislation in a manner compatible with the ECHR as far as possible (section 3), where this cannot be achieved higher courts may issue a declaration of incompatibility. That is to say, they can proclaim legislation to be in contravention of ECHR rights. Although this has no automatic consequences, it is likely to result in pressure for reform and gives the judiciary the power to expose shortcomings by government in the human rights field. Furthermore, the courts have the power to award any of the full range of remedies where a human rights violation is found to have occurred.

[2]Before considering the extent to which the judiciary has come into conflict with the executive and legislature, you should briefly explain the powers given to judges by the HRA to rule upon the compatibility of measures with the ECHR.

The courts have proven willing to issue declarations of incompatibility in respect of a number of legislative provisions.[3] The first such instance came in **R (on the application of H) *v* Mental Health Review Tribunal for North and East London Region**

[3]You should ensure that you provide examples of declarations of incompatibility issued by the courts in order to show that you are aware of instances of possible conflict between the judiciary and legislature or executive.

[2001] EWCA Civ 415 where the Court of Appeal determined that sections 72–3 of the Mental Health Act 1983 were incompatible with Articles 5(1) and 4 of the ECHR. In **Wilson *v* First County Trust** [2003] EWCA Civ 633, the House of Lords declared a provision of the Consumer Credit Act 1974 to be incompatible with the ECHR, and in **Bellinger *v* Bellinger** [2003] issued a declaration of incompatibility in relation to transsexuals' rights.

A notable area of conflict between courts and government has been in relation to anti-terrorism provisions.[4] Section 23 of the Anti-Terrorism, Crime and Security Act 2001, made provision for the Home Secretary to order the detention of foreign nationals suspected of involvement in terrorist activities indefinitely and without charge. The government entered a derogation under the ECHR on the grounds that the threat of terrorism constituted an emergency threatening the life of the nation. The issue came to a head in the case of **A and others *v* Secretary of State for the Home Department** [2004] UKHL 56, where the House of Lords declared the relevant provision to be incompatible with Article 5's right to liberty and Article 14 (non-discrimination in protection of rights) on the principal ground that it was discriminatory and illogical – any concern over the threat of terrorism would surely necessitate that the provision be applied to UK and foreign nationals alike, who were both capable of terrorist activity. Furthermore, any subject of a derogation order was free to leave the country (and potentially engage in terrorism against the UK from abroad), undermining the argument that the provision was necessary to protect against the terrorist threat.

[4]This is an area which you might wish to explore in greater depth, particularly in an extended piece of work on this subject. The example provided here is one of the most notable instances of the judiciary finding itself at odds with the government of the day over one of its policies due to the human rights implications.

The cases referred to above would appear to indicate growing tension between the courts and government over human rights issues. However, it is very rare for a court to issue a declaration of incompatibility. Section 3 of the HRA obliges them to interpret legislative provisions to conform with the ECHR insofar as this is possible, and the broad nature of the rights protected by the ECHR gives them much scope for interpretation. In the overwhelming majority of cases brought under the HRA, the courts have either found that there is no prima facie contravention of the ECHR, or have been able to interpret the applicable legislation under section 3 in a manner compatible with the Convention.[5] For example, in **Brown *v* Stott** [2001] 2 WLR 817 the Privy Council held that Article 6's guarantee of a fair trial was not an absolute right and dismissed

[5]This is a very important point which you need to make in order to provide a balanced discussion. You must not focus solely on instances of conflict between the judiciary and executive or legislative, but must demonstrate that such instances are far from representing the norm.

arguments that section 172 of the Road Traffic Act 1988 contravened it. Similarly, in **R *v* Benjafeld and others** [2001] 3 WLR 75, both the Court of Appeal and House of Lords dismissed arguments that powers of confiscation enjoyed by the state were incompatible with the ECHR.

The courts have used section 3 of the HRA in a number of cases to interpret statutory provisions in a manner which will not bring them into conflict with the ECHR. For example, **in R *v* A** [2001] 2 WLR 1546, a challenge was launched to restrictions placed upon the admission of certain evidence in rape trials by section 41 of the Youth Justice and Criminal Evidence Act 1999, which the House of Lords tackled by interpreting the provision in a manner compatible with the ECHR. In **Mendoza *v* Ghaidan** [2002] EWCA Civ 1533, the Court of Appeal used section 3 to interpret a right conferred upon partners to inherit statutory tenancies under the Rent Act 1977 to extend to same-sex partners.[6] A final example can be found with **R *v* Secretary of State for the Environment, Transport and the Regions, *ex parte* Holding & Barnes plc and others** [2001] 2 WLR 1389, where aspects of the planning system were alleged to contravene Article 6's right to a fair trial. The court disagreed, finding the planning system to be entirely compatible with Article 6.

[6]You should make reference to some instances where the courts have interpreted legislation to conform to the ECHR. There is scope to provide more detailed discussion of the cases cited in an extended piece of work.

In conclusion, the statement is arguably misleading. Undoubtedly, the HRA has given the judiciary a tool with which it can rule upon the compatibility of legislative and executive actions with the ECHR, and indeed it has made effective use of its power to issue declarations of incompatibility in some prominent cases. However, through the mechanism of judicial review the courts have always been in the position of ruling upon the legal validity of government actions more generally. The HRA has not led to a flood of cases in which the courts have found the ECHR to have been breached. In fact, such findings have been very few and as some of the cases referred to illustrate, the courts attempt to find compatibility with the ECHR wherever possible, and for the most part appear to do so.[7]

[7]This is a reasoned, logical conclusion which flows naturally from the discussion contained in the essay.

✓ Make your answer stand out

- Refer to a range of case law in order to illustrate the courts use of declarations of incompatibility and section 3 to interpret statutory provisions to conform to the ECHR.
- Read – Kavanagh, A., 'Judging the Judges under the Human Rights Act: Deference, Disillusionment and the 'War on Terror', *Public Law*, 2009, pp. 287–304 – for some critical insights into the judiciary's approach to human rights issues which have arisen in relation to anti-terrorism legislation to which you can make reference in your answer.

! Don't be tempted to . . .

- Focus only on instances of cases where the courts have issued declarations of incompatibility.

Question 4

Discuss the significance of the major reforms introduced by the Constitutional Reform Act 2005.

Answer plan

→ Briefly explain that the changes brought about by the Constitutional Reform Act 2005 formed part of the government's constitutional reform agenda and are especially significant for their impact upon the separation of powers within the UK.

→ Discuss the changes introduced to the role of the Lord Chancellor.

→ Discuss the creation of the new Supreme Court to replace the House of Lords as the highest domestic court.

→ Discuss the changes introduced to the judicial appointments process.

→ Conclude by commenting upon the constitutional significance of the Act.

Diagram plan

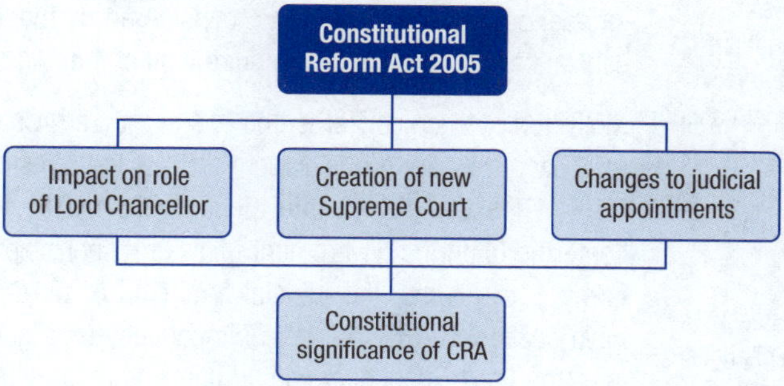

A printable version of this diagram plan is available from www.pearsoned.co.uk/lawexpressqa

Answer

The Constitutional Reform Act 2005 formed part of the Labour government's constitutional reform agenda enacted during its first two terms in office. The Act impacts upon the court apparatus and judiciary of the UK legal system and has been of particular significance for the considerable impact which it has been perceived as having on the separation of powers in the UK. In terms of the major reforms introduced by the Act, arguably three matters are of such significance to warrant explanation and comment.[1] Firstly, the Act impacted considerably upon the role and status of the Lord Chancellor within the judicial system. Secondly, the Act created a new Supreme Court for the UK which has replaced the Judicial Committee of the House of Lords as the final appellate court within the domestic legal system. Thirdly, the Act introduces new provisions to govern appointments to the judiciary. Each of these reforms introduced by the Constitutional Reform Act will now be considered in turn.

[1]The introductory paragraph sets the scene for the remainder of the essay. It clearly shows what are considered to be the most important reforms introduced by the Constitutional Reform Act and provides a structure to be followed in answering the question.

Prior to the Constitutional Reform Act, the role of Lord Chancellor was especially controversial due to his concurrent involvement in all three powers, through serving as a cabinet minister, speaker of the House of Lords and head of the judiciary all at the same time. He could sit in judgment upon cases brought before the Judicial Committee of the House of Lords and was also capable of exercising considerable influence on judicial appointments. One of the main concerns over the former overlapping functions of the Lord

Chancellor, apart from its violation of the doctrine of the separation of powers, was that it seriously impinged upon the principle of the independence of the judiciary,[2] considered by most constitutional scholars to constitute a core requirement of the rule of law.

[2]The introductory paragraph sets the scene for the remainder of the essay. It clearly shows what are considered to be the most important reforms introduced by the Constitutional Reform Act and provides a structure to be followed in answering the question.

Motivated by such concerns, the role of the Lord Chancellor is radically altered by the provisions of Part 2 of the Constitutional Reform Act.[3] While the official title of Lord Chancellor remains and is conferred upon the government minister responsible for the administration of justice, the judicial functions of the Lord Chancellor have ceased to exist. While in his capacity as a government minister the Lord Chancellor will by convention sit within the Houses of Parliament, he is no longer required to be a member of the House of Lords under section 2 of the Act. When taking upon the post of Lord Chancellor, combined with that of Secretary of State for Justice, Jack Straw became in 2007 the first MP to hold the title of Lord Chancellor. The Lord Chancellor no longer holds judicial office and has been replaced as head of the judiciary by the Lord Chief Justice, under section 7(1) of the Act. The removal of the judicial functions of the Lord Chancellor serves to reinforce the independence of the judiciary. This is underlined by provisions such as section 3 which obliges the Lord Chancellor, as well as other government ministers, to uphold the independence of the judiciary. The Lord Chancellor, even if he happens to be a member of the House of Lords, no longer holds the post of Speaker within that chamber of Parliament.[4] Due to changes initiated by section 18 and schedule 6, the members of that body now independently select their own speaker, bringing it in line with the House of Commons. This arguably reinforces the perception that although Parliament, in practice, tends to be dominated by the government of the day, it ought to retain at least some degree of independence from government.

[3]This paragraph effectively explains the main changes to the role of the Lord Chancellor. It is important to stress their relevance by reference to the extent to which they strengthen the independence of the judiciary.

[4]This point is easy to overlook, but is worth mentioning also in the context of changes to the role of Lord Chancellor.

Part 3 of the Constitutional Reform Act is concerned with the new Supreme Court for the UK, which section 23 creates. Under section 40, the Supreme Court's jurisdiction is essentially that formerly exercised by the House of Lords, serving as the ultimate appellate court for the UK.[5] Despite its name, it has no special constitutional role in the absence of a codified constitution. The first members of the court were those serving as Lords of Appeal in Ordinary at the time of its commencement of business on 1 October 2009. Although the creation of the Supreme Court to some extent appears

[5]This is a key point to be made about the new Supreme Court. In terms of its functions, there is little to distinguish it from the House of Lords.

to have been a cosmetic exercise, given the fact that it simply takes upon a role previously exercised by the House of Lords comprised of the same judges, there is at least one notable difference. Whereas the Lords of Appeal in Ordinary, the 'Law Lords' who sat upon the Judicial Committee of the House of Lords, were also entitled to sit and vote in the legislative chamber of the House of Lords, this privilege is not afforded to members of the new Supreme Court. Section 137 provides that any judge of the Supreme Court is disqualified from sitting or voting in the House of Lords while he holds judicial office.[6] This change is notable in that it removes the overlap which previously existed between the judiciary and legislature and serves to strengthen the separation of powers model in the UK, reinforcing the independence of the judiciary from the politically driven legislative process.

[6]This is an obvious significant change brought about by the act and ought to be mentioned. It reinforces the argument made at the outset of the answer: that the act has impacted considerably upon the separation of powers and independence of the judiciary.

There are detailed provisions in the Constitutional Reform Act concerning judicial appointments processes.[7] The main objective of these new provisions has been to strengthen the independence of appointments processes and minimise the influence of government over these. Prior to the Act, the Lord Chancellor had a huge input into decisions over judicial appointments. Appointments to the High Court and lower courts were made by the Queen on his advice, and those to the Court of Appeal and House of Lords on the advice of the Prime Minister, who acted in turn on the Lord Chancellor's advice. Section 61 of the 2005 Act created an independent Judicial Appointments Commission which is charged with the responsibility of recommending suitable candidates to fill judicial vacancies which arise. Although the Lord Chancellor may reject the first nomination for a post, he cannot substitute his own choice of nominee or reject more than one nominee per post. Supreme Court appointments will be effectively chosen by the Lord Chancellor from a list put forward by a temporary appointments commission formed for this purpose. Although some scope remains for government influence over judicial appointments, the changes brought about by the Act clearly provide for a much greater degree of independence in judicial appointments.

[7]You are unlikely to have time to explain these various provisions in any technical detail, but the important point is that you emphasise the role of the newly created Judicial Appointments Commission and relate this back to the importance of the independence of the judiciary.

In conclusion, the major reforms introduced by the Constitutional Reform Act 2005 are of huge significance. Their impact upon the role of the Lord Chancellor, functions of Supreme Court judges and judicial appointments considerably strengthen the separation of powers within the UK and reinforce the independence of the judiciary.[8]

[8]This is a logical conclusion which relates back to the argument advanced at the outset of the answer and which has been reinforced throughout the following discussion.

✓ Make your answer stand out

- Clearly emphasise the importance of the Constitutional Reform Act in terms of its impact upon the separation of powers and independence of the judiciary. For some critical insights on these matters, you may find it helpful to read: Lord Windlesham, 'The Constitutional Reform Act 2005: Ministers, Judges and Constitutional Change, Part 1', *Public Law*, 2005, p. 806.
- Demonstrate a clear understanding of the situation which existed before the reforms introduced by the Act came into force, in order to reinforce its significance.

! Don't be tempted to . . .

- Concentrate your answer simply on the changes made to the role of the Lord Chancellor;
- Attempt to reel off numerous provisions of the Act, rather than focusing on the few most significance changes it has brought about.

5

Personnel within the English legal system

How this topic may come up in exams

Examination questions will typically require you to demonstrate an understanding of the process by which judges, solicitors and barristers are appointed or become qualified, and the main functions which they perform. Specifically you may be asked to comment upon the composition of the judiciary or consider the case for a unified legal profession. You might also be tested on your understanding of the function of lay participants – magistrates and juries – in the legal system, their relative merits, and the process by which they are selected. You may also be asked to assess the role of the government's law officers.

Attack the question

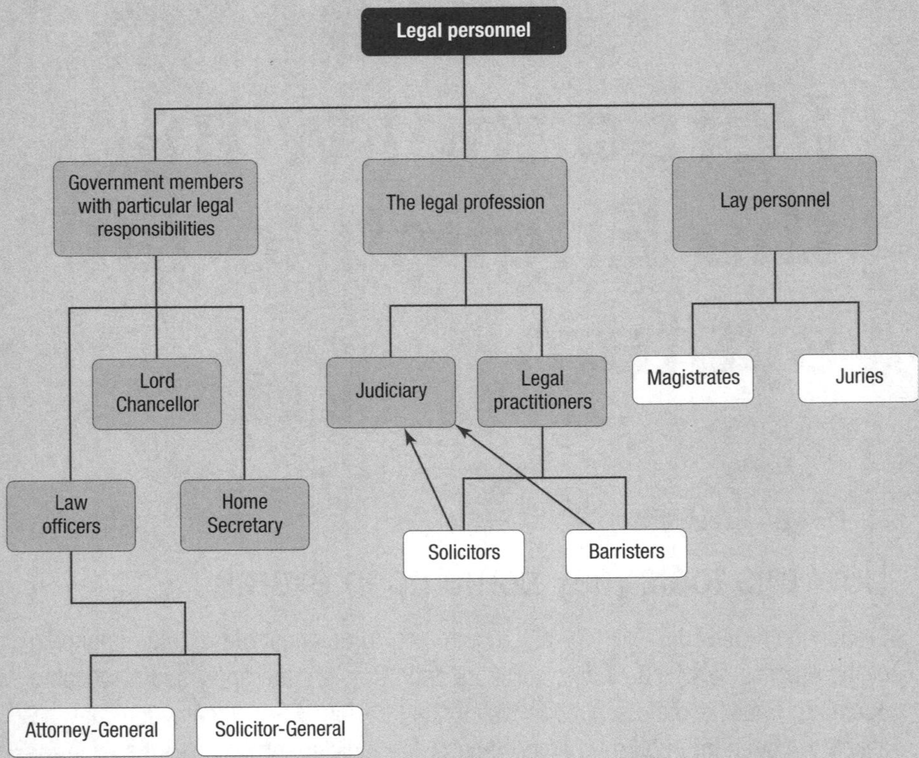

A printable version of this diagram plan is available from www.pearsoned.co.uk/lawexpressqa

Question 1

(A) What requirements must a candidate for the judiciary satisfy?

(B) Discuss the extent to which the current judiciary is representative of society.

Answer plan

- ➜ Briefly explain how judicial appointments are made.
- ➜ Explain what qualifications must be satisfied by candidates for judicial posts, ensuring that you mention some of the recent reforms which have broadened the pool from which appointments must be made.
- ➜ Make some observations upon the current composition of the judiciary with reference to gender, race, age and background.
- ➜ Briefly refer to some of the initiatives which have, or may, impact upon levels of diversity among the judiciary.

Diagram plan

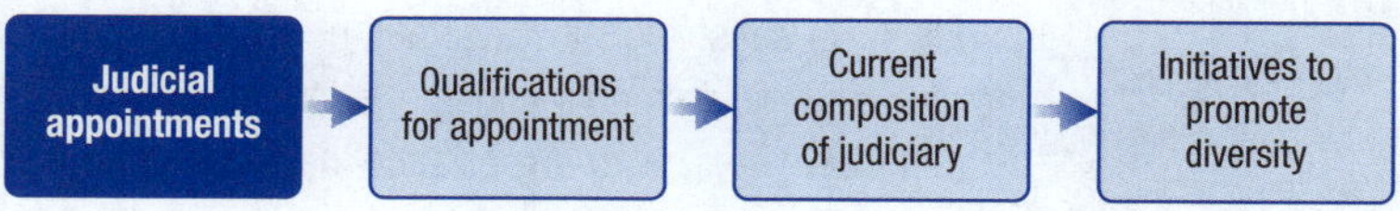

A printable version of this diagram plan is available from www.pearsoned.co.uk/lawexpressqa

Answer

The Constitutional Reform Act 2005 created the Judicial Appointments Commission, which is the principal body responsible for most judicial appointments.[1] It is responsible for soliciting applications for judicial vacancies and evaluating the merits of candidates for posts, before putting forward a nominated candidate for confirmation or rejection by the Lord Chancellor. As the Lord Chancellor may only reject one candidate for each vacant post, his role in the appointments process is clearly limited and the Judicial Appointments Commission's choice of candidates to fill vacant posts will generally stand. A more complicated process governs appointments to senior judicial posts, where temporary commissions are formed to consider the merits of candidates. For appointments to the Supreme Court, the Lord Chancellor is

[1]Before considering the qualifications to be satisfied by candidates for the judiciary, it is helpful to briefly explain how judicial appointments are made by way of background to your answer. The role of the Judicial Appointments Commission is particularly relevant, as it has played an important role in developing some of the necessary qualifications.

presented with a choice of candidates from which a vacancy can be filled. For any candidate to be considered for appointment to a judicial post, however, certain qualifications must be satisfied.

The qualifications for holding judicial office essentially fall into two categories. Firstly are those qualifications which any potential judge must be able to satisfy.[2] Under section 63(3) of the Constitutional Reform Act, judicial appointees are required to be of 'good character'. The Judicial Appointments Commission has set out guidelines which will inform its judgments upon the question of whether candidates are of 'good character'. These include consideration of the criminal convictions, insolvency history and disciplinary records of candidates. Candidates for judicial office must also be citizens of the UK, Ireland or a commonwealth country, and be under the judicial retirement age of 70. To assess candidates for vacancies, the Judicial Appointments Commission has also identified five core qualities and abilities which are required for judicial office. These consist of intellectual capacity, personal qualities, an ability to understand and deal fairly, authority and communication skills and efficiency.

In addition to satisfying these various general qualifications, specific statutory requirements apply to each judicial post concerning the minimum degree of experience necessary for candidates seeking that particular post.[3] Until relatively recently, eligibility for appointment to judicial posts was based on the number of years during which a candidate had enjoyed rights of audience. As a result, barristers accounted for the overwhelming majority of new appointments to the judiciary. However, the Tribunals Courts and Enforcement Act 2007 made eligibility for more posts dependent upon a candidate's number of years' post-qualification experience as opposed to rights of audience.[4] Thus, more solicitors will now be eligible for consideration for appointment to judicial posts. Due to provisions of the 2007 Act, legal executives are now also able to apply for certain judicial posts, as are government lawyers. The pool of potential judicial appointees, therefore, is wider than it has ever been before. Generally speaking, a candidate for judicial office must have a minimum of five to seven years' post-qualification experience at the level for which they are seeking a judicial position. Longer minimum periods of qualification are required for appointments to the more senior judicial posts.[5]

[2]It is useful to distinguish judicial qualifications into those which apply generally to all posts and those specific to particular posts.

[3]You need to demonstrate that different levels of experience are required for different judicial posts within the court hierarchy, in addition to the general qualifications required of all candidates for judicial office.

[4]This is a very important point to make. It shows awareness of relatively recent developments but is directly relevant to the issue of the composition of the judiciary to be addressed later in the answer.

[5]Within the constraints of an exam setting it is not necessary to describe the various minimum periods of qualification required for appointment to each judicial office. The key point is that you demonstrate that you are aware of the existence of these. You could perhaps provide an example, say, of the minimum requirements for appointment to a senior court, such as the Supreme Court or Court of Appeal.

It is widely acknowledged that the judiciary within the UK are not particularly representative of the wider society. The composition of the judiciary is regularly subject to criticism on the grounds that it is disproportionately white, male, middle class and middle aged. Some commentators have also called into question the political values which they feel are held by most judges. Statistically, there is little case for disputing the narrow composition of the judiciary.[6] The judiciary is overwhelmingly white. In 2004, only 3% of judges came from ethnic minority groups despite the fact that ethnic minorities accounted for 8% of the population of the UK. The gender imbalance within the judiciary is also evident. Although the population is approximately split evenly by sex, women only held 16% of judicial posts in 2004. In terms of senior posts, they were even less well represented, holding just 9% of those positions. The narrow class background from which judges are drawn is blatantly obvious when it is considered that since 1997, approximately 80% of the holders of judicial office received a public school education. The average age of judges is 58, confirming that judges are by and large middle aged. Having considered the statistical evidence, it is difficult to refute the commonly held perception that judges are indeed white, male, middle class and middle aged.

[6]You can most effectively illustrate the extent to which the judiciary is not representative of wider society through the citation of some relevant statistics.

It can be asked whether it particularly matters that the judiciary are unrepresentative of the wider society.[7] In his famous work, *The Politics of the Judiciary*, Griffith suggests that the narrow range of backgrounds from which members of the judiciary are drawn has resulted in the existence of a judiciary which is biased in favour of conventional and established interests, and cites a number of areas of the law where he perceives the courts as having given effect to such interests. At the same time, defenders of the judiciary would argue that notwithstanding their unrepresentative composition, the judiciary are fiercely independent and exercise balanced judgments upon sensitive political matters. In support of this view they might make reference to various examples in the area of judicial review where the courts have held to account the actions of governments of both political persuasions. Arguably, the major concern over the unrepresentative composition of the judiciary is that it threatens to undermine public confidence in the judicial system. If the population at large are unable to relate to the judiciary because they are not perceived to reflect the diversity of the population, a resulting

[7]This is a relevant point to raise. If the judiciary is unrepresentative, it is worth considering briefly why this might matter before looking at how it might be made more representative.

perception that the judiciary lacks legitimacy would not be surprising. Reinforcing such arguments, in a 2001 article concerned with the underrepresentation of women in the judicial ranks, Baroness Hale argues that a more representative judiciary is necessary for imperatives associated with the promotion of equal opportunities and bolstering the judiciary's legitimacy.

[8]You should conclude your answer by briefly considering whether any steps have been taken to improve the diversity of the judiciary. At this point you can relate back to your earlier discussion of the qualifications necessary for judicial appointment, as recent changes in that respect offer some prospects of improving the diversity of those appointed to judicial office.

Some steps have been taken to improve the diversity of the judiciary.[8] Under section 64 of the Constitutional Reform Act, the Judicial Appointments Commission must have regard to the need to encourage diversity in judicial appointments. In pursuit of this, the Commission may undertake various initiatives, for example, launching campaigns to encourage under-represented groups to apply for judicial posts. The Lord Chancellor can also issue guidance on promoting diversity within the judiciary. It should not be overlooked that recent changes to necessary qualifications for appointment to judicial posts will hopefully also go some way towards improving diversity within the judiciary. By widening the pool of potential candidates, whereby more solicitors (or even legal executives) – who comprise a more diverse group than do barristers – are likely to assume judicial posts, gradually there should be more women, ethnic minorities and those with non-public school educational backgrounds holding judicial office.

✓ Make your answer stand out

- Demonstrate how the judicial appointments process has been opened up to allow for a wider pool of potential categories of people to be eligible for appointment to judicial posts.
- Refer to academic debates upon the composition of the judiciary in considering the importance of a diverse bench, for example the discussion provided by Dame Brenda Hale, 'Equality and the Judiciary: Why Should We Want More Women Judges?', *Public Law*, 2002, p.489.
- Consider how the diversity of the judiciary might be enhanced.

! Don't be tempted to . . .

- Describe in detail the minimum qualifications applicable to each single judicial post;
- Treat the two parts of the question as two mutually exclusive questions.

Question 2

'Solicitors and barristers share in common basic legal qualifications and the fact that they work in the law. However, that is where their similarities end.' Discuss in relation to the roles performed by solicitors and barristers respectively.

Answer plan

- Briefly explain the division of the legal profession within the UK.
- Explain the different routes through which solicitors and barristers qualify.
- Explain the nature of the work undertaken by solicitors and the environment within which they work.
- Explain the nature of the work undertaken by barristers and the environment within which they work.
- Conclude by commenting upon the extent to which the roles performed by solicitors and barristers respectively are different.

Diagram plan

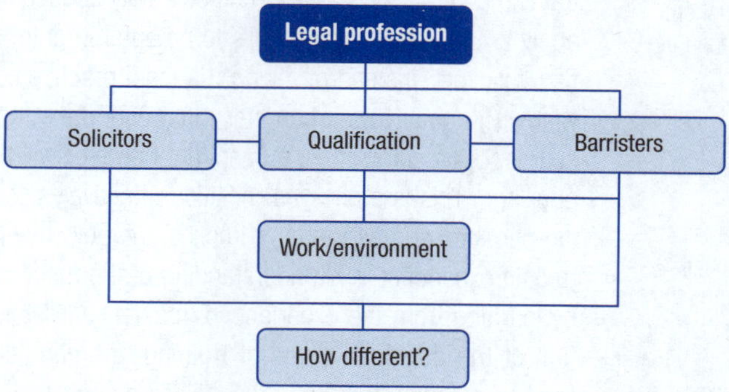

A printable version of this diagram plan is available from www.pearsoned.co.uk/lawexpressqa

Answer

Compared to many jurisdictions the UK is somewhat unusual in lacking a single legal profession. The distinction between the roles of solicitors and barristers is of historic origin, and to this day, the two professions are distinct from one another in their routes to qualification, the nature of the work they perform and the environments within which they operate.[1]

The normal route for entry to either of the legal professions begins with the requirement of either a qualifying law degree, or a degree in another subject followed by the successful completion of the graduate diploma in law (formerly known as the common professional examination). This requirement can be dispensed with in some circumstances but these are rare and exceptional. Following completion of this stage, the routes to qualification of solicitors and barristers proceed down different paths as the quotation implies.[2]

To qualify as a solicitor, a student must first complete the legal practice course before obtaining a training contract. The training contract is effectively the apprenticeship stage of training and involves spending two years as a trainee solicitor, ordinarily in a firm of solicitors, but the training contract might alternatively be served with a government department or public sector body. During the training contract, the trainee solicitor will gain practical experience of the work undertaken by solicitors, but will also complete several days of practical skills courses. After successful completion of the training contract, a trainee becomes a fully fledged solicitor and can apply to the Master of the Rolls to be entered onto the roll of qualified solicitors. Instead of taking the legal practice course, a person wishing to qualify as a barrister must undertake the bar vocational course. Upon completion, an aspirant barrister will need to obtain a pupillage. This is a one-year position effectively assisting a practising barrister, and as the term implies, the objective is for the 'pupil' to gain experience and understanding of the functions of a barrister by learning from the experienced 'master' barrister. Upon completion of the pupillage stage of training, the candidate is called to the bar, meaning that he is recognised as qualified to practise as a barrister. Trainee barristers must join one of the four inns of courts and must dine there 12 times before being eligible to be called to the bar. The route to qualification is clearly very different for solicitors and barristers. However, post-qualification both professions are expected to undertake continuing training and education on an annual basis.[3]

It has been suggested that solicitors perform a 'general practitioner' role within the provision of legal services.[4] They are involved in the provision of all forms of legal service, covering such diverse forms

[1]By alluding to the nature of the main differences between the two professions at the outset, you set the scene nicely for the main contents of the answer to follow.

[2]It is important that you show the similarities and differences in the qualifying routes for both professions. You are able to refer back to the question here in agreeing that in terms of qualifying routes, solicitors and barristers only share basic legal qualifications in common, after which they must pursue different paths. You should ensure that you explain both the formal qualifications and necessary training which must be satisfied by solicitors and barristers.

[3]This is a useful point to make as it illustrates the fact that training does not end upon qualification. If you have time you might explain in a little more detail the specific continuing professional development requirements of each profession.

[4]This is a very important point. You need to illustrate the diverse range of services provided by solicitors as this is a key factor distinguishing them from barristers.

of work as conveyancing, probate, drafting contracts, provision of advice to suspects in police custody and advocacy. In practice, an individual solicitor is likely to specialise in one or a few areas of law. Solicitors enjoy considerable direct contact with their clients. Most solicitors spend much of their time concerned with various forms of paperwork undertaken for private clients, with only a minority of solicitors being involved in advocacy. The traditional role of solicitors has been challenged by some key changes in recent years.[5] In 1985, solicitors lost the monopoly which they had long held upon conveyancing, this being opened up to non-solicitors. However, on the other hand, solicitors have seen their rights of appearance in the courts substantially increased. Although traditionally solicitors would represent defendants in most criminal proceedings, as the overwhelming majority of cases were dispensed with in the Magistrates Courts, barristers effectively had a monopoly on advocacy in higher courts. However, the Courts and Legal Services Act 1990 conferred greater rights of audience upon solicitors, which were then increased by section 36 of the Access to Justice Act 1999, as a result of which solicitors now enjoy full rights of audience, subject to having the necessary qualifications and training. Increasingly solicitors are now undertaking advocacy work.

[5]Credit should be given for coverage of this issue. By referring to some of the ways in which the traditional role of solicitors has undergone change, you evidence awareness of wider debates over the future roles of the legal profession and can refer back to this in your conclusion.

Solicitors are able to form partnerships,[6] and since 2001 have been able to form limited liability partnerships, which they are increasingly doing. With the exception of a small number of solicitors working alone, solicitors invariably work within a firm of solicitors, which range from huge commercial firms in London employing thousands of staff to smaller practices where the staff number single figures. The Law Society is the professional body of solicitors, although the regulation of solicitors is now the responsibility of the Solicitors Regulatory Authority.

[6]The difference between solicitors and barristers is further highlighted by reference to the environments within which they work. By clearly explaining the working environment of solicitors here, you can contrast this to that of barristers later in your answer.

Unlike solicitors, barristers only undertake advocacy and related work, such as the preparation of materials for court proceedings.[7] In contrast to the perception of the solicitor as a 'general practitioner, the barrister is very much a 'specialist'. Furthermore, most barristers specialise in particular areas of law. After 10 years of practice, a barrister may apply to become a Queen's Counsel (QC), a title which is used to distinguish an elite group of the most highly regarded barristers. Unlike solicitors, barristers enjoy only limited direct access to clients. Traditionally, clients are referred to a

[7]In explaining the nature of the work undertaken by barristers, you should be able to refer back to points you have already made about solicitors to reinforce the differences between them.

barrister through a solicitor. The ban on direct access to clients was relaxed in 2004, but direct access is restricted and is only permitted where a barrister has been in practice for three years. Barristers are bound by the 'cab rank' rule, whereby they are obliged to take on any case which they are asked to unless they are already committed to another case for the time in question.

Unlike solicitors, barristers may not form partnerships. They are instead required to be self-employed.[8] However, barristers are based in premises shared with other barristers known as chambers. A barrister, once qualified, must obtain a tenancy within a chambers in order to practise. Although each individual barrister is self-employed, each chambers will have a shared clerk of chambers who will be responsible for ensuring the smooth running of the chambers and for allocating cases to barristers. The professional body of barristers is the Bar Council, with the regulation of barristers being undertaken by the Bar Standards Board.

[8]Again, you are able to contrast the working environment of barristers with that of solicitors to reinforce the major differences between the professions.

Solicitors and barristers undoubtedly are very much distinct from one another. They qualify through different routes, are regulated by different bodies, work in different environments and undertake different work. The quotation, thus, bears much truth. However, there has been a growing debate in recent years over possible moves towards a fusion of the two professions and measures such as the granting of full rights of audience to solicitors may be taken as evidence of increasing overlap between the professions. That said, there clearly remain such significant differences between them that the creation of a unified legal profession would constitute a very radical step indeed.[9]

[9]Having considered the major differences between solicitors and barristers, it is helpful to add some context to this in your conclusion by referring to debates over possible fusion of the two professions. You can refer back to your earlier discussion of changes to the role performed by solicitors in considering the extent to which there has been some convergence between the professions.

✓ Make your answer stand out

- Make reference to the increased rights of audience now enjoyed by solicitors to illustrate the extent to which there is now greater overlap between the legal professions.
- Ensure that your answer covers not only the differences in the necessary training of, and nature of work undertaken by, solicitors and barristers, but also the different nature of their working environments.
- Provide greater context to your answer by reading Abel, R.L., 'The Decline of Professionalism', *Arbitration*, 1987, v. 53, n. 3, pp. 187–208, and making reference to the historical and social background to some of the distinctions between the two legal professions.

! Don't be tempted to . . .

- Explain the main features of the two professions without making any comparison between them.
- Become sidetracked by considering the arguments over merging the legal professions.

Question 3

Discuss the case for a merged legal profession to replace the separate status of barristers and solicitors.

Answer plan

→ Briefly explain the major differences between the nature of the work undertaken by barristers and solicitors.

→ Discuss the arguments in favour of a merged legal profession.

→ Discuss the arguments against a merged legal profession.

→ Conclude by commenting upon whether you consider the case for a merged legal profession to be sufficiently compelling.

Diagram plan

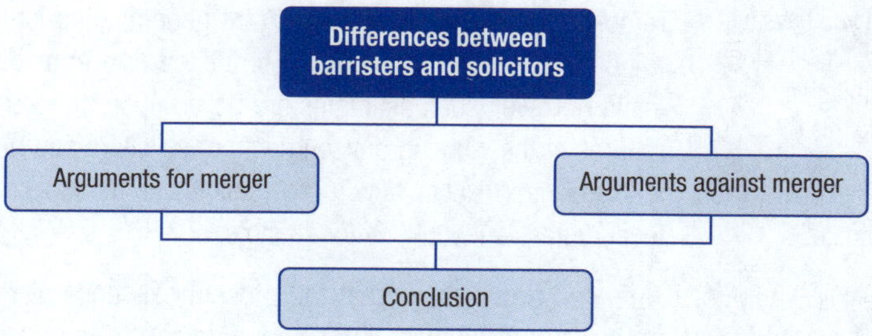

A printable version of this diagram plan is available from www.pearsoned.co.uk/lawexpressqa

Answer

The legal profession within the UK is divided into two significantly different branches, solicitors and barristers.[1] They have different routes to qualification, their working environments are different, they have their own professional and regulatory bodies and whereas solicitors are engaged in the provision of the full range of legal services, barristers only undertake advocacy work. Notwithstanding these significant differences, there has been a growing debate over the merits of creating a single unified legal profession. Recent developments, such as the greater rights of audience afforded solicitors by the Courts and Legal Services Act 1990 and Access to Justice Act 1999 have arguably added further momentum to this debate.

[1]Begin your answer by providing some context, demonstrating the extent to which solicitors and barristers are very different in some key respects.

A major argument for creating a unified profession is that this will reduce the cost of litigation.[2] The traditional restriction upon the ability of potential litigants to approach barristers directly means that ordinarily a solicitor will be contacted in the first instance, who will probably undertake some work upon the case in hand before, when appropriate, instructing a barrister who will represent the client in court proceedings. The client is, thus, essentially required to pay two lawyers for work on the same matter. It has been suggested that the creation of a unified legal profession could minimise the costs faced by potential litigants, who would be able to approach the same person to undertake all of the work in a shorter period of time as any duplication would also be removed. It has been suggested that generally barristers are likely to be cheaper than solicitors due to the lesser overheads which they incur. However, such estimates are based upon the current differing natures of the working environments of solicitors and barristers and it is less clear exactly how more economical the services of a single legal profession would be for litigants.[3]

[2]This is a prominent argument that you should refer to.

[3]Here you counter-balance the argument you have just considered by highlighting its possible limitations. You should do this for each argument throughout considered in your answer where appropriate.

A related argument is that the present existence of two separate professions produces inefficiency due to the unnecessary duplication of much work.[4] Prior to a barrister becoming involved in a particular case, a solicitor will already often have undertaken a considerable amount of preparatory work. Often the barrister will have actually had very little input into the case prior to the time at which it reaches court and will have to familiarise himself with all the relevant information and materials which have already been prepared

[4]This argument is closely connected to the one considered previously. You should make connections between the various arguments where you can. They are not mutually exclusive.

and understood by the solicitor. The existence of a single legal profession would remove this duplication as the same person who began work on the case could take it through to its conclusion in litigation. Duplication aside, it is also sometimes felt that barristers are insufficiently involved in the preparatory work for cases, meaning that they are perhaps sometimes insufficiently acquainted with a case to argue its merits in court.[5] Many clients only meet their barrister for the first time at the 'last minute', immediately before a case commences in court.

[5]This is a key point that can be drawn from the more general argument. Be prepared to try and identify these where they exist and clearly state them.

The above arguments only really apply where litigation is concerned.[6] The enhanced rights of audience afforded solicitors by the Access to Justice Act 1999 mean that increasingly solicitors will be able to steer cases to and through court litigation. A more general argument for a unified profession is that currently much talent goes to waste[7], with law students having to choose their career path at a very early stage, potentially depriving each profession of the talents of those who have embarked upon the other career path. This argument is now harder to sustain in respect of solicitors who may be effective advocates, as it has become much easier for solicitors to take upon advocacy work that was once solely the domain of barristers. However, barristers are very much limited to advocacy work and any competences they may have for other forms of legal work currently go unrecognised and unusable. The argument can be made that other countries do not tend to divide the legal profession as the UK does, but this is hardly a good reason in itself why the UK should not do so.

[6]Here you are recognising the limitations of some of the arguments that you have considered. This demonstrates that you are taking a balanced approach to the question.

[7]Again, here is an argument that you can take and subject to a counter-argument.

It is argued that the existence of separate legal professions allows for specialisation.[8] However, solicitors are generalists in performing the full range of legal services. Whereas barristers are specialists in advocacy, the gradual extension of advocacy rights for solicitors appears to undermine the importance of specialism. In any event, even within a unified legal profession lawyers would be likely to continue to specialise in particular forms of services or areas of law, just as they do now.

[8]You are now addressing the arguments against the creation of a unified profession, yet are continuing to subject each argument to critique.

A related argument is that the importance of good advocacy demands that there be a specialist body performing this service.[9] However, there is no evidence that solicitors who currently perform advocacy are less competent than barristers. Advocates must be able to satisfy minimum periods of training and/or qualification. Within a unified legal profession there is likely to be a body of lawyers who specialise in advocacy. There is no reason why the quality of advocacy would decline.

[9]Again, you present a key argument and effectively counter-balance it with a relevant point.

It has been suggested that accessibility of advocates would be threatened by the creation of a single profession as many top barristers could move to join a few large elite commercial firms, who would dominate the advocacy market.[10] However, a market would inevitably continue to exist for more affordable advocacy services, and while access to the most high profile advocates may be restricted by economic factors, this is arguably already the case with leading barristers being far more expensive than their lower profile peers.

[10]Some of the arguments to be considered are based on a degree of speculation. While this may be a ground for criticism of them, you may also need to think speculatively in order to rebut or accept them.

A final argument against the creation of a single legal profession is that it may threaten the independence of advocates.[11] Barristers are bound by the 'cab rank' principle and may not form partnerships, whereas neither rule would be likely to apply to those practising advocacy as part of a single legal profession. However, this argument is overstated as barristers currently deploy certain devices to circumvent the 'cab rank' principle and thousands of solicitors employed by partnerships are gradually taking on greater advocacy rights.

[11]Here you are able to effectively rebut an argument by reference to some factual evidence, in this case the increased advocacy role undertaken by solicitors.

Strong arguments can be advanced both for and against the creation of a unified legal profession. Although the arguments in favour of retaining the status quo are not entirely convincing, many of the arguments for merger concern benefits for litigants from reduced duplication of work and costs. Reforms granting greater rights of audience to solicitors have, arguably, gone some way towards addressing some of these concerns and it may be asked whether there is any need to proceed to a complete merger of the professions. Given the radical step which a merger would constitute, arguably the case for such a move should be more compelling than it appears to be.[12]

[12]This is a logical conclusion which relates back to the opening paragraph's explanation of the significant differences between the two branches of the profession, and the balanced discussion which followed of the various arguments over merging them.

Make your answer stand out

- Add some context to your answer by highlighting at the outset the significance of the differences between the two branches of the legal profession.
- Incorporate some reference to reforms which have closed the gap between the respective roles of barristers and solicitors in the provision of advocacy services.

Don't be tempted to . . .

- List the various arguments for and against the creation of a single unified legal profession as a series of bullet points;
- Try and cover every argument you may have read on this debate if this risks you having insufficient time to properly explain the most compelling arguments.

Question 4

Discuss the main functions of those members of the government with particular responsibility for the administration of justice.

Answer plan

→ Briefly explain who the government's law officers are and which government members have particular responsibility for the administration of justice.

→ Consider the main responsibilities of the Lord Chancellor/Secretary of State for Justice.

→ Consider the main responsibilities of the Home Secretary.

→ Consider the main responsibilities of the Attorney-General and Solicitor-General and their relationship with one another.

→ Make reference to the arguments that have been made concerning the possible politicisation of the Attorney-General's functions and proposals for reform.

Diagram plan

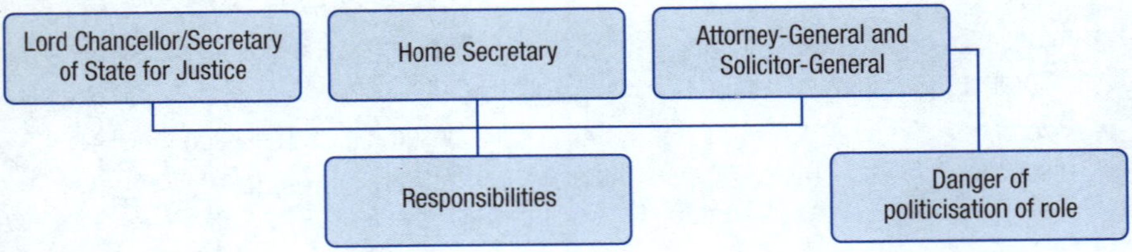

A printable version of this diagram plan is available from www.pearsoned.co.uk/lawexpressqa

Answer

The Attorney-General and Solicitor-General are generally referred to as the government's law officers.[1] They are government members drawn from either House of Parliament and appointed by the Prime Minister. In addition to these, although many government ministers have legal functions of some form, two have responsibilities that are particularly central to the administration of justice. These are the Lord Chancellor and the Home Secretary.

Historically, the Lord Chancellor's position compromised the principle of the separation of powers, him simultaneously sitting within the executive as a cabinet member, the legislature as speaker of the House of Lords, and the judiciary as its head capable of sitting on cases brought before the Judicial Committee of the House of Lords. However, the Constitutional Reform Act 2005 removed the latter two of these functions.[2] The Lord Chancellor may now be drawn from either House of Parliament, and in 2007 Jack Straw became the first MP appointed to the post. Today, the Lord Chancellor heads the Ministry of Justice and is more commonly referred to by his other title, Secretary of State for Justice. The Lord Chancellor and his ministry have overall responsibility for the operation of the legal system in general, which includes the organisation and management of the courts and tribunals, the administration of legal aid and judicial appointments.[3] The Ministry of Justice also has specific responsibility for criminal law legislation and constitutional reform. Recently, it took on responsibility for prisons and the probation service, areas which had until then been within the remit of the Home

[1]You should begin your answer by stating which government members have particular responsibility for the administration of justice.

[2]In explaining the functions of the Lord Chancellor, you should briefly explain the major changes that have taken place to his role relatively recently. This serves to reinforce that you understand his modern day functions by also showing what functions he no longer performs.

[3]This, in essence, summarises the key responsibilities of the Lord Chancellor and the Ministry of Justice today. In an examination setting you are unlikely to have the time to embark upon a detailed discussion of any of these.

Office.[4] While the Lord Chancellor retains much responsibility for the administration of the court system, the effect of the 2005 Act is that he no longer has any judicial role.

Despite losing responsibility for prisons and the probation service, the Home Secretary continues to be a key governmental figure as far as the administration of justice is concerned in particular as a result of the fact that he retains overall responsibility for the police.[5] The Home Secretary is also responsible for various crime related matters, such as government policy on drugs and the national identity card scheme. Since losing its responsibility for prisons and probation the Home Office's priorities have increasingly focused upon counter-terrorism, national security, immigration and asylum. The Home Secretary's responsibilities are very much of an executive nature and do not tread upon judicial territory.

The Attorney-General is the government's main legal adviser on both matters of domestic and international law. The Solicitor-General serves as his deputy, although since section 1 of the Law Officers Act 1997 permits the Solicitor-General to perform any of the functions of the Attorney-General,[6] the two can in practice agree upon a suitable division of labour between themselves.

As noted, the Attorney-General is the government's principal legal adviser.[7] He is responsible for advising the government upon the legal implications of government action or policy. This can occasionally lead to the Attorney-General becoming embroiled in a degree of controversy where the validity or objectivity of his advice is called into question. This occurred over the government's decision to participate in the invasion of Iraq in 2003, when the then Attorney-General, Lord Goldsmith, advised the government in a well publicised memo that there was justification under international law for the action, advice which was regarded by many as representing a u-turn from advice he had reportedly given earlier in which doubt was cast upon the legality of the government's intended course of action. The lingering assumption was that the Attorney-General changed his advice as a result of political considerations.

The Attorney-General is responsible for representing the government in major litigation, both domestically and internationally. He may also take action to restrain vexatious litigants and can intervene in the public interest in certain family and charity cases.[8] The

[4]This is a relevant point which evidences awareness of recent developments and leads into the next paragraph's treatment of the Home Secretary.

[5]This is the main point to be made in respect of the Home Secretary's responsibilities for the administration of justice.

[6]You should begin your answer by stating which government members have particular responsibility for the administration of justice.

[7]This is arguably the principal function of the Attorney-General and must be mentioned. Reference to the case of Iraq is useful in demonstrating that you are aware of situations in which the Attorney-General has advised the government on controversial matters.

[8]You are unlikely to have time within an examination setting to discuss in great detail the various functions of the Attorney-General. You should attempt to outline these briefly and focus upon those that are particularly interesting, topical or controversial to evidence wider understanding of the Attorney-General's role.

various prosecutorial bodies fall under the oversight of the Attorney-General, most notably the Crown Prosecution Service, whose head, the Director of Public Prosecutions, is directly answerable to the Attorney-General.

The Attorney-General enjoys various specific powers in relation to the criminal justice process, which are exercised in the public interest. A varied range of offences, as diverse as those covered by the Genocide Act 1969 and the Highways Act 1980, require the Attorney-General's consent for prosecution to commence, and the Attorney-General may also grant immunity from prosecution in certain circumstances.[9] He may also intervene to stop prosecutions in certain cases. Where media coverage of a trial risks jeopardising the right to a fair trial, the Attorney-General may bring contempt of court proceedings. Whenever there has been an acquittal in a criminal case, the Attorney-General can refer any relevant points of law to the Court of Appeal. Significantly, the Attorney-General can also appeal to the Court of Appeal against what he considers are lenient sentences handed down to those convicted of certain criminal offences. This power only applies, however, in respect of more serious offences and must be exercised within 28 days of the sentence having been imposed. The importance of this power is underlined by the fact that about 80 cases were referred to the Court of Appeal under this power during 2008 and approximately three quarters saw an increase to the original sentence.[10]

There has been some concern that some of the Attorney-General's functions may become politicised due to the fact that the post-holder is a government member.[11] For example, the need for the Attorney-General's consent for prosecution to commence in certain cases may be compromised by political considerations. If the example is taken of the police investigation into the 'cash for honours' scandal during 2006–7 in which the Prime Minister himself was questioned by police, should the Attorney-General have been presented with the decision over whether to initiate any prosecution, it would have been difficult to dispel any suggestion that his decision was politically motivated. (In the event, the police concluded there was insufficient evidence to commence any proceedings.)

[9]You need to make it clear that the Attorney-General enjoys specific powers in relation to the prosecution process and that you understand what the most noteworthy of these powers entail. Where possible, cite examples to illustrate situations where these powers may arise.

[10]Here you are focusing upon a particular power enjoyed by the Attorney-General and citing statistical evidence to illustrate its significance.

[11]You should conclude your discussion of the role of the Attorney-General by considering the charges which have been levelled at the possible politicisation of his role, and proposals to remove some of his powers where these may give rise to allegations of being subject to political influence. Refer to some practical examples to reinforce the issues raised.

Controversially, in 2007 the Attorney-General decided not to sanction prosecution against BAE Systems over possible bribes to the Saudi Arabian royal family in order to procure a contract. In response to concerns over the risk of politicisation of the Attorney-General's role, the government put forward proposals in a 2008 white paper to remove his power to decide whether prosecution should proceed in individual cases except for the most exceptional and serious of matters. The Director of Public Prosecutions would become responsible for making the decision whether to prosecute in virtually all cases. Such a reform would, arguably, be welcome as it would remove any danger or perception of political considerations shaping the prosecution process and strengthen public confidence in the criminal justice process.

✓ Make your answer stand out

- Make reference to the debate over the risk of politicisation of the role of the Attorney-General. Your answer can be strengthened by making reference to the discussion provided in the government green and white papers, *The Governance of Britain: A Consultation on the Role of the Attorney-General* (2007) and *The Governance of Britain: Constitutional Renewal* (2008). This reinforces awareness of recent developments.
- Illustrate the functions of the personnel covered by the question by citing examples of particular measures which they have been responsible for.
- Refer to the importance of the separation of powers in relation to the roles performed by the Lord Chancellor and Attorney-General.

! Don't be tempted to . . .

- Attempt to explain every single responsibility of each of the personnel covered by the question;
- Interpret the question narrowly and cover only one or two of the personnel that are relevant to your answer.

Question 5

Explain the role performed by lay magistrates and the process by which they are appointed. To what extent are lay magistrates representative of society?

Answer plan

- Explain that lay magistrates are non-legally qualified, part-time judges who preside over cases in the Magistrates Courts.
- Outline the main categories of cases which lay magistrates hear and the limited sentencing powers which they enjoy.
- Explain the eligibility criteria for appointment as a lay magistrate.
- Explain the process by which magistrates are appointed and the training which they receive.
- Conclude by commenting upon the narrow range of backgrounds from which lay magistrates are invariably drawn.

Diagram plan

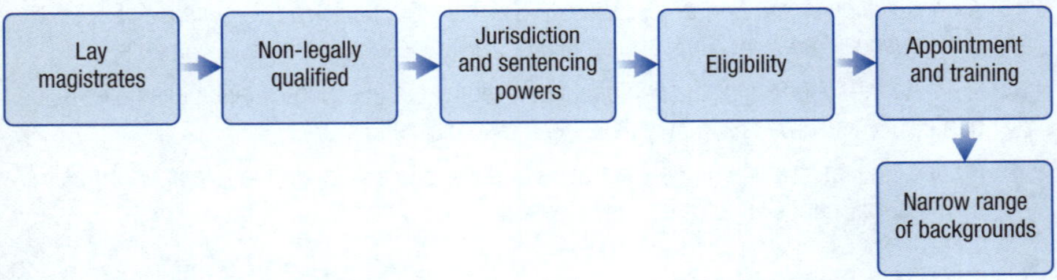

A printable version of this diagram plan is available from www.pearsoned.co.uk/lawexpressqa

Answer

Lay magistrates are non-legally qualified, part-time judges who preside over cases heard in the Magistrates' Court.[1] Their involvement in the administration of justice dates back to the Justices of the Peace Act 1361. Lay magistrates are not salaried, but may receive expenses to reimburse them for costs incurred in the performance of their duties. There are approximately 28,000 lay magistrates currently sitting in about 700 different courts. They normally sit in panels of two or three, and each lay magistrate is expected to sit for a minimum

[1] Your introductory paragraph should briefly summarise the non-legally qualified, non-salaried, voluntary nature of lay magistrates. This leads into the following paragraphs' explanation of their jurisdiction and the manner by which they are appointed.

of twenty-six and a half days each year. Being non-legally qualified, lay magistrates rely considerably upon the assistance of the justices' clerk, who is a legally qualified officer of the court and will advise them on any legal issues which they need further guidance upon, as well as the extent of their sentencing powers.

[2]Although you do not need to go into great detail on the jurisdiction enjoyed by magistrates, the crucial point is that you make clear that they are primarily concerned with the administration of the criminal law, in particular lower level criminal offences. This paragraph gets this point over clearly and also demonstrates an awareness of magistrates' powers as far as sentencing offenders is concerned.

Although lay magistrates have limited jurisdiction over civil matters, for example exercising licensing powers, they are primarily concerned with the administration of the criminal law.[2] All trials for summary offences are heard in the Magistrates' Court and it can also hear those 'triable either way' offences, listed in schedule 1 to the Magistrates' Courts Act 1980 or contained under various individual statutes. The vast majority of criminal cases are in fact concluded in the Magistrates' Court. Essentially, magistrates are concerned with relatively minor offences, and approximately 50% of their time is spent on motoring offences. Lay magistrates have limited sentencing powers, although these were increased by the Criminal Justice Act 2003 to a maximum of 12 months' imprisonment for a single offence and 65 weeks where more than one consecutive custodial sentence is imposed for multiple offences. If it is felt that a particular defendant is deserving of a tougher sentence, sentencing will need to be passed over to the Crown Court where judges enjoy the full range of sentencing powers. Magistrates also have the responsibility of granting bail and issuing search warrants in certain circumstances.

[3]In explaining the process by which lay magistrates are appointed you should begin by setting out the eligibility criteria.

There are relatively few requirements to be satisfied by a person wishing to be appointed as a lay magistrate.[3] Candidates for the magistracy must be under the age of 65 at the time of appointment, although serving magistrates may continue to sit until the age of 70, they must live within 15 miles of the area for which they will serve and must be available to sit for a minimum of $26\frac{1}{2}$ days annually. Although magistrates do not technically retire, they are placed upon the 'supplemental list' once they reach the age of 70 which means that they are no longer eligible to sit on the magistrates' bench. Magistrates may be dismissed earlier on certain specified grounds listed under section 11 of the Courts Act 2003, such as misconduct. In 1998 a 'job description' for magistrates was introduced, which sought to outline the qualities necessary of a magistrate. These included good character, social awareness, maturity and sound temperament, commitment and reliability. Certain categories of people are excluded from eligibility to serve as magistrates.[4] These are those whose status may lead to conflicts of interest or bias in performing the role, such as members of the police, traffic wardens, those convicted of criminal offences and bankrupts. Others are precluded from serving because their status undermines their ability to serve effectively, namely members of the armed forces and those with certain disabilities.

The appointment of lay magistrates is formally made by the Lord Chancellor on behalf of the Queen, under section 10(1) of the Courts Act 2003, although appointment procedures may soon fall under the remit of the Judicial Appointments Commission which was created by the Constitutional Reform Act 2005. Appointments are made following consultations with local advisory committees, the membership of which is appointed by the Ministry of Justice. Local advisory committees nominate candidates for vacancies.[5] In putting forward names for appointment, they are to have regard to the composition of the area for which the magistrates are to be appointed, in order to ensure a relatively representative lay bench. Local advisory committees will sometimes advertise available posts, for which various locally active groups, such as political parties, trade unions and community groups may put forward names.

Upon appointment, lay magistrates receive relatively little training.[6] Although it is a statutory requirement under section 19 of the Courts Act 2003 that the Lord Chancellor arrange for suitable training, the training which new magistrates receive is rather basic, covering issues such as procedure, chairing hearings, jurisdiction and sentencing powers. Training places special emphasis upon the equal treatment of those who come before them in court.

A major criticism of lay magistrates is that they are drawn from a narrow sector of British society. Although there is a roughly even number of men and women sitting as lay magistrates, they do tend to be middle aged, white and come from professional backgrounds. Politically, the lay magistracy is thought to be more conservative than the population at large.[7] Arguably, more needs to be done to diversify the composition of the lay magistracy if they are to enjoy public confidence in their ability to perform their functions effectively and not be seen as 'out of touch' with the realities of everyday life

[4]This builds upon the previous point. It is helpful if you are able to explain briefly the rationale for such classes of people being ineligible for appointment as a lay magistrate.

[5]Local advisory committees play an important role in the appointment process and it is important that they are not overlooked in your answer. You might relate the point made here about the kinds of groups which put forward names for appointment to the lay bench to the issue discussed later of the narrow composition of the bench.

[6]Although training comes upon appointment, it is worth mentioning in your answer and should receive some credit. By briefly alluding to the limited training given to lay magistrates you can reinforce their status as non-legally qualified adjudicators.

[7]This is a very good point on which to conclude your answer. By raising the narrow range of backgrounds from which the composition of the lay bench is drawn, you are able to indirectly raise questions about the process of appointment. Depending upon time constraints you may be able to make more of this issue and possibly make some proposals for reforms which might help to diversify the composition of the lay magistracy.

experienced by others. However, it is arguable that to some extent the very nature of the lay magistrate's role can be used to account for the narrow composition of the bench. For example, older people are more likely to be retired from full-time employment and have the necessary time to devote to the work of a magistrate. Professionally employed people are also more likely to either be able to take time off work, or have retired earlier. By contrast, those employed in working class jobs have traditionally found it more difficult to take the time off work necessary to take on roles such as that of a lay magistrate. Although there is a right to be released from work to undertake the duties of magistrate, contained in section 50 of the Employment Rights Act 1996, there is no obligation upon the part of employers to pay employees during this time, a problem more likely to affect those employed in lower paid occupations. Although increasing the diversity of lay magistrates is not likely to be an easy task, the importance of doing so was underlined by the fact that the Auld Review made some suggestions for ways in which the composition of the lay bench may be diversified, and in 1999 a campaign was launched to diversify recruitment to the lay bench.

✓ Make your answer stand out

- Make reference to debates over the perceived narrow range of backgrounds from which lay magistrates are appointed.
- Consider the merits of the functions performed by lay magistrates and whether the role of the magistracy ought to be reformed.

! Don't be tempted to . . .

- Confuse lay magistrates with District Judges, who are legally qualified full-time judges who sit in the Magistrates' Courts;
- Attempt to set out every individual matter over which magistrates have jurisdiction. You will not have time and it will suffice to summarise their jurisdiction more generally.

Question 6

Explain how juries are selected and their function in criminal trials.

Answer plan

- ➜ Explain that juries are used in all criminal trials heard in the Crown Court and a very limited range of civil cases.
- ➜ Explain who is eligible to serve as a juror.
- ➜ Explain the process by which juries are selected.
- ➜ Explain who is ineligible for jury service and who may be granted exemption or deferral.
- ➜ Explain the function of the jury in criminal trials and the process by which they reach their decisions.

Diagram plan

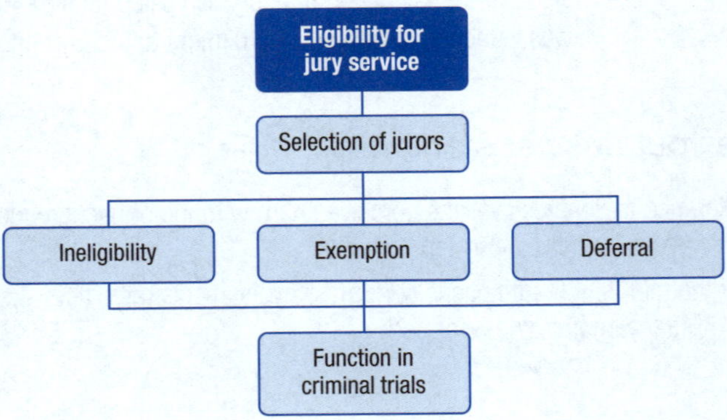

A printable version of this diagram plan is available from www.pearsoned.co.uk/lawexpressqa

Answer

The jury system has deep historical roots, and has been described by Lord Devlin as 'the lamp that shows freedom lives'. Juries are used in all criminal trials held in the Crown Court, as well as a few civil cases relating to defamation, malicious prosecution, false imprisonment or fraud. According to Slapper and Kelly, 409,807 people were summoned for jury service in 2004. However, only

1% of criminal trials are heard before a jury in the Crown Court. There has been considerable recent debate over the merits of the use of juries.[1] The Auld Review made recommendations enacted in the Criminal Justice Act 2003 which broadened the pool of eligible jurors, as well as allowing for dispensation with jury trial where a case involves complex financial arrangements (section 43) or there is a serious risk of jury tampering (section 44)

[1]It can provide useful context to your answer if you make reference to the scale upon which juries are used within the criminal justice process at the outset. You might also refer to the ongoing debate over the merits of the system of trial by jury.

Eligibility for jury service is governed by section 1 of the Juries Act 1974, as amended by the Criminal Justice Act 2003. Anyone on the electoral roll aged 18–70 and resident in the UK for the previous five years is generally eligible.[2] Mentally disordered persons and those with certain criminal convictions and sentences are disqualified from service. The Jury Central Summoning Bureau administers summonses to jurors randomly selected from the electoral register. At this stage, ineligible persons or those who feel that they ought to be exempted from, or have deferred until a later stage, jury service are able to report this fact for further consideration. Although jury service is regarded as a civic duty and no payment is made as such, jurors are entitled to claim expenses for travel, meals, time taken off work and other incidental expenses, such as childcare.

[2]The first stage in explaining the process by which juries are selected is to set out the eligibility criteria for jury service.

Before each trial commences in the Crown Court, the court officer produces a list of available jurors from which a jury will be selected by ballot in open court, following which the 12 selected will be sworn in. There is some scope for the defence and prosecution to challenge jurors[3] where they are regarded as unsuitable to sit on the case in hand, although they must show good reason for doing so. This will normally arise where the defendant is known to a juror. Where possible, jurors may be asked to 'stand by', which requires no reasons to be given. Attorney-General guidelines apply to this practice and although the theory is that a juror asked to 'stand-by' is only provisionally removed from the case depending upon the suitability of other possible jurors, the usual availability of alternatives mean that in practice it is a simpler means of excluding a particular juror. In exceptional cases, jurors can be vetted prior to being confirmed,[4] through checking police and special agency records. There is no statutory framework to govern the vetting of potential jurors, although Attorney-General guidelines seek to restrict the practice to serious cases, for example those involving terrorism and national security.

[3]Although this can easily be overlooked, it is highly relevant to this question to make reference to the process by which jurors might be challenged by either side in court as this is one means by which otherwise eligible jurors selected at random can be 'de-selected' prior to the commencement of a trial. If you have time, you may discuss some of the controversies which can arise from this practice.

[4]Jury vetting raises a similar issue to the previous point. Again, there are controversial issues which it gives rise to that may be given further consideration if time constraints in an exam setting do not militate against this.

Certain categories of persons are ineligible for jury service. Prior to the Criminal Justice Act 2003, several categories were exempted from jury service,[5] such as the clergy and those involved within the administration of justice like practising lawyers and police officers. However, the pool of those exempted was felt to be too wide and now only those with certain mental disabilities or certain forms of criminal conviction are disqualified. While the rationale for the previous exemption of those working within the administration of justice was based upon fears of bias, the House of Lords stated in **R *v* Abdroikov** [2007] 1 WLR 3538, CA that such people were no more prone to bias than anyone else. The random selection of juries should theoretically ensure that any biases among jurors balance themselves out. Exemption or deferral from jury service may also be granted at the discretion of the Jury Central Summoning Bureau, guidance upon which is provided in sections 9 and 9A of the Juries Act 1974.[6] A relatively flexible approach is taken towards requests for deferral of jury service, and it is usual for such requests to be accommodated to take account of a person's work commitments, childcare needs, pre-arranged holidays or other legitimate business which precludes him or her from performing jury service at the time when called. Exemption from service is now only possible where a person has already performed jury service within the previous two years, under section 8 of the Juries Act, or where the person considered is currently in military service. A judge may also excuse a person from jury service where he has doubts as to that person's ability to perform the role of juror effectively, for example, because of difficulty in understanding the English language.

[5]You need to explain who is not eligible to serve on a jury. You can demonstrate awareness of recent changes to the law here by showing how the pool of eligible jurors has been widened by legislative changes.

[6]You can conclude your treatment of the selection of jurors by explaining the scope for excusal or deferral from service once selected. In building upon the previous point, it is important that you show that although deferral is granted in a range of circumstances, exemption from jury service is rare.

Within a criminal trial the function of a jury is simply to decide upon the question of guilt: is the defendant guilty of the offence(s) with which he is charged? It has been established since **Bushell's Case** (1670) 124 ER 1006 that the jury are the sole judges of fact. As juries are comprised of lay people, most of whom will have very little understanding of the law, the judge is responsible for summarising the relevant legal issues for the jury. It is very important that the judge does this in an appropriate manner, as any incorrect summary of the law may give rise to an appeal against conviction on a matter of law. The decision to be reached by a jury is a matter for the jury alone and there have been cases where improper judicial pressure upon the jury for a particular verdict has been criticised.[7] For

[7]Explaining the basic function of the jury in a criminal trial is relatively straightforward, but there are issues which may affect the jury's performance of this function which merit some discussion. Judicial directions to the jury are one such matter and you can demonstrate awareness of this controversial area by referring to some of the cases in which judicial directions to the jury have resulted in criticism.

example, in **R *v* Wang** [2005] 1 WLR 661, the House of Lords held that a judge can never tell a jury to convict a defendant. In **R *v* McKenna** [1960] 2 WLR 306, it was improper for a judge to threaten to lock a jury up overnight if they did not return a verdict within ten minutes. The jury's discussions are behind closed doors and strictly confidential. Any breach of this confidentiality may give rise to an action for contempt of court, under section 8 of the Contempt of Court Act 1981. In **Attorney-General *v* Scotcher** [2005] 1 WLR 1867, confidentiality was breached by a juror's later letter discussing the case. Ordinarily, for a defendant to be convicted there must be a guilty verdict which is shared by at least ten jurors, although where the jury has decreased in size to ten members, a verdict agreed upon by nine can suffice. Juries are not required to give any explanation for the verdicts which they reach. They must simply pronounce whether they find the defendant to be guilty or not of the offence that he has been charged with.[8]

[8]This is a critical point and one of the key criticisms of the jury system. It is also an appropriate point on which to conclude the answer, marking the final act of the jury.

✓ Make your answer stand out

- Make reference to proposals for reform to the jury system, such as those contained in Sir Robin Auld's 2001 review of the criminal justice system.
- Make reference to some of the case law in which controversies have arisen in relation to aspects of the jury system.

! Don't be tempted to . . .

- Become engaged in the debate over the overall merits of using juries to try criminal cases;
- Simply list the eligibility criteria for jury service by way of explanation of the selection of juries.

Question 7

Discuss the arguments for and against the abolition of juries.

Answer plan

- ➜ Briefly explain the role performed by juries and refer to recent debates over their merits.
- ➜ Discuss the main arguments for the abolition of juries.
- ➜ Discuss the main arguments against the abolition of juries.
- ➜ Conclude upon the merits of the jury system.

Diagram plan

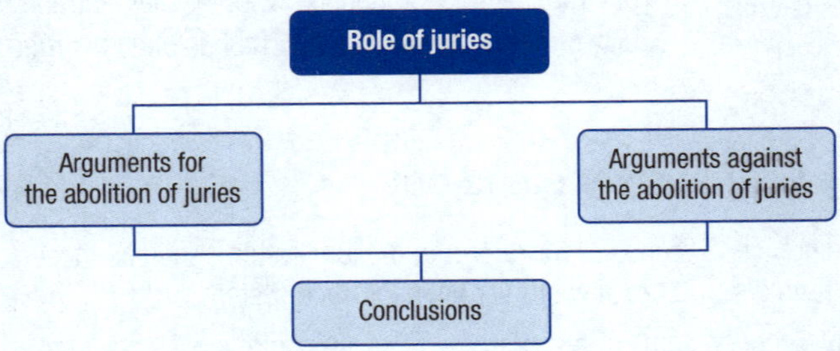

A printable version of this diagram plan is available from www.pearsoned.co.uk/lawexpressqa

Answer

Juries are randomly selected from the electoral register and are principally used in criminal trials heard in the Crown Court, charged with responsibility for determining the guilt of the defendant.[1] There have been ongoing debates for some time as to the merits of the jury system. Sir Robin Auld's review of the criminal courts gave some attention to juries and his proposals led to the abolition of many of the previous grounds for exemption from jury service, as well as removing the need for juries to be used where a serious risk exists of jury tampering or the case involves complex financial arrangements (sections 43–44, Criminal Justice Act 2003).

[1] You should provide a little context to your answer in the first paragraph by briefly stating the principal function of jurors and referring to recent debates over the merits of the jury system. It is appropriate to focus your discussion upon the use of juries in criminal trials given that this is primarily where they are used.

Some of the arguments that have been advanced for the abolition of juries are not particularly convincing.[2] For example, it has been claimed that it would be both cost and time efficient to dispense with their use. However, the counter-argument can be made that such considerations should be irrelevant to decisions over how to try cases where the interests of justice and individual liberty are at stake. It has also been argued that juries may find certain trials distressing, for example those involving offences against children. In some high profile cases, for example the James Bulger murder case, jurors have required post-trial counselling. However, such cases account for a small minority of those coming to trial and while perhaps a reason to limit the kinds of cases which juries hear, it does not constitute a good argument for the abolition of juries *per se*. The verdicts of juries are not accompanied by any explanation, which it is alleged makes it difficult to formulate appeals against conviction. However, it would be impractical to expect a group of lay people to draft a reasoned justification of their findings. Furthermore, the alternative argument is that the very nature of juries' verdicts endows them with certainty and creates no risk of misunderstanding.[3]

[2]In discussing the arguments for the abolition of juries, it makes sense to begin with the less convincing arguments before building up to the strongest arguments, upon which you can more effectively conclude the case for abolition.

[3]Some of the arguments for and against the abolition of juries are opposites of one another. You should emphasise this when applicable, as here.

Although the above arguments are not particularly convincing, other arguments lend greater support to the case for the abolition of juries. Jurors are lay people who will ordinarily have very little understanding of the law. As a consequence of this limited competence, many jurors may find it difficult to understand complex cases or the full nature and implications of their functions as jurors.[4] This risk was highlighted in **R *v* Young** [1995] QB 324, where the jury held sessions with a ouija board in an attempt to contact the victim in a murder case. The Roskill Committee (1986) concluded that in complex cases the interests of justice were not best served by jury trial. However, several studies have suggested that juries are generally capable of comprehending complex cases, for example fraud. On a related point, it has been submitted that their limited competence makes juries more prone to being influenced by others.[5] The trial judge, prosecution and defence counsel and other more vocal jurors can all potentially exert considerable influence, or even intimidation, over jurors.

[4]This is one of the major criticisms of the use of juries and you must ensure that you discuss this in your answer. There are various bodies of research which you could refer to in your discussion, such as the findings of the Roskill Committee.

[5]This is another key criticism of the use of juries. You might be able to find some case examples where jurors in reaching their verdict have acted under influence exerted by others to reinforce this point.

Another criticism of juries is that their random, lay composition will often result in a lack of objectivity which leads to them reaching what might be regarded as perverse verdicts.[6] These arise where a jury acquits a defendant who has no defence for his actions in law, but with whom the jury has some sympathy, for example because they feel the law he has fallen foul of is an unjust one. It is a statistical fact that juries acquit a higher proportion of defendants than magistrates do, with Home Office research suggesting acquittal in jury trials is twice as likely. The biases of individual jurors may produce juries that are more sympathetic or hostile to a defendant than an objective understanding of the case would warrant. Research into acquittals by Baldwin and McConville suggested that up to a quarter of them were questionable. Although supporters of jury trial would argue that the biases of individual jurors should theoretically balance one another out, this will not always be the case as the random selection of the jury can as easily produce an unrepresentative cross-section of society as it can a representative sample. The most recently considered arguments suggest that a fair case can be made for the abolition of the jury system. They emphasise quite clearly the limited capabilities of lay people to adjudicate properly on what may be difficult legal questions free of prejudice or influence. As will be seen, however, the ability of juries to render perverse verdicts has often been acclaimed as a virtue of the jury system.

[6]This is the final key criticism of the use of juries which you should include in your answer. Again, there are various examples of research into the area which you can cite to reinforce this point.

Defenders of the jury system maintain that it generates public participation within the legal system.[7] Trial by one's peers is a longstanding feature of the English legal system. Although research has found that most jurors have a positive experience of, and attitude towards, jury service, whether lay involvement in the legal system is particularly beneficial is debatable given some of the perceived weaknesses of the jury system referred to above and the highly important task with which they are charged. It would never be suggested that lay people should be involved in the provision of medical treatment! The argument that the prejudices of twelve people will mitigate one another has already been called into question above.

[7]As with the criticisms of juries, you should begin your discussion of the arguments in favour of retaining juries with any arguments you consider to be unconvincing. You should ensure that you make reference to the public participation argument as it is one of the most often cited.

A final possible argument in support of the preservation of the jury system is that as ordinary people jurors are able to judge according to their conscience,[8] meaning that on occasion they can effectively serve as a barometer of public opinion against what may be perceived as unduly harsh consequences of the law. For example, in

[8]This argument should be supported by reference to relevant examples from case law. You should ensure that you refer to the downside of this argument, which is the risk that jurors fail to effectively discharge their duty to judge a defendant according to the relevant law.

[9]The balance of the arguments considered in the answer tend to tilt in favour of the case for abolition of juries, although not overwhelmingly so. The conclusion reflects this and makes the relevant point that juries are such a longstanding feature of the legal system that it is difficult to foresee their abolition without much greater consideration of their merits first taking place.

R v Ponting [1985] Crim LR 318, a civil servant had passed confidential information to the media which exposed the government over the misleading of Parliament. To many this disclosure was in the public interest and Ponting was acquitted of breaching the Official Secrets Act in what was widely perceived to be a politically motivated prosecution.

In conclusion, some strong arguments can be made for the abolition of juries, principally those relating to their limited competence and lack of objectivity. The reasons for maintaining their use, while not without any merit, do not appear particularly compelling. However, that juries have endured for so long in common law systems suggests that their abolition will only ever occur after far greater analysis has taken place of their merits.[9]

✓ Make your answer stand out

- Refer to some of the recent debates over the merits of the jury system and some of the changes to have taken place to the extent to which they are used, for example sections 43–44 of the Criminal Justice Act 2003.
- Where relevant, refer to case examples, statistical evidence or research studies to reinforce your arguments.
- Read and make comment upon the arguments over the merits of juries discussed by Darbyshire, P., 'The Lamp that Shows that Freedom Lives – Is It Worth the Candle?', *Criminal Law Review*, 1991, p. 740.

! Don't be tempted to . . .

- Discuss each single argument that appears in any textbook discussion of the merits of the jury system;
- Reach your conclusion based upon the number of arguments which you consider for each side of the debate.

6

Appeals and judicial review

How this topic may come up in exams

Examination questions on appeals are likely to focus specifically upon either the civil or criminal appeals process and test your understanding of the circumstances in which appeals can be made from lower court decisions and the criteria governing them. Within an ELS syllabus, any question on judicial review is likely to be fairly general and may test understanding of the judicial review procedure including standing of applicants and bodies susceptible to judicial review, the grounds upon which judicial review may be sought, and the remedies available following a successful judicial review action.

Attack the question

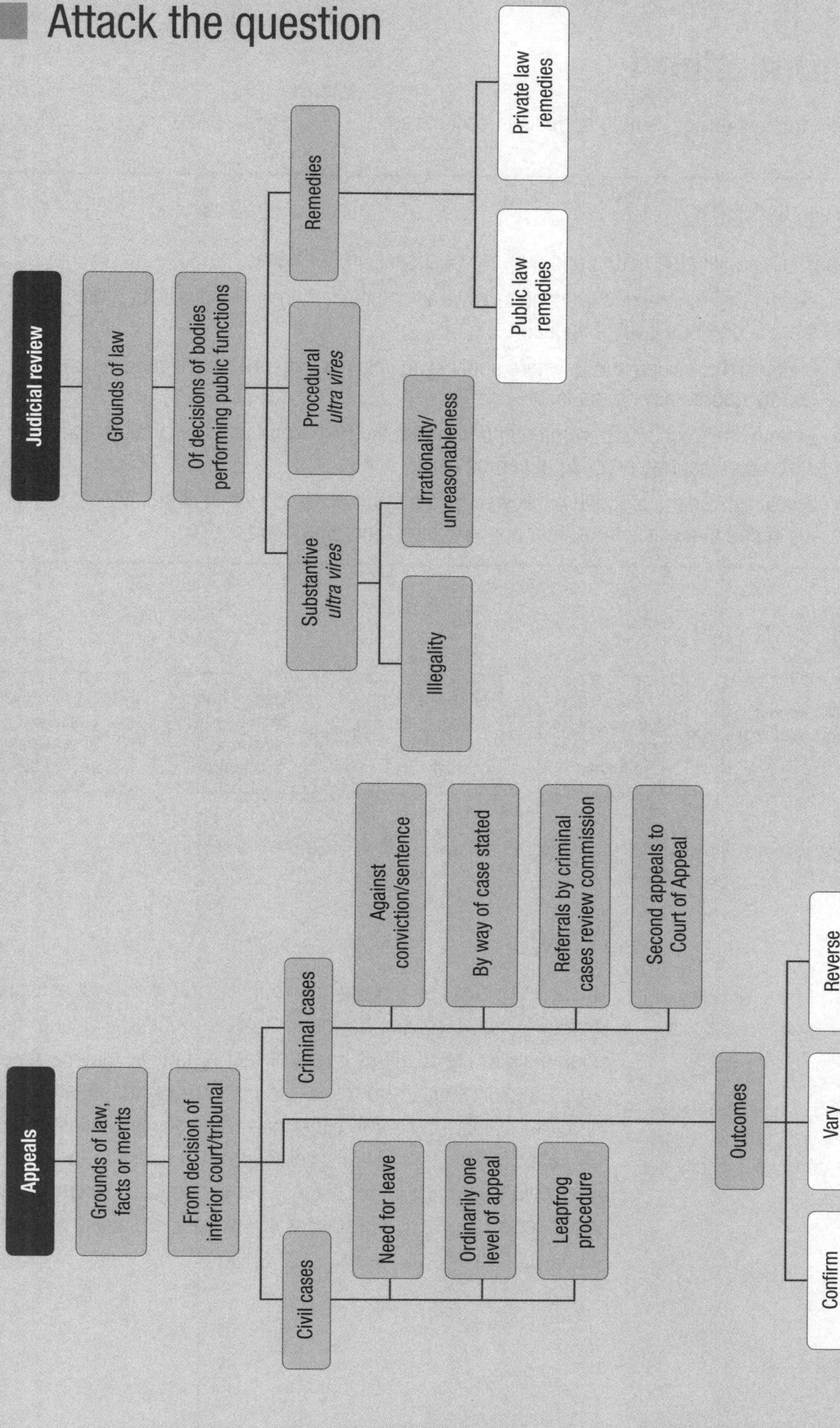

A printable version of this diagram plan is available from www.pearsoned.co.uk/lawexpressqa

Question 1

Explain the system governing appeals in civil cases.

Answer plan

- Briefly explain the nature and purpose of appeals in civil cases.
- Explain the general requirement for leave to be obtained to appeal and that ordinarily there is only one level of appeal.
- Briefly explain when and to where appeals against decisions of the Magistrates and County Courts may be made.
- Explain the procedure governing appeals from the High Court and the circumstances in which the 'leapfrog procedure' can be used.
- Briefly explain the procedure followed by the Court of Appeal when hearing appeals and the scope that exists for further appeals to the Supreme Court.

Diagram plan

A printable version of this diagram plan is available from www.pearsoned.co.uk/lawexpressqa

Answer

The main purpose of appeals procedures is to provide a mechanism through which incorrect decisions can be rectified.[1] Wrong decisions may be the result of errors of fact or law, or may be flawed due to a court's failure to follow the correct procedures in hearing the case. Within a civil case either party may appeal against a decision, although in response to a considerable increase in the number of appeals the Access to Justice Act 1999 introduced reforms which sought to reduce the circumstances in which appeals could be made.

[1] At the very outset of your answer you should briefly explain the nature and purpose of appeals. This will provide helpful background before you go on to explain more substantive points.

[2]Before embarking upon explanation of the different routes of appeal in different cases, you should demonstrate your knowledge of the fundamental principles which govern the civil appeals process as these generally apply across the board irrespective of where a case is appealed from or on what grounds.

[3]This is an important principle governing civil appeals and it is therefore important that you mention it, while indicating where exceptions to this rule may be made.

[4]Most civil cases are initially heard in the County Court or High Court. You would not be expected to entertain any real discussion of appeals from civil rulings of the Magistrates' Court, although in order to be comprehensive, a brief comment upon these could be made.

[5]It is essential that you demonstrate an understanding of the circumstances in which appeals from County Court and High Court decisions can be made, given that these account for most civil appeals.

A couple of important principles apply to civil appeals in general. As a result of section 54 of the Access to Justice Act 1999, permission to appeal is now required in almost all cases and must be obtained from either the court of first instance or the appellate court.[2] Permission to appeal will normally be given where the appellant has a realistic chance of success or there is some other compelling reason why the appeal should be heard. In exceptional circumstances, permission to appeal is not required. These are those in which individual liberty is at stake, such as habeas corpus applications and secure accommodation orders for children, being regarded as sufficiently serious to dispense with the ordinary requirement for leave to appeal. Motivated by the desire to reduce the number of civil appeals, section 55 of the Access to Justice Act provides that there will normally be only one level of appeal in civil cases.[3] Second appeals should be rare, and under section 55 the Court of Appeal will only hear a case that has already been heard on appeal by a lower court if it considers that the appeal will raise an important point of principle or practice, or there is some other compelling reason for it to hear the case.

The Magistrates' Court has very limited civil jurisdiction relating to family and licensing matters.[4] Subject to satisfying leave requirements, appeals on family matters will be made to the Family Division of the High Court and appeals on licensing matters to the Crown Court.

The vast majority of civil cases will commence in either the County Court or High Court depending upon the subject matter and monetary value of any claim. Where a case has been heard in the County Court and either party is dissatisfied with its ruling, subject to receiving permission to appeal, that party may appeal to the Court of Appeal on the basis of errors of fact or errors of law on the part of the County Court. Likewise, where a case has commenced in the High Court, there is a route of appeal to the Court of Appeal on the same grounds[5] subject to permission to appeal having been granted by either the High Court or Court of Appeal.

Appeals by the Court of Appeal (CA) will ordinarily be heard by one judge although in some circumstances one judge may hear an appeal sitting alone. Appeals seldom take the form of a re-hearing of the case by the CA. Instead the CA will usually review the ruling of the inferior court on the basis of the notes made by the judge in the original hearing and other relevant documentary evidence. The Court of Appeal effectively has three options in terms of the decision which it is entitled to reach.[6] It may affirm the decision of the inferior court, essentially indicating its agreement with the validity of that decision. Where the CA agrees with part, but not all of the decision of the inferior court, it may vary its decision, thus allowing the appeal in part. This may arise, for example, where the CA agrees with the inferior court's decision on liability but not the remedy which it imposed. In such an event, the Court of Appeal may confirm the decision whilst perhaps reducing the damages awarded to a claimant. Where the inferior court's decision is felt to be incorrect, the Court of Appeal may allow the appeal and reverse the earlier decision. An appeal may only be allowed because a decision is wrong, unjust or has been reached in circumstances where there have been procedural irregularities. The CA cannot allow an appeal simply because it is of the belief that it may have reached a different decision, in the absence of any of the aforementioned grounds for allowing an appeal.

There is some scope for further appeals to be made from decisions of the Court of Appeal to the Supreme Court on questions of law.[7] However, leave to appeal must be obtained from either court. In reality, very few cases are heard annually by the Supreme Court and in the overwhelming majority of cases the Court of Appeal will in practice be the final appellate court.

There is a special procedure, known as the 'leapfrog procedure', which enables certain cases to be appealed directly from the High Court to the Supreme Court, thus bypassing the Court of Appeal.[8] The 'leapfrog procedure' is governed by sections 12–15 of the Administration of Justice Act 1969. To be able to make use of the procedure and appeal directly to the Supreme Court from the High Court, all parties to the case must consent and under section 12(3) of the 1969 act the High Court judge who heard the original case must certify that the appeal is either on a point of law which relates wholly or mainly to the construction of a provision of a

[6] As the major appellate court for civil cases, you should ensure that you provide an explanation of the possible outcomes of appeals to the Court of Appeal. This follows on logically from your earlier explanation of the main principles governing appeals, the grounds on which they can be made and to where.

[7] Although this point does not need to be laboured, you should mention the fact that appeals can be made from the Court of Appeal to the Supreme Court, as this is a higher court within the court hierarchy.

[8] The 'leapfrog procedure' is a very important mechanism for speeding up appeals and you should ensure that you demonstrate a clear understanding of the rationale for this procedure and the rules which govern its application. A clear explanation of this is likely to receive credit from the examiner.

statute or statutory instrument and has been fully argued and considered, or on a question of law where the High Court judge was bound by a Court of Appeal or Supreme Court precedent and the matter had been fully considered in the relevant previous Court of Appeal or Supreme Court judgments. The rationale for the 'leapfrog procedure' is to save on time and cost in court proceedings in those circumstances where because of the effect of judicial precedent, the Court of Appeal is unlikely to be able to satisfactorily resolve a case appealed from the High Court, which will probably require ultimate recourse to the Supreme Court anyway. No appeal can pass directly from the High Court to the Supreme Court without the aforementioned certification from the trial judge. The trial judge enjoys discretion over the granting of this certificate and there is no right to appeal against his decision in respect of this. It should also be noted that even if the requirements imposed by the Administration of Justice Act 1969 are satisfied, leave to appeal will still need to be obtained from the Supreme Court.

✓ Make your answer stand out

- Make reference to the impact upon the civil appeals process of the Access to Justice Act 1999.
- Explain clearly the importance of the 'leapfrog procedure' for appeals against decisions of the High Court.

! Don't be tempted to . . .

- Simply provide an overview of the court hierarchy which details to which courts appeals can be made from lower courts.

Question 2

Discuss the range of circumstances in which verdicts in criminal cases may be appealed against.

Answer plan

- ➜ Consider the routes of appeal from decisions of the Magistrates' Court.
- ➜ Consider the routes of appeal from decisions of the Crown Court.
- ➜ Consider the circumstances in which the Court of Appeal will hear second appeals.
- ➜ Consider the ability of the Court of Appeal to admit fresh evidence and the possible outcomes of appeals heard by the Court of Appeal.
- ➜ Conclude upon the extent to which the English legal system provides a range of opportunities for appealing criminal convictions or sentences.

Diagram plan

A printable version of this diagram plan is available from www.pearsoned.co.uk/lawexpressqa

Answer

The overwhelming majority of criminal cases are concluded in the Magistrates' Court. Appeals are only made against the decisions of the court in 1% of cases and may take one of four forms.[1] Firstly, although not strictly speaking an appeal, a case may be retried by the Magistrates' Court itself to rectify any errors made by the court in the original hearing. Section 142 of the Magistrates' Courts Act 1980 permits such a retrial, before a different bench, where the interests of justice warrant this and the sentence imposed upon an offender can be varied. This procedure has been credited with leading to a reduction in the number of actual appeals to the higher courts. Secondly, a defendant may appeal as of right to the Crown Court on the grounds of having either been wrongfully convicted

[1]It is worthwhile noting that it is rare for an appeal to be made against a decision of this court. However, you should begin your answer by considering the scope which exists for appealing against verdicts and sentences imposed by the Magistrates' Court, as all criminal cases commence here.

or handed a sentence that is unduly harsh, although a defendant who pleaded guilty may only appeal against his sentence. Appeals must be made within 28 days and the appeal will take the form of a re-hearing of the facts by the Crown Court which enjoys the power to impose any sentence which could have been imposed by the Magistrates' Court. There is the potential for sentences to actually be increased by the Crown Court, although this is comparatively rare, with evidence pointing to a tendency for tougher sentences to be handed down by magistrates.[2] Thirdly, either prosecution or defence may appeal by way of case stated to the High Court on the grounds that the Magistrates' Court has made an error of law or exceeded its jurisdiction. Up to three judges from the Queen's Bench Division will sit to confirm, reverse or vary the Magistrates' decision, or give their opinion on a point of law to the Magistrates' Court. They may also issue other orders, for example to require a re-hearing of the case in the Magistrates' Court. This is effectively a means of appeal on limited grounds, but it was established in **R *v* Mildenhall Magistrates' Court, *ex parte* Forest Heath DC** [1997] 161 JP 401 that a Magistrates' Court can refuse to state a case for the High Court where it feels it would be frivolous to do so. Finally, although not an appeal as such on the part of a convicted defendant, under the terms of the Criminal Appeals Act 1995, the Criminal Cases Review Commission can refer a case to the Crown Court if it feels a particular conviction or sentence is unsafe. This will then be regarded as an appeal, although it is very rare for the CCRC to refer cases heard in the Magistrates' Court.

[2]Where appropriate, you can draw upon your wider knowledge of appeals processes to make points such as this to illustrate your understanding of the impact of appeals processes in practice.

Appeals against convictions or sentences handed down by the Crown Court can be made along similar grounds that they can from the Magistrates' Court.[3] Either party can appeal by way of case stated to the Queen's Bench Division of the High Court, just as they can from the Magistrates' Court. From there further appeal to the Supreme Court may be possible, but only where the Divisional Court certifies that the case raises a question of law of public importance and leave is obtained from the Supreme Court. A defendant can appeal to the Court of Appeal on grounds of an error of fact or law, or against the sentence imposed by the Crown Court. Leave to appeal must be obtained from either the Crown Court or the Court of Appeal. According to Slapper and Kelly, approximately 8,000 such appeals are launched annually. The overwhelming majority are

[3]The routes of appeal from Crown Court decisions are similar to those that exist for appeals from the Magistrates' Court, so you should focus your discussion here on aspects of the appeals process more relevant to appeals from the Crown Court, such as appeals to the Court of Appeal.

against sentence as opposed to conviction, arguably encouraged by the fact that the Court of Appeal may not increase a sentence imposed by the Crown Court. Although only a defendant can appeal to the Court of Appeal, either party is entitled to appeal onwards to the Supreme Court on a point of law although this is only possible if permission is given by either court and the Court of Appeal certifies that the case involves a matter of general importance. The Criminal Cases Review Commission can also refer cases heard in the Crown Court to the Court of Appeal where a conviction or sentence is regarded as unsafe. This has led to several notable cases being effectively re-visited by the Court of Appeal, among the most publicised of which was the case of Derek Bentley whose conviction for murder was set aside by the Court of Appeal in 1998, over 45 years after his execution.[4]

[4]Some discussion of the role played by the Criminal Cases Review Commission is worthwhile when you are considering appeals to the Court of Appeal. You can illustrate its importance in relation to addressing miscarriages of justice by citing practical examples, and will receive credit for doing so.

It was established in **Taylor *v* Lawrence** [2002] EWCA Civ 90 that in exceptional cases a second appeal may be brought to the Court of Appeal even though a previous appeal has been rejected.[5] The case itself concerned new evidence which had come to light following an earlier appeal, casting doubt upon the validity of its outcome. However, to bring a second appeal it must be clearly established that a significant injustice has probably been done, the circumstances are exceptional and there is no alternative remedy. In reality, second appeals are likely to be extremely rare occurrences, but their availability provides an important additional safeguard against the perpetration of miscarriages of justice.

[5]This is an important point to make and builds further upon the earlier discussion of ways in which the law on criminal appeals has developed in response to miscarriages of justice. It evidences an awareness of relatively recent changes in the law.

Ordinarily, an appeal hearing by the Court of Appeal will take the form of a review of the original case. However, section 23(1) of the Criminal Appeals Act 1968 allows it to admit fresh evidence 'if they think it necessary or expedient in the interests of justice'.[6] Essentially, this will be where the newly available evidence casts doubt upon the reliability of the original ruling. There is a series of factors which the Court of Appeal is to have regard to in considering whether the admission of evidence will satisfy the requirements of section 23(1). Under section 2 of the Criminal Appeals Act 1968, an appeal should be allowed wherever the Court thinks a conviction is 'unsafe'. The appeal ought to be dismissed if there is no reason to question the original ruling. Alternatively, the Court of Appeal can order a new trial to be held and this is an option which it may choose where there are some reservations over the original

[6]As the main court responsible for hearing criminal appeals you should comment upon some of the key features of appeal hearings before the Court of Appeal. The ability of the CA to admit fresh evidence is particularly relevant to your answer and can be cited to reinforce the earlier points made in relation to the role which the appeals process plays in addressing miscarriages of justice.

decision, perhaps as a result of procedural factors, but the CA is not minded to simply overturn that decision.

There is clearly a range of opportunities for criminal convictions and sentences to be appealed against, leading Slapper and Kelly to comment that when compared to other jurisdictions it is 'unusual' to find 'as many opportunities for appeal and challenge as exist in the English system'.[7]

[7]This brings your answer to an end nicely, evidencing awareness of the wider context of criminal appeals.

✓ Make your answer stand out

- Provide some discussion of the role of criminal appeals in addressing miscarriages of justices.
- Refer to the role played by the Criminal Cases Review Commission in bringing appeals against criminal convictions.
- In a more critical extended essay you might consider in more detail the purposes of criminal appeals and whether the current system for appeals achieves these. A useful discussion of such issues is provided in Spencer, J.R., 'Does Our Present Criminal Appeal System Make Sense?', *Criminal Law Review*, 2006, p. 677.

! Don't be tempted to . . .

- Simply provide an overview of the court hierarchy which details to which courts appeals can be made from lower courts;
- Describe individual miscarriages of justice in detail.

Question 3

How does an action for judicial review differ from an appeal? Who is entitled to bring an action for judicial review and which bodies are susceptible to judicial review?

Answer plan

- Explain briefly what judicial review is.
- Outline the main differences between an appeal and a judicial review action.
- Explain the criteria which govern eligibility to bring an application for judicial review..
- Explain the criteria which govern the susceptibility of bodies to judicial review actions.

Diagram plan

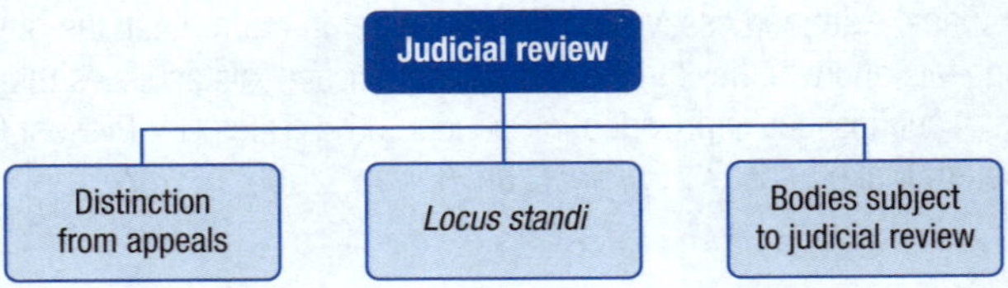

A printable version of this diagram plan is available from www.pearsoned.co.uk/lawexpressqa

Answer

[1]Before launching into an explanation of the differences between judicial review and appeals, you should briefly explain what judicial review is. This will set the scene for you to then go on to distinguish it from the appeals process. You should state what the main function of judicial review is and briefly refer to the grounds upon which an application for judicial review can be brought.

Judicial review refers to the process by which the decisions and actions of public bodies are subject to the oversight of the courts to ensure that they have been exercised in accordance with the law.[1] Applications for judicial review are made to the Queen's Bench Division of the High Court, which is responsible for exercising a supervisory jurisdiction over governmental and public bodies. Judicial review is essentially concerned with ensuring that public bodies do not act outside of the powers with which they have been conferred by statute and this consists of checking that they do not make decisions or take action which they are not permitted to (substantive *ultra vires*) and comply with all relevant procedures throughout their decision-making processes (procedural *ultra vires*). Judicial review plays an important function within the doctrine of separation of powers and in upholding the rule of law, being the primary means through which the executive branch of government is held to account for the legality of its decisions and actions by the judiciary. Applications for judicial review have increased considerably in recent years, Slapper and Kelly estimating the number of applications to have grown from in the region of 500 in 1980 to over 5,000 in 1998.

[2]The question asks you firstly how judicial review differs from an appeal. The main differences concern the grounds upon which an action may proceed and the basis for the courts' powers. You should clearly explain these. Although you have been asked about differences between the two, it is desirable to refer to the degree of overlap between the two concepts in order to illustrate the degree to which they differ.

A judicial review action differs from an appeal in some very fundamental respects.[2] Unlike the appeals process, judicial review is not concerned with the merits of the decisions which the court is asked to review. The sole purpose of judicial review is to examine the legality of a decision. If it is lawfully made, the fact that its merits may be questionable is irrelevant. This differs to the appeals process where the merits of a particular decision will often be the grounds for appeal against it. A second distinction relates to the legal basis for the powers exercised by the court in hearing applications for judicial review and appeals respectively. Whereby appeals procedures are grounded in statutory provisions, the origins of the courts' powers to subject public bodies to judicial review lie in the common law. Despite these fundamental differences, there is nonetheless a degree of overlap between judicial review and appeals. The same occurrence can potentially give rise to both an appeal and grounds for judicial review. For example, while there will ordinarily be a route of appeal from the decision of a statutory tribunal, its decisions may also be subject to judicial review if they exceed the tribunal's powers or do not comply with the appropriate procedural requirements.

[3]The second part of the question asks you who can bring an application for judicial review. It is crucial that you are able to explain the concept of *locus standi*. Depending upon the time that you have available you should refer to relevant case law to illustrate how the 'sufficient interest' test has been applied in practice.

An application for judicial review can only be brought by a party which enjoys *locus standi*, that is sufficient standing to bring the case to court. For purposes of judicial review, *locus standi* has been defined by the Supreme Court Act 1981, section 31(3) which defines this as 'a sufficient interest in the matter to which the application relates'.[3] The Supreme Court Act 1981 has now been renamed as the Senior Courts Act 1981 (see the Constitutional Reform Act 2005). The logic of this test is to prevent against frivolous applications for judicial review being made, thus reserving the courts' time for hearing worthwhile cases. Whether a particular applicant or group of applicants will be able to establish a sufficient interest in a particular matter is essentially something to be decided on a case by case basis by the courts, although clear *locus standi* is likely to be satisfied when the private law rights of the party bringing the action are threatened. It was established in **R *v* Inland Revenue Commissioners, *ex parte* National Federation of Self-Employed and Small Businesses** [1982] AC 617 that the merits of the case can be taken into account when deciding whether the test for *locus standi* is satisfied.

The courts have taken a relatively flexible approach to the issue of *locus standi*, so, for example, pressure or interest groups may be able to demonstrate a sufficient interest in a matter with which they are principally concerned in order to be able to bring an application for judicial review. The Attorney-General will always have *locus standi* to bring an application for judicial review, and consequently he is able to permit 'relator' actions to be brought in his name where there may be doubts as to whether a party seeking to bring an application will be able to satisfy the *locus standi* test.[4] An example of a relator action can be found, for example, in the case of **R *v* Secretary of State for Employment, *ex parte* Equal Opportunities Commission** [1994] 1 WLR 910.

[4]Some credit should be given for mentioning the *locus standi* enjoyed by the Attorney-General, as his role can be very important in judicial review proceedings where would-be applicants may be unable to demonstrate *locus standi*.

To be amenable to judicial review proceedings, a body must be responsible for performing a public function.[5] Government departments and agencies will clearly be amenable to judicial review, whereas bodies which are entirely of a private nature will not. However, it has been established for some time that where private bodies perform important public functions they will be amenable to judicial review. In the case of **R *v* Panel on Takeovers and Mergers, *ex parte* Datafin plc** [1987] QB 815, it was established that although the Panel on Takeovers and Mergers was essentially a privately constituted body, it performed an important public function and thus could be subject to judicial review. Similarly, the Advertising Standards Agency was deemed to be amenable to judicial review when the court in **R *v* Advertising Standards Agency Ltd, *ex parte* Insurance Services plc** [1990] 2 Admin LR 77 held that the ASA performed an important public function which if it did not exist would need to be performed by the Office of Fair Trading. This factor was central to its amenability to judicial review. In accordance with this approach various self-regulatory bodies have been held to be subject to judicial review proceedings, such as the Bar Council.

[5]The final part of the question asks which bodies are susceptible to judicial review. The key concept to be discussed here is that of a 'public function' being performed on the part of the body concerned. You should refer to a range of appropriate cases to illustrate how this concept has been applied in practice, the *Datafin* case being especially significant in highlighting the susceptibility of private bodies to judicial review where they perform a public function.

Despite its relatively broad approach to the question of which bodies can be subjected to judicial review, certain bodies have been clearly determined as being exempt. For example, religious bodies are generally not deemed to perform a public function, so entities such as the Chief Rabbi have been held exempt from judicial review, their functions being regarded as essentially religious in nature and not more broadly public. Domestic tribunals of a voluntary nature are also not regarded as performing a public function. Interestingly, in the case of **R *v* Parliamentary Commissioner for Standards, *ex parte* Al Fayed** [1997] EWCA Civ 2488, it was held that the Parliamentary Commissioner for Standards was not subject to judicial review as the office functioned as part of the proceedings of Parliament, which were immune from judicial review. Thus, judicial review can be seen as applicable to a relatively, but not too narrowly, restricted class of bodies.

✓ Make your answer stand out

- Demonstrate not only the differences between judicial review and appeals, but also the degree of overlap which they share.
- Make reference to the fact that the Attorney-General always enjoys *locus standi* for judicial review purposes.
- Consider the extent to which the test for standing in judicial review cases is broader or narrower than in some other forms of actions by reading and making reference to Ligere, E., '*Locus Standi* and the Public Interest: A Hotchpotch of Legal Principles', *Journal of Planning and Environment Law*, 2005, p. 292.

! Don't be tempted to . . .

- Embark upon an explanation of the procedure for judicial review;
- Confuse the differences and similarities between judicial review and appeals;
- Make the assumption that only public bodies can perform public functions, thus excluding all private bodies from susceptibility to judicial review.

Question 4

'A broad range of activity on the part of public bodies may potentially fall foul of the law.' Discuss with reference to the grounds of judicial review.

Answer plan

- → Briefly explain the purpose of judicial review and that there are three broad grounds upon which a public body may be subjected to judicial review.
- → Discuss the scope which exists for challenging actions of public bodies upon grounds of illegality.
- → Discuss the scope which exists for challenging actions of public bodies upon grounds of irrationality.
- → Discuss the scope which exists for challenging actions of public bodies upon grounds of procedural impropriety.
- → Conclude by commenting upon the extent to which the judicial review process places broad checks upon the exercise of power by public bodies.

Diagram plan

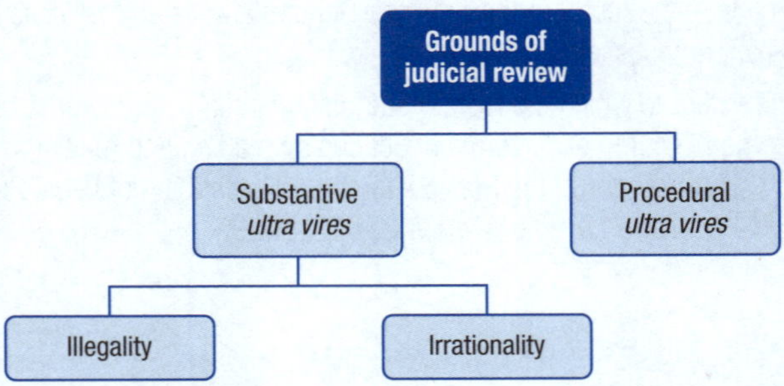

A printable version of this diagram plan is available from www.pearsoned.co.uk/lawexpressqa

Answer

Judicial review is the ultimate mechanism used by the courts to hold public bodies to account for their actions and decisions. The purpose of judicial review is to ensure that public bodies act in conformity with the law. It is common to base the grounds of judicial review upon the concepts of substantive and procedural *ultra vires*. The former arises where a body makes a decision or takes an action which it is not lawfully permitted to, thus acting outside of its powers. The latter arises where a body fails to follow the appropriate procedures in its decision-making process.[1] Although the grounds of judicial review are often grouped under these two broad headings, they can also be ordered under the three headings outlined by Lord Diplock in **Council of Civil Service Unions *v* Minister for the Civil Service** [1985] AC 374, namely illegality, irrationality and procedural impropriety.[2] The former two headings both refer to forms of substantive *ultra vires*, whereas the latter simply refers to procedural *ultra vires*.

The term 'illegality' encompasses those relatively clear cut instances of substantive ultra vires in which a public body exercises a power which it does not have.[3] For example, in **R *v* Secretary of State for the Home Department, *ex parte* Leech (No. 2)** [1994] QB 198 it was held unlawful for a prison governor to censor a prisoner's correspondence with his solicitor in the absence of any such power within the legislation governing such matters. However, not all cases of substantive *ultra vires* are so straightforward and the notion of 'irrationality' is applied to those scenarios where a public body is conferred with a broad discretionary power which it exercises in such a manner that it would be regarded as so irrational that no rational decision maker could have acted in such a manner.[4] Although not expressly prohibited by any statutory provision, it would not be a means of exercising the power reasonably contemplated by Parliament when conferring the power. The courts can use their powers of review to restrain such unreasonable exercises of broad discretionary power. This heading of judicial review has its origins in the case of **Associated Provincial Picture Houses *v* Wednesbury Corporation** [1948] 1 KB 223 from which the concept of unreasonableness derived.[5] The contribution of that case was to rule that any decision which was so unreasonable that no reasonable authority could make it would be regarded as ultra vires. There are several apparent instances where a body exercising discretionary powers is likely to fall foul of the test for unreasonableness or irrationality and thus have acted *ultra vires*.

[1]It is worthwhile to make this distinction between the grounds of judicial review at the outset, these being the most common classifications utilised for the grounds of judicial review.

[2]Because substantive *ultra vires* covers both straightforward instances of bodies exceeding their jurisdiction and those cases where discretionary powers are exercised in a manner that cannot have been taken to have been envisaged when the powers were conferred upon the respective bodies, it may be helpful in order to sustain a clear argument to adopt the terms set out by Lord Diplock to break down the grounds of judicial review.

[3]You need to explain that public bodies may not exceed the powers which they are given, and if they do so this will constitute a straightforward case of unlawful activity.

[4]Explaining the concept of irrationality or unreasonableness should constitute a significant part of your answer as there are several ways in which it is possible to demonstrate its presence in a decision or action of a public body.

[5]You should make reference to the landmark *Wednesbury* case as providing the origins of the concept of reasonableness/rationality as a ground upon which applications for judicial review could be grounded, in light of the fundamental importance of the case.

Exercising a discretionary power for improper purposes will constitute an unlawful action.[6] This occurred in **R *v* Derbyshire County Council, *ex parte Times Supplements*** (1990) COD 139, where an authority's treatment of the concerned publishers was motivated by earlier criticism directed at it by the publisher's publication. Additionally, a body subject to judicial review may not take into account irrelevant considerations in exercising a discretionary power. Thus, in **R *v* Somerset County Council, *ex parte* Fewings** [1995] 3 All ER 20 the exercise of regulatory powers to ban deer hunting on Council owned land was deemed to be unlawful based upon the Council having employed irrelevant considerations in the exercise of this power. A person or body conferred with a discretionary power is obliged to exercise that power and not to fetter that discretion by delegating this power to another. A decision that results from fettered discretion is likely to be unlawful, as **British Oxygen *v* Minister of Technology** [1971] AC 610 illustrates.

[6]You will improve your answer if you are able to highlight some of the specific cases in which an exercise of a discretionary power is likely to be deemed *ultra vires* due to its lack of reasonableness. Acting for improper purposes, taking into account irrelevant considerations and fettering discretion can all be highlighted with supporting examples from case law.

A failure to comply with required procedures will also render decisions or actions of public bodies *ultra vires*. Public bodies exercising discretionary powers must comply with the requirements of natural justice.[7] There are two notable rules, the rule against bias (*nemo judex in sua causa*, meaning that nobody should be a judge in his own cause) and the requirement of a fair hearing (*audi alteram partem*, meaning to hear the other side). The rule against bias essentially requires that nobody should make a decision in respect of a matter in which he has a direct interest, which could give rise to charges of bias. For example, in **Dimes *v* Grand Junction Canal Proprietors** (1852) 3 HL Cas 759, the Lord Chancellor sat in judgment on a case concerning a company in which he owned a substantial number of shares and ruled in their favour. This was held to compromise his ability to exercise independent judgment on the case and he was declared disqualified from sitting on the bench in this case. More recently, in **R *v* Bow Street Metropolitan Stipendiary Magistrate, *ex parte* Pinochet Ugarte (No. 2)** [1999] COD 139, a court ruling in respect of the extradition of the former Chilean dictator Pinochet to face charges related to human rights abuses had to be set aside due to the fact that one of the judges hearing the case, Lord Hoffman, had close links to Amnesty International, a human rights pressure group which had been heavily involved in calls for Pinochet to face exportation and trial.

[7]In explaining the procedural grounds for judicial review, you must ensure that you evidence an understanding of the rules of natural justice. Use case law examples to show these being enforced in practice.

The requirements of a fair hearing will vary with the circumstances of each case, but a failure to satisfy what is reasonable in the circumstances will give rise to the charge that the public body concerned has acted procedurally *ultra vires*. Many statutory procedural requirements are now imposed in respect of public decision-making processes. These sometimes include the imposition of a requirement to enter into consultation with those to be affected by particular decisions, the provision of notice of pending decisions, the provision of an opportunity for affected persons to make representations to a decision-making authority, and the provision of reasons for decisions that have been taken. Although these procedural requirements vary from one situation to another, a failure to comply where obliged would posit strong grounds upon which an application for judicial review could be lodged.

[8]Your conclusion should flow naturally from your explanation of the different grounds of judicial review. By showing the broad grounds which exist you are able to conclude upon its importance in strengthening the accountability owed by public bodies for their actions.

Judicial review is undoubtedly an important mechanism through which the courts are able to hold public bodies to account for their actions and ensure that they act within the law.[8] The grounds of judicial review are sufficiently broad enough to support the courts' ability to perform this function. Not only are the courts able to nullify the decisions or actions of public bodies that are clearly taken in excess of their powers, but they are also able to remedy situations where broad discretionary powers are exercised in a manner so unreasonably or irrational that they cannot be taken to have been envisaged upon the part of the discretion conferring authority. Furthermore, the procedural grounds of judicial review reinforce the importance of standards of fairness within decision-making processes.

✓ Make your answer stand out

- Explain the different kinds of actions which may give rise to the unlawful exercise of a discretionary power.
- Use a good breadth of case law examples to illustrate the different grounds of judicial review in action.

! Don't be tempted to . . .

- Confuse judicial review actions with appeals;
- Explain the grounds of judicial review narrowly without elaborating upon the various kinds of actions which may give rise to their invocation.

Question 5

What remedies are available from the courts in a successful judicial review action?

Answer plan

→ Briefly explain the potential importance of appropriate remedies following a successful judicial review action.

→ Explain the public law remedies which may be awarded following a successful judicial review action, illustrating situations in which their award may be appropriate.

→ Explain the private law remedies which may be awarded following a successful judicial review action, illustrating situations in which their award may be appropriate.

→ Conclude by commenting upon the extent to which the courts are able to effectively utilise remedies that are appropriate to the situation at hand.

Diagram plan

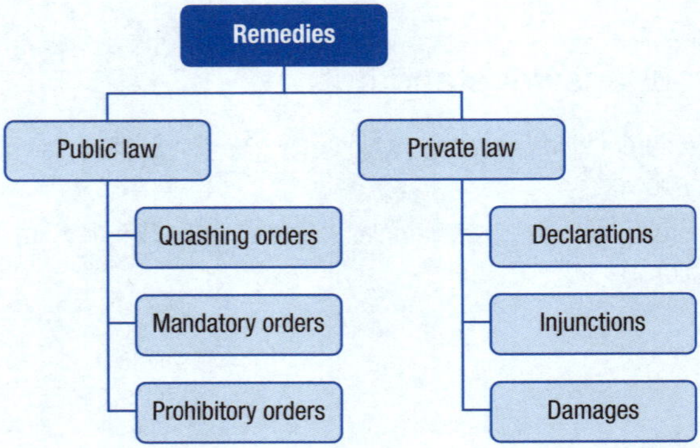

A printable version of this diagram plan is available from www.pearsoned.co.uk/lawexpressqa

Answer

The objective of judicial review is to ensure that public bodies or those performing a public function are held to account for the conformity of their actions with the law. Where such bodies have acted unlawfully, the provision of appropriate remedies to aggrieved citizens serves as an important aspect of the supervisory jurisdiction exercised by the courts.[1] Unlawful actions by public bodies can potentially have devastating effects upon the rights and interests of private bodies and individuals, thus necessitating the award of remedies that are suited to each situation to rectify any harm caused to the party affected by the wrongdoing of a public body. The remedies potentially available following a successful judicial review action can be divided into two categories, public law remedies and private law remedies.

[1]In your introduction you should emphasise the importance of appropriate remedies in judicial review proceedings by relating their role to the principal objective of judicial review, holding public bodies to account for the legality of their actions.

The prerogative orders available from the Queen's Bench Division are public law remedies that are only available following successful applications for judicial review.[2] They are discretionary in nature and cannot be executed against the crown. Three prerogative orders are available. Firstly, there are quashing orders, formerly known as *certiorari*. The effect of a quashing order is to quash a decision that has been taken by a public body when that decision has been taken *ultra vires*. It is an effective means of nullifying an unlawful decision so as to deprive it of any legal effect. Quashing orders are the most commonly awarded remedy in judicial review actions and will be appropriate wherever the simple effect of quashing a decision will suffice to put an end to any harm being caused to the affected party. An example of the award of a quashing order can be found in the case of **Ridge *v* Baldwin** [1964] AC 40, where the dismissal of a police chief constable was found to have breached the rules of natural justice. The quashing order was used to declare the dismissal null and void, thus effectively meaning that the dismissal was treated as never having occurred.

[2]You should ensure that you clearly explain the different prerogative orders that are available and emphasise that these remedies are unique to judicial review actions. You should explain the effect of each of the prerogative orders and can demonstrate your understanding of their application by providing examples from case law of situations in which they have been awarded.

Secondly, mandatory orders, formerly known as mandamus, can be used in order to compel a public body to perform a particular action. They are addressed at wrongful failures to act, as well as acts not performed in the manner which they should have been, and serve to ensure that public authorities perform their statutory duties. A mandatory order may be combined with a quashing order, so that where a body has taken a decision unlawfully, that decision is quashed and the body is ordered to take the decision again, in accordance with the law.

The third category of prerogative orders are prohibiting orders, formerly known as prohibition. The effect of a prohibiting order is to prevent an unlawful decision being taken by an authority or tribunal. It is a useful measure that can be employed to ensure that a body does not proceed to act in a manner which will constitute an excess of its jurisdiction or a breach of natural justice. An attempt to obtain a prohibiting order by then Labour leader, Michael Foot, failed in the case of **R *v* Boundary Commission for England, *ex parte* Foot** [1983] 1 QB 600. By contrast, a prohibiting order was successfully obtained to prevent the continuation of committal proceedings in **R *v* Telford Justices, *ex parte* Badham** [1991] 2 WLR 866. Essentially, the prerogative orders are directly concerned with the validity of the decision-making process employed by bodies exercising public functions, involving as they do the courts intervening to quash decisions that have been taken unlawfully, ordering bodies to fulfil their legal duties and preventing them from acting in a manner which would constitute unlawful action on their part.[3]

[3]It will strengthen your answer if you are able to make some comment upon the nature of the prerogative orders as judicial remedies.

Whereas the prerogative orders are confined to judicial review proceedings and are concerned with the manner of decision-making processes on the part of public bodies, several remedies stemming from the private law may be employed by the courts in judicial review proceedings. The main private law remedies of potential relevance in judicial review proceedings are declarations, injunctions and damages.[4]

[4]In the context of judicial review you do not need to provide some coverage of all remedies available in private law, but focus upon those which are of relevance as remedies that can have some application in this context. Building upon your earlier discussion of public law remedies, you should explain clearly the nature of declarations and injunctions, demonstrating your understanding of their application by referring to examples of their award in judicial review actions.

Following an application for judicial review the court may grant a declaration. This is a definitive statement of the law in relation to the matter brought before it. A declaration was granted by the court in **Congreve *v* Home Office** [1976] QB 629, a case which resulted from the decision of the Home Office to revoke annual television licences after just eight months. The court declared that this would be unlawful. A declaration is unlike other remedies in that it has no direct impact upon the decision of a public body and provides no substantive redress for any harm caused to the applicant. Its possible benefit lies in the ability of the court to helpfully clarify the legal effects of a particular situation, although a declaration cannot be legally enforced in itself. A court can also award an injunction following a successful application for judicial review. For example, in **Attorney-General *v* Fulham Corporation** [1921] Ch 440, an injunction was granted to prevent a local authority from continuing to provide a laundry service for residents as it only had the power under statute to establish laundries at which residents could perform their own washing tasks.

Interim injunctions can be awarded pending a full court hearing where there is evidence of an imminent risk of loss to the applicant and there are no suitable alternative remedies. Until relatively recently it was thought that interim injunctions were unavailable against the crown. However, this was dispelled when it was ruled that the crown is equally subject to interim injunctions, in **M *v* Home Office** [1993] All ER 537. Whereas declarations and injunctions are private remedies which can be awarded in public law proceedings, damages remain a purely private law remedy and to be entitled to claim them following a judicial review action, the applicant will need to be able to demonstrate that he has suffered some form of loss or harm accruing from the commission of a private wrong.[5] As a result, in judicial review proceedings damages are never available as a remedy in their own right, but may be awarded in conjunction with other remedies, where those remedies are insufficient to rectify any loss suffered by the applicant, for example a declaration that the decision which forms the basis for the action is unlawful.

[5]It is important that you explain the main difference between the availability of damages and other private law remedies in judicial review proceedings as this is rather significant in that damages are likely to be available in a narrower range of situations than declarations or injunctions will be.

In conclusion, in hearing applications for judicial review the courts have a broad range of remedies which they can effectively employ to respond to any injustice caused by unlawful decisions and actions of public bodies. The only real difficulty arises in respect of the limited scope for damages to be awarded, which may mean that some applicants are not appropriately compensated for harm accruing from the conduct of public bodies.[6]

[6]Your conclusion should follow on logically from the earlier parts of the answer. The answer here has outlined a number of remedies which are available in judicial review proceedings, illustrated by case law examples, and this is therefore a logical conclusion to draw.

✓ Make your answer stand out

- Illustrate the application of different remedies by making reference to relevant examples from case law.
- Explain, where appropriate, the factors which may influence the court's decision to award a particular remedy.

! Don't be tempted to . . .

- Simply explain what remedies can be awarded by the courts without illustrating their use;
- Discuss remedies generally, as opposed to their application in the context of judicial review.

7 The criminal law process

How this topic may come up in exams

Examination questions on this topic may relate to police powers to stop, search, and arrest suspects, the rules applicable to the detention and questioning of suspects and taking of evidence. Your understanding of police powers may be assessed through the use of the essay or problem questions. Your understanding of the criminal trial procedure may also be assessed, and you should be particularly prepared to answer questions relating to the rules applicable to the grant or refusal of bail, plea bargaining, the admission and exclusion of evidence and the factors which inform the sentencing of offenders following conviction.

Attack the question

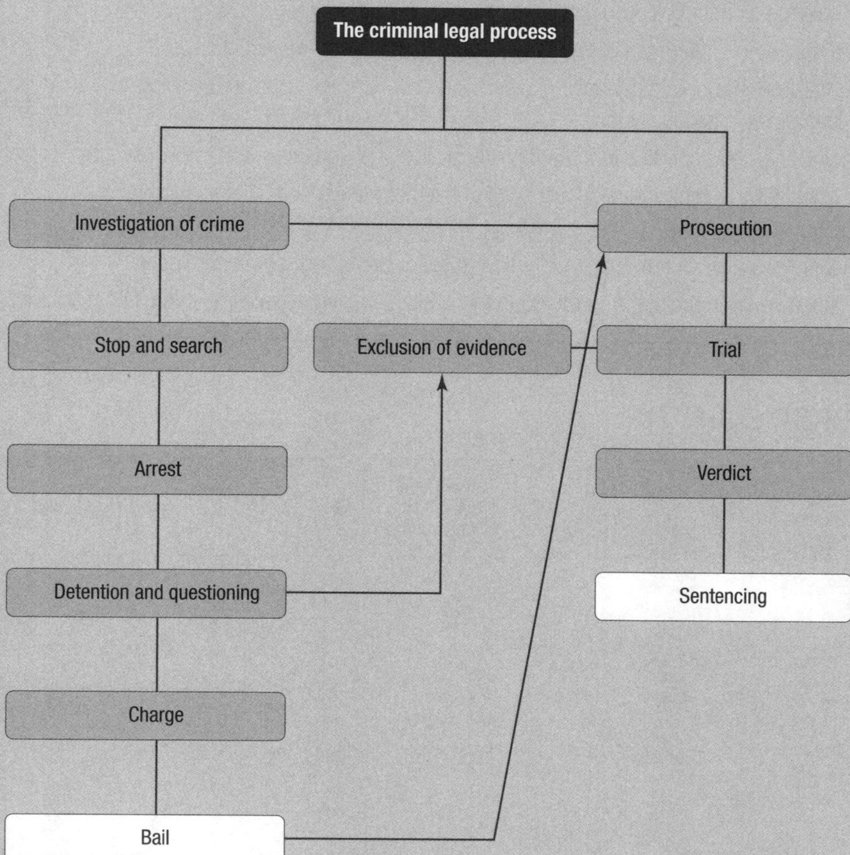

A printable version of this diagram plan is available from www.pearsoned.co.uk/lawexpressqa

Question 1

Discuss the safeguards which protect suspects against inappropriate police behaviour during questioning at the police station following arrest.

Answer plan

→ Briefly explain the need for suspects to be protected against inappropriate police interrogation techniques.

→ Explain the importance of time limits upon the detention of suspects.

→ Briefly explain the importance of the requirements which apply to the treatment of detainees in police custody.

→ Consider the importance of the tape-recording of police interviews with suspects.

→ Consider the importance of suspects' entitlement to consult a legal adviser.

→ Comment upon the abolition of the so-called 'right to silence' and the extent to which this decreases the protection afforded to suspects against self-incrimination.

→ Briefly explain the ability of the courts to exclude evidence which is of dubious reliability.

Diagram plan

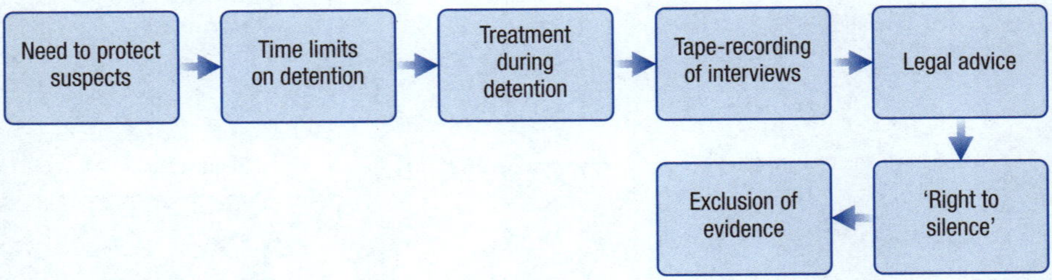

A printable version of this diagram plan is available from www.pearsoned.co.uk/lawexpressqa

Answer

Police questioning of suspects detained at the police station is a key means of obtaining evidence as part of the criminal investigation process, yet without appropriate regulation there is a danger that in some instances police may adopt unscrupulous methods when questioning suspects as a result of their urge to secure confessions or irrefutable evidence. The use of such practices have come to light through a number of miscarriages of justice to have emerged in which confessions have been secured from suspects through the application of oppressive interrogatory methods.[1] The Police and Criminal Evidence Act 1984 (PACE) provides a series of provisions which prima facie affords important safeguards to protect suspects from inappropriate police conduct.

Sections 40–43 of PACE limit the period for which a suspect may be detained for questioning[2], requiring that regular reviews take place after six hours, then at nine-hour intervals when further authorisation for detention must be granted. Detention beyond 24 hours requires the authorisation of a superintendent, and beyond 36 hours of the Magistrates' Court, although after 96 hours a suspect must be charged or released. The requirement of regular reviews ensures that a case must be made for continuing to detain a suspect for questioning, especially beyond 36 hours where a magistrate must be satisfied that continued detention is necessary.

The detainment of suspects for questioning is regulated by Code of Practice C[3] which specifies standards of accommodation which detainees are to be kept in, requires the provision of regular meals and regular breaks from questioning including adequate sleep. These requirements are important in order to ensure that suspects are able to remain fit and alert for questioning, minimising the danger of their unwittingly incriminating themselves during questioning.

Section 60 of PACE requires that all police interviews be tape-recorded. Theoretically, this provides a safeguard against oppressive interrogation techniques of suspects, although there has been some debate over the extent to which this has proven the case in practice.[4] Video-taping of interviews has been piloted which has the potential to improve the safeguards afforded to detainees when being questioned, interviews being clearly visible. However, it is costly and is unlikely to become a standard practice in the foreseeable future. In general, the courts appear to have attached much significance to compliance with recording requirements on the part of the police. For example, in **R *v* Canale** [1990] 2 All ER 187, where the evidence of an interview had not been contemporaneously written up, the court declined to admit it.

[1]You can provide some useful context to your answer by making reference to the importance of safeguards in protecting against miscarriages of justice. If you have time you might cite some specific examples of miscarriages of justice to have arisen from improper police conduct during questioning.

[2]Although the question asks about safeguards to protect suspects during police questioning, time limits upon the detention of suspects nonetheless serve to prevent the indefinite questioning of suspects and ensure that a case must be made for questioning to continue beyond specified periods of time.

[3]There is scope to outline these requirements in greater detail. Again, these requirements are relevant to the protection of suspects during questioning as they safeguard against the mistreatment of detainees resulting in them being more susceptible to incriminating themselves when under interrogation from the police.

[4]This point could be explored further if you have the time. There is certainly some evidence to suggest that tape-recording of interviews has not led to an end in heavy-handed interrogation tactics on the part of the police. By making reference to possible video-recording of interviews, you evidence awareness of recent developments and debates in this area.

Section 58 of PACE entitles any detained person to consult with a legal adviser privately and free of charge. The right to legal advice is widely recognised within most legal systems, and forms part of the right to a fair trial guaranteed by Article 6 of the European Convention on Human Rights. Appropriate legal advice can provide suspects with important protection against police tactics during interrogation which might otherwise lead them to unwittingly incriminate themselves. All detainees are entitled at a minimum to speak to a member of the Criminal Defence Service over the telephone, although any detainee who is to be interviewed by the police can have present a legal adviser during questioning even if the offence which he is being questioned in relation to is relatively minor. Although the right to consult a legal adviser can be denied where there is reasonable cause to suspect this will lead to other suspects being alerted, this should only apply in exceptional circumstances. The courts have shown that they are wary of admitting evidence obtained from suspects where legal representation has been denied. For example, in **R *v* Samuel** [1988] QB 615, evidence of a suspect's confession was held inadmissible where he had been denied access to legal advice. However, in cases such as **R *v* Alladice** (1988) 87 Cr App R 380, the courts have admitted evidence notwithstanding the denial of access to a legal adviser on the ground that it would not have affected the suspect's evidence in the circumstances.[5]

[5]It is essential that you discuss the right to legal advice and the possible impact of a suspect being denied legal advice, in light of some conflicting case law on this matter.

Historically, suspects could claim the benefit of the so-called 'right to silence', that is to say, their failure to answer police questions could not entitle juries to draw any adverse inferences against them during trial. However, section 34 of the Criminal Justice and Public Order Act 1994 now permits a jury to draw inferences as they deem appropriate from a suspect's refusal to answer police questions. This has been the subject of much controversy, although it was held in **Murray *v* UK** (1996) 22 EHRR 29 that this provision does not breach Article 6 of the ECHR. While the abolition of the so-called 'right to silence' has been regarded by some as a weakening of the protection afforded to detainees against self-incrimination during questioning, in practice, very few detainees avail themselves of it and commentators such as Zander have suggested that its value was overstated.[6] Furthermore, adverse inferences may not be drawn where a suspect has been denied legal advice (section 34(2A)), and the courts have identified a number of cases in which adverse inferences should not be drawn.

[6]Much can be made of the abolition of the so-called 'right to silence' and the consequences of this for the protection which it affords to a suspect during questioning. There has been much academic debate upon the issue, which you could usefully make reference to.

A final safeguard against inappropriate police treatment of suspects during questioning can be found in section 76(2) of PACE, which enables the courts to refuse to admit evidence of confessions which have been extracted by oppression.[7] This ought to deter the police from using unscrupulous methods as part of the interrogation process. For example, shouting at a suspect who had denied involvement in an offence over 300 times will constitute oppression (**R *v* Paris, Abdullahi and Miller** [1993] 97 Cr App R 99). Furthermore, section 78(1) enables the courts generally to exclude any prosecution evidence where it appears that in the circumstances it would have an adverse effect on proceedings that it ought not to be admitted. This provision can be invoked to prevent the admission of evidence which has been obtained by the police where serious breaches of safeguards have taken place, for example, the denial of legal advice to a suspect, mistreatment in custody or a failure to comply with other procedural safeguards.

[7]Ensure that you don't overlook the provisions which enable the courts to refuse to admit police evidence where its reliability is in question. This is a 'final' safeguard as even where the police fail to comply with the other provisions which attempt to protect suspects, the courts are still able to decline to admit evidence which emerges from inappropriately conducted police interrogations.

In conclusion, there is a series of useful safeguards which go some way towards ensuring that suspects are protected against inappropriate police behaviour. The prescription of time limits for detention, minimum conditions which detainees are entitled to be kept within, recording of interviews, and the right to legal advice all theoretically minimise the risk of the police mistreating suspects in order to extract confessions or other evidence. The courts' power to exclude unreliable evidence is particularly important as a means of responding to situations in which the police have not complied with the relevant provisions designed to protect suspects being questioned in custody.

✓ Make your answer stand out

- Make reference to relevant research findings upon the relative value of safeguards such as the 'right to silence', the tape-recording of interviews and access to legal advice.
- Consider any gap between the protection given to suspects by PACE provisions in theory and in practice.
- Place the issues into context by making reference to miscarriages of justice and the need for safeguards to be adequate to protect against these occurring.

! Don't be tempted to . . .

- Focus narrowly upon the process of questioning suspects without paying attention to broader issues, such as the exclusion of improperly obtained evidence.

Question 2

Discuss the general powers enjoyed by the police to stop and search suspects in public and the safeguards which apply to these powers.

Answer plan

→ Explain the balance that needs to be struck between competing interests in relation to stop and search powers.

→ Make reference to the common law position in relation to stop and search by the police.

→ Explain the power conferred upon the police by section 1 of PACE.

→ Explain the requirements imposed on the police by section 2 of PACE.

→ Explain the restrictions placed upon the police's ability to search suspects in public and the requirements imposed upon them in relation to recording stops and searches.

→ Make reference to the increased powers of stop and search conferred upon the police by various recent legislative provisions.

Diagram plan

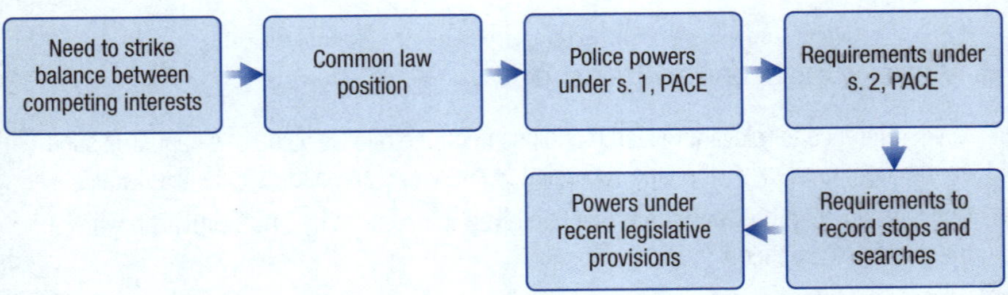

A printable version of this diagram plan is available from www.pearsoned.co.uk/lawexpressqa

Answer

The ability of the police to stop and search individuals whom they may suspect of criminal activity gives rise to a series of competing tensions in respect of which the law needs to strike an appropriate balance. On the one hand, the police must be given powers that are sufficient to enable them to undertake legitimate investigations to perform their primary function to prevent and detect crime, yet there is also a need to protect against unnecessary interferences with individual liberty arising from abuse of police powers. In specific relation to the exercise of stop and search powers by the police, there has been ongoing concern for some time that ethnic minorities are discriminated against[1], with statistical evidence pointing to disproportionately higher use of these powers against Black and Asian people, especially in London.

[1]You can provide useful context to your answer by citing evidence of discriminate use of stop and search powers, which underlines the importance of having effective safeguards against abuse of these powers.

At common law it has long been established that the police have no power to detain suspects short of arresting them.[2] This was demonstrated in the case of **Kenlin v Gardiner** [1967] 2 QB 510 where it was held that the police had no power to detain a group of boys for questioning prior to arrest. However, where a police officer merely pursues a suspect in an attempt to ask questions as opposed to physically detaining them, this has been held to amount to a trivial interference with liberty as opposed to an instance of unlawful detention (**Donnelly v Jackman** [1970] 1 WLR 562). Although the police are entitled at common law to ask questions of members of the public, there is no corresponding obligation on the part of the public to answer as the case of **Rice v Connolly** [1966] 2 QB 414 established, although failure to answer questions when accompanied by abusive behaviour on the part of the person questioned may be held to constitute obstruction of a police officer (**Ricketts v Cox** (1982) 74 Cr App R 298).

[2]It is worthwhile briefly outlining the common law position in relation to stopping suspects. This serves to reinforce the significance of PACE provisions.

Police powers to stop and search suspects were placed upon a statutory footing by the Police and Criminal Evidence Act 1984 (PACE), which seeks to provide the police with the powers necessary to effectively perform their functions whilst ensuring that adequate safeguards are placed upon the exercise of these powers to protect against abuse. Under section 1, a police officer may search a person or vehicle in a public place for stolen or prohibited articles[3], which as a consequence of changes made by the

[3]You need to explain clearly the power conferred upon the police by section 1 and the safeguards attached to it.

Criminal Justice Act 2003 now extends to articles intended for use to cause criminal damage. A person may be detained for the purpose of conducting such a search. A search may only be undertaken if the police officer has reasonable grounds for suspecting that he will find one of the articles referred to. Guidance on what constitute 'reasonable grounds' for suspicion is to be found in Code of Practice A.[4] Paragraph 2.2 of the code states that 'reasonable grounds' will be dependent upon the circumstances of the individual case. However, it goes on to add that there must be an objective basis for a police officer's suspicion which is based upon facts, information or intelligence relevant to the likelihood of finding an article of the kind covered by section 1 of PACE. The need for an objective basis for a search prevents police officers from acting out of irrelevant considerations or carrying out stop and searches on a mere whim. Ordinarily, a reasonable suspicion cannot be based purely on personal factors such as race, age or the fact that the individual concerned is known to have previous criminal convictions. This should minimise the risk of particular groups being discriminately singled out for stop and searches, although statistical data unfortunately suggests that discrimination on the part of the police continues in this respect. There is, however, some scope for a reasonable suspicion to exist in the absence of specific information, paragraph 2.3 of the code providing the example of a police officer encountering someone on the street at night who is obviously attempting to hide something.

[4]You can only effectively illustrate the safeguards which accompany section 1 by referring to the guidance offered by code A, in particular in relation to 'reasonable grounds' for suspicion.

As a further safeguard, section 2 of PACE sets out a series of minimum standards that must be satisfied by a police officer before a search takes place of a person or vehicle.[5] The police officer must identify himself, provide the name of the station at which he is based and explain the grounds upon which he is going to undertake the search. If the officer is not in uniform, he must provide documentary evidence of his identity. These standards serve as important safeguards against police abuse of stop and search powers by providing a degree of accountability on the part of police officers for their actions. Significantly, the Court of Appeal ruled in **R *v* Bristol** [2007] EWCA Crim 3214 that the failure of a police officer to provide the necessary information under section 2 when undertaking a stop and search will render it unlawful.

[5]Section 2 provides several safeguards which apply to stop and search powers and should be outlined.

Under section 117 of PACE, a police officer may use 'reasonable force' where necessary in order to exercise his powers.[6] Thus, while it may be necessary to employ some force to facilitate a search where a suspect refuses to cooperate with police, the requirement that force be 'reasonable' protects against the excessive use of force, some degree of proportionality being required on the part of the police. Furthermore, where a person is subject to a search in public section 2(9) of PACE provides that the only clothing which can be removed is outer clothing including coats, jackets or gloves, thus affording some protection to the dignity of the searched individual.

[6]You should refer to the fact that force may be used in order to perform a stop and search, but that this is qualified by the need for it to be 'reasonable', this providing a further example of PACE attempting to strike a balance between empowering the police and protecting the rights of suspects.

Wherever the police stop and search a person in public, that person's name, address and ethnicity must be recorded together with the reason for the stop and search and its outcome. A copy of the record must be provided to the suspect. If not searched, the person's ethnicity must be noted and a receipt given. The police are empowered under section 1(6) to seize any stolen or prohibited articles discovered as a result of a search, and must make a written record at the time detailing these unless exceptionable circumstances exist which make this wholly impracticable. These recording requirements are an important means of ensuring police actions are justified and accounted for.[7]

[7]Ensure that you do not overlook the recording requirements imposed by PACE. These provide a further safeguard against abuse of power.

While PACE provisions appear to attempt to strike a reasonable balance between empowering the police to perform their essential functions and providing necessary safeguards against abuse of these powers, a number of recent legislative provisions have introduced new powers to stop and search in relation to particular offences which arguably enhance police powers in this area further,[8] for example, under the Criminal Justice and Public Order Act 1994 and the Terrorism Act 2000.

[8]If you have time you could make more of this point, by providing examples of some of the areas in which police powers of stop and search have been increased, for example in relation to stopping vehicles en route to festivals and terrorist suspects. You might offer further comment upon the extent to which such powers undermine the balanced framework for stop and search contained in PACE.

✓ Make your answer stand out

- Provide context to your answer by referring to the disproportionate use of stop and search powers against certain groups in society, making reference to the findings detailed in Miller, J., 'Stop and Search in England: A Reformed Tactic or Business as Usual?', *British Journal of Criminology*, 2010, v. 50, n. 5, pp. 954–74.
- Make reference to the growth of stop and search powers under various recent pieces of legislation, and the extent to which this may undermine the balanced framework provided by PACE for the exercise of stop and search powers.

! Don't be tempted to . . .

- Confuse stop and search powers with other powers possessed by the police, for example searches of suspects in custody and searches of premises.

Question 3

Discuss the extent to which the rules on the granting of bail strike a balance between protecting the rights of defendants and the wider interests of society.

Answer plan

→ Briefly explain what bail is.

→ Explain the various tensions which arise in the bail process and the need to have regard to competing objectives.

→ Explain which bodies are empowered to grant bail.

→ Discuss the statutory presumption in favour of bail and the circumstances in which bail may be refused.

→ Discuss the scope which exists for a grant of bail to be made subject to conditions.

→ Conclude upon the extent to which the current law strikes an appropriate balance between protecting the rights of defendants and wider interests of society.

Diagram plan

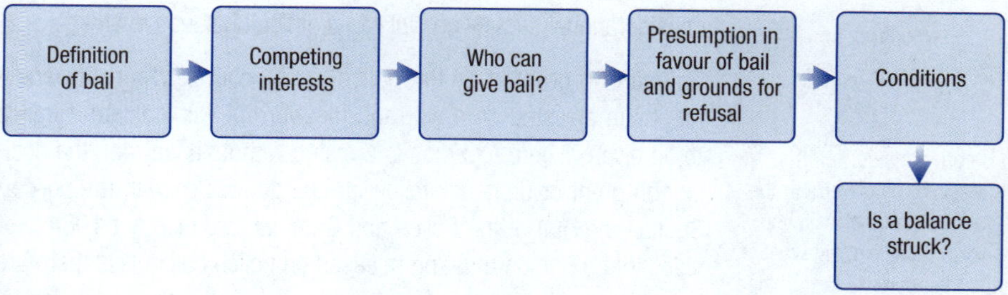

A printable version of this diagram plan is available from www.pearsoned.co.uk/lawexpressqa

Answer

[1]You should begin your answer by briefly demonstrating that you understand what bail is.

'Bail' refers to the release from custody of a person charged with a criminal offence pending and during trial.[1] Bail may be subject to conditions and may be dependent upon the willingness of another person to act as a surety whereby a sum of money is put down which will be forfeited if the defendant absconds or breaks bail conditions.

[2]You should provide some contextual background to your answer by illustrating the competing interests which come into play when decisions are made to grant or refuse bail. It will be helpful to refer to statistical evidence relating to such matters as the number of offences committed by those on bail or instances of defendants failing to attend court. This goes to the very heart of the question and reinforces the need for the law on bail to strike a balance between various competing interests.

Decisions over the grant or refusal of bail need to balance some very important competing interests.[2] On the one hand, a fundamental principle of English law is the presumption of the innocence of the accused until proven otherwise in a court of law. The increasing influence of human rights standards also requires that individual liberty, guaranteed by Article 5 of the European Convention on Human Rights, be protected unless there are compelling reasons for it to be compromised. Remanding defendants in custody takes a burden on the already overcrowded population, approximately 16% of the prison population consisting of those held on remand awaiting trial and yet to be convicted of an offence. This is arguably of special concern given that during the 1990s, of those remanded in custody awaiting trial for summary offences, 50% ultimately received non-custodial sentences and 25% were acquitted. However, granting bail comes with its own series of problems. 12% of those bailed fail to appear for their trial, a factor which led then Attorney-General Lord Goldsmith to call in 2005 for a crackdown on those who 'skip bail', at a time when 60,000 warrants were outstanding for failure to appear in court. Those on bail may also commit further offences or possibly interfere with prosecution witnesses or obstruct the course of justice. Approximately 50,000 offences are committed annually by those on bail, which have included some high profile instances of rape and serious assault offences. In light of these considerations, the law on bail has a difficult balance to strike.

Bail can be granted by the police or the courts. Where a person has been arrested on a warrant, the warrant will indicate if bail is to be given. Where a person is arrested without a warrant, the decision to grant or deny bail following charge resides with the police.[3] Section 38(1)(a) of the Police and Criminal Evidence Act 1984 provides that a person must be released on police bail unless there are reasonable grounds for doubting the name and address given by the person, for believing detention to be necessary to prevent the accused harming himself, others or property, or for believing that he will fail to appear in court or that his detention is necessary to prevent interference with the course of justice. Although broad, these considerations can only be used to deny bail where the custody officer has reasonable grounds for believing in their applicability. In practice, bail is overwhelmingly granted, with 83% of those charged with indictable offences and 88% of those charged with summary offences being bailed in 1990. If the police deny bail, the accused should be brought before the Magistrates' Court as soon as possible. The granting of bail by the courts is primarily governed by the Bail Act 1976,[4] and a duty is imposed on the courts to consider bail at each subsequent hearing, underlying the importance of the defendant's liberty pending any conviction. This is reinforced by the existence of rights of appeal against decisions to refuse bail.

Section 4 of the Bail Act 1976 contains a statutory presumption in favour of bail. Bail should be generally granted unless serious considerations militate against it. These are outlined in schedule 1 to the Act[5] and are that the court is satisfied that there are substantial grounds for believing that the defendant will abscond, offend while on bail, interfere with witnesses or obstruct the course of justice. These reflect the main problems associated with the granting of bail and are arguably therefore very logical. Bail may also be denied where it is felt custody is warranted for the defendant's own protection, where he has previously failed to answer bail, or the court requires further information in order to make a reasoned decision. The court must take into account all relevant factors when making its decision. Further grounds for the denial of bail were added by the Criminal Justice Act 2003, sections 14–15, these being where

[3]Before considering the specific rules governing the grant or denial of bail, you should firstly explain who has the power to grant bail. The role of the police in this respect should be explained first as they are responsible for considering bail in the first instance. It is helpful to cite figures on the granting of bail to demonstrate the extent to which it is readily given or otherwise.

[4]You should explain the continuing role of the courts in the bail process in order to illustrate the clear importance attached to bail.

[5]It is essential that you explain the presumption which exists in favour of bail and outline the grounds upon which bail can be denied. This goes to the heart of the question and involves considering the extent to which an appropriate balance is struck by the law. You should point out that the grounds for the denial of bail relate directly to the main undesirable consequences which bail tends to give rise to.

the defendant committed the present offence while on bail or has absconded previously in the same proceedings.

Arguably, the law appears to strike a reasonable balance by making a presumption in favour of bail, while enabling its denial where there is reason to believe that its grant may have one of the undesirable effects most closely associated with bail. That the overwhelming majority of defendants are granted bail would seem to reinforce this point. The law's relative flexibility is evidenced by the outcome of the attempt of section 25 of the Criminal Justice and Public Order Act 1994 to deny bail to those charged with serious offences who have previous convictions for other serious offences.[6] The provision was challenged in **Caballero *v* UK** (2000) 30 EHRR 1 by a defendant denied bail when charged with rape in 1996 due to his having a manslaughter conviction from 1987. This was deemed to breach Article 5(3) of the European Convention on Human Rights and was amended by the Crime and Disorder Act 1998, so that bail could be granted in such cases where the court is satisfied that 'exceptional circumstances' justify this. Thus, even where a very serious offence is committed by a defendant with a serious previous conviction, bail is no longer automatically excluded as a possibility.

[6]The impact of section 25 of the Criminal Justice and Public Order Act was controversial. By discussing the outcome of this attempt to restrict bail you are able to illustrate in action a key tension between competing values and the extent to which the law has struck a balance in respect of defendants charged with serious offences.

Conditions may be imposed upon bail.[7] There are no statutory limitations upon what conditions may imposed, but they commonly include curfews or residency requirements, regular attendance at a police station, or the surrender of a passport. The objective of conditions is to minimise the risk of re-offending, absconding or interfering with witnesses or the course of justice without having to remand the defendant in custody.

[7]You should explain the scope which exists for conditions to be imposed on bail grants and how these may help to resolve some of the tensions which arise when deciding whether to award bail or not.

In conclusion, the law on bail appears to generally balance well the competing interests at stake.[8] There is a presumption in favour of bail, but the problems associated with bail are recognised in the provisions which enable bail to be denied where there are solid grounds to do so. Ultimately bail is awarded to the vast majority of defendants and the scope which exists for conditions to be placed upon grants of bail make it easier to strike an appropriate balance between protecting the individual liberty of those yet to be convicted of an offence and having regard to other legitimate concerns.

[8]This conclusion flows logically from the discussion contained in the essay which has portrayed the law as essentially balanced between the competing objectives.

✓ Make your answer stand out

- Provide some context to your answer by illustrating the tensions which arise in the bail process with reference to relevant statistical evidence.
- Make reference to attempts to reduce the availability of bail.

! Don't be tempted to . . .

- Simply regurgitate the main provisions of the Bail Act 1976;
- Focus only upon either court bail or police bail.

Question 4

Discuss the factors which inform a judge's approach to sentencing a convicted defendant.

Answer plan

→ Briefly outline the main categories of sentence open to a judge to impose upon a convicted defendant and the factors which constrain a judge's discretion.

→ Explain the purposes of sentencing which judges are to be guided by.

→ Consider the use of sentencing guidelines to assist judges when sentencing.

→ Consider the increased control placed upon sentencing by legislation, such as the imposition of fixed or minimum sentences for certain offences, or requirements which must be satisfied for certain sentences to be imposed.

→ Explain the role formerly played by the Home Secretary in the imposition of life sentences, and how this has now been reformed.

→ Conclude upon the extent to which the law affords judges sufficient flexibility to impose sentences suited to the offence.

Diagram plan

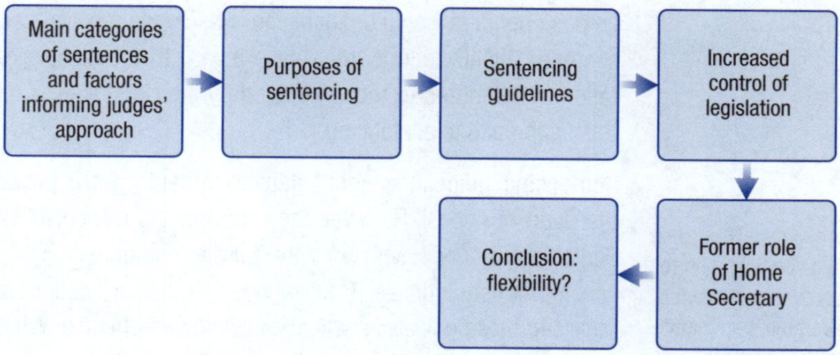

A printable version of this diagram plan is available from www.pearsoned.co.uk/lawexpressqa

Answer

Following the conviction of a defendant, there are four main categories of sentence which a judge may choose to impose.[1] The ultimate sanction is that of the imposition of a custodial sentence, but sentences may also take the form of fines, various community sentences and other miscellaneous sentences. A judge's approach towards sentencing in any given case is constrained by a variety of factors.[2] Legislation prescribes certain sentences for particular offences, taking the form of minimum or maximum sentences. There are also sentencing guidelines which judges ought to have regard to when deciding upon the appropriate sentence in any given case, and reference is also to be had to the purposes of sentencing which are to be found in statute. Over time, judicial discretion upon sentencing matters has become increasingly regulated by legislation.

Section 142 of the Criminal Justice Act 2003 prescribes a number of recognised purposes of sentencing.[3] Firstly, sentencing should serve to punish offenders, that is to say there should be a degree of retributive effect in sentences, the idea being that any sentence should fit the crime committed. Secondly, sentencing should be designed to reduce crime. This applies both to individual offenders, deterring them from re-offending, and the general public, who may be deterred from committing similar crimes through the imposition of exemplary sentences upon offenders. Thirdly, sentencing should give consideration to the reform and rehabilitation of offenders, an

[1] While useful in your introduction to refer to the main types of sentence which a court can impose, the question does not ask for a detailed explanation of these and so is not necessary.

[2] It is helpful in the introduction to briefly outline the main factors which impact upon a judge's approach to sentencing as this enables you to highlight the key issues to be covered in the remainder of the answer.

[3] The question is not concerned specifically with the purposes of sentencing, but these are a factor which judges must have regard to and should thus be mentioned.

objective which has been of increased interest recently. The fourth objective of sentencing is the protection of the public, hence dangerous offenders would ordinarily be expected to receive a custodial sentence. Finally, courts must have regard to the making of reparation by offenders to those affected by their offences, a relatively fresh approach to sentencing.

Sentencing guidelines until relatively recently were provided by the Court of Appeal. However, they are now the responsibility of the Sentencing Council, set up by the Coroners and Justice Act 2009, which produces guidelines for judges.[4] Courts are obliged to have regard to these guidelines when sentencing an offender. While these guidelines provide a degree of discretion for judges to operate within, they suggest appropriate starting points for sentence levels for particular offences and direct the courts to consider relevant aggravating or mitigating factors which may warrant the imposition of a higher or lower sentence than the ordinary suggested starting point.

[4]Sentencing guidelines are a paramount consideration for judges sentencing offenders. If you have time, you might provide more detailed discussion of the background to the creation of the SC to replace the Sentencing Guidelines Council and the Sentencing Advisory Panel.

Judicial discretion is significantly curbed in those areas where legislation has been used to carefully control sentencing by the courts.[5] The Magistrates' Courts is restricted to imposing custodial sentences of 12 months in respect of any offence (section 154, Criminal Justice Act 2003), although it may under section 3 of the Powers of Criminal Courts (Sentencing) Act 2000 send a defendant to be sentenced in the Crown Court if it deems that a tougher sentence than it has the jurisdiction to impose is warranted. Subject to any specific restrictions imposed in respect of certain offences, the Crown Court is able to make use of the full range of available sentences. There are no limits to its ability to impose fines, although in so doing it must take account of the seriousness of the offence committed and the means of the defendant to pay (section 167, Criminal Justice Act 2003). Minimum sentences have been created for a number of offences, one example being that applicable to certain firearms offences under section 287 of the Criminal Justice Act 2003. Although maximum sentences exist for many offences, they are rarely imposed in practice. Mandatory sentences are carried by some offences, the most notable example being that of murder, for which nothing less than a life sentence will suffice.

[5]A major point to be made is the extent to which judicial discretion has been curbed as a result of legislative provisions which pertain to the sentencing process. You can illustrate this effectively through the use of the examples cited.

Despite evidence of increased regulation of sentencing policy by legislation, there are several legislative provisions designed to guard against a hasty resort to sentences which may be harsher than are

[6]This is a useful point to make in order to provide a balanced account of the impact of legislation on the sentencing process.

warranted by the offence committed.[6] For example, under section 152 of the Criminal Justice Act 2003 a court should not pass a custodial sentence unless it considers the offence is so serious that only this sentence can be justified. Section 153 of the same Act provides that custodial sentences should be for the shortest term commensurate with the seriousness of the offence. In determining the seriousness of an offence, section 143 directs the court to have regard to the culpability of the offender, harm caused by the offence and the offender's previous criminal record. Thus, while legislation has been increasingly used to control the imposition of sentences by judges, it has been used to discourage the rash imposition of harsh sentences in some circumstances as well as ensuring that minimum or specified sentences are imposed in others.

[7]If you have the time, there is scope for more detailed discussion of the extent to which the sentencing of offenders has given rise to some fierce political debates and the ensuing implications for the doctrine of separation of powers.

A major area of controversy in sentencing policy has arisen from attempts to politicise the process. Crime is a significant area of political concern and successive governments have sought to portray themselves as tough on criminal offenders.[7] One example can be found with the Crime (Sentences) Act 1997, section 2 of which prescribed mandatory life sentences for those convicted of a second serious offence, such as manslaughter, rape or certain offences against the person. Criticism of the provision followed cases such as **R *v* Turner** [2000] Crim LR 492, where a life sentence was imposed following a conviction for grievous bodily harm with intent because the defendant had been convicted of manslaughter thirty years earlier. Although section 2 allowed courts to decline to impose a life sentence where of the opinion that there were exceptional circumstances to justify this, this was interpreted rigidly until the case of **R *v* Offen and others** [2001] 1 WLR 253 where the Court of Appeal ruled that mandatory life sentences were not intended to apply to defendants not posing a future risk to the public.

Another example of the danger of politicisation of the sentencing process is found in the role formerly played in the setting of tariffs for life sentences of those convicted of murder by the Home Secretary. This was found to breach Article 5(1) and 5(4) of the European Convention on Human Rights in **Stafford *v* UK** (2002) 35 EHRR 1121, and was subsequently removed. Section 269 of the Criminal Justice Act 2003 created instead a three-tier system of life sentences within which after considering specified starting points, judges are able to apply aggravating and mitigating factors.

[8]This conclusion flows logically from the discussion contained within the answer which alludes to several factors which influence the approach taken towards the sentencing of offenders by judges in individual cases.

In conclusion, the sentencing of those convicted of an offence is not an automated process.[8] Whereas legislation has increasingly sought to control the process, judges retain a degree of flexibility within which they can operate in light of guidance which they are given and must have regard to.

✓ Make your answer stand out

- Provide some discussion of attempts to politicise sentencing and the importance of the separation of powers within the context of sentencing by the courts.
- Emphasise the increased control over judicial approaches to sentencing exerted by legislation with reference to examples from specific statutory provisions.
- Consider the value of sentencing guidelines in achieving policy objectives by reading and referring to Wasik, M., 'Sentencing Guidelines in England and Wales – state of the art?', *Criminal Law Review*, 2008, p. 253.

! Don't be tempted to . . .

- Spend a lot of time explaining the purposes of sentencing;
- Spend a lot of time outlining the various types of sentences which the courts may impose.

Question 5

'The removal of the "right to silence" by the Criminal Justice and Public Order Act 1994 has had relatively little impact upon the protection afforded to defendants when being questioned.' Discuss.

Answer plan

- ➜ Briefly explain what is meant by the 'right to silence' and the pre-1994 legal position on its protection.
- ➜ Explain the impact of sections 34–37 of the Criminal Justice and Public Order Act 1994.
- ➜ Consider the rationale for the changes introduced by the 1994 Act.
- ➜ Consider how the 1994 changes have been built upon by subsequent legal developments.
- ➜ Conclude upon the extent to which the abolition of the 'right to silence' has had an impact upon the protection afforded to defendants when being questioned.

Diagram plan

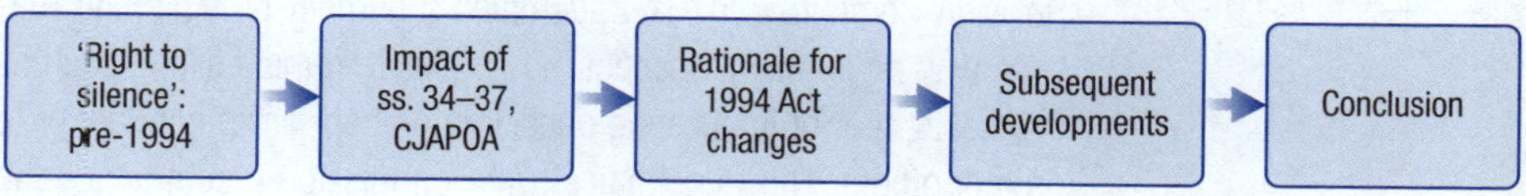

A printable version of this diagram plan is available from www.pearsoned.co.uk/lawexpressqa

Answer

The 'right to silence' refers to the ability of suspects to refuse to answer questions during police questioning or when on trial without a jury being entitled to draw any adverse inferences from this silence.[1] Prior to provisions introduced by the Criminal Justice and Public Order Act 1994, although juries in practice might draw adverse inferences from a defendant's failure to answer any questions, judges were obliged to tell them that they should not do so. It is slightly misleading to say that the 1994 Act abolished the right to silence as no defendant can be compelled to answer any questions if he does not want to; however, the effect of the change to the law was that a defendant's silence could have adverse consequences for his defence which previously the law did not permit.

[1]At the outset of your answer you should explain what the 'right to silence' entailed, thus setting the scene nicely for you to move on to consider the impact upon this of the provisions of the 1994 Act.

[2]You should briefly explain the main provisions of the 1994 Act which permitted courts to draw adverse inferences from a suspect's silence.

Sections 34–37 of the 1994 Act provide four circumstances in which a suspect's silence will entitle a court to draw any inferences they deem appropriate from this silence.[2] These are where a suspect fails to mention something during police questioning later relied on as part of his defence and which he could reasonably have been expected to mention, where a suspect fails to give evidence or answer questions during trial, where a suspect fails to account after arrest for objects, substances or marks on his clothing, and where a suspect fails to account for his presence at a place after arrest. The 1994 Act clearly introduces a wide range of circumstances in which a jury can draw adverse inferences from a defendant's silence.

[3]In considering the real impact of the abolition of the 'right to silence', it is important to engage with the debate over the merits of the right. This will enable you to consider whether the effect of the 1994 Act was to remove a hugely significant right, or was relatively inconsequential.

Prior to the introduction of the 1994 Act there was much debate over the merits of the traditional 'right to silence' enjoyed by suspects.[3] Defenders of the right claimed that it was an important safeguard for suspects to protect themselves against self-incrimination during police questioning, particularly where interrogation involves oppressive techniques. While critics of the right to silence argued that the innocent had nothing to fear from its abolition if they simply answered truthfully police questions, the Criminal Law Revision Committee in 1972 identified a number of legitimate reasons why an innocent suspect may prefer to remain silent, such as confusion, fear of implicating oneself in embarrassing conduct or to protect others. The Runciman Royal Commission recommended in 1993 that adverse inferences should not be permitted to be drawn from silence under police questioning. The main rationale behind the abolition of the right to silence would appear to have been the concern with suspects frustrating criminal investigations through non-cooperation with the police when being questioned. The Home Secretary at the time of the Act, Michael Howard, argued that hardened criminals disproportionately availed themselves of the right to frustrate the criminal justice process, wasting police time and making it more difficult to convict offenders. A particular concern was the use of 'ambush' defences by defendants, whereby they would launch last-minute defences not mentioned during questioning which the prosecution would then have insufficient time to investigate in order to rebut in court.

However, while these appear prima facie logical grounds for wanting to remove the right to silence, the fact is that various studies – such as those conducted by Zander (1979) and Sanders *et al.* (1989)

– have demonstrated that very few suspects remain silent during questioning, as few as 2% in the Sanders study.[4] This undermines any argument that there are huge gains to be made from abolishing the right to silence, especially where this may weaken the protection which the right potentially can afford to innocent suspects. However, it also suggests that any protection afforded to defendants by the right to silence was minimal given the relatively little use made of it. In this sense, it could be argued that the impact of the provisions of the 1994 Act, in practice, ought to be minimal.

The extent to which adverse inferences may be drawn from a defendant's silence has been the subject of debate in a number of post-1994 cases.[5] Although it was held in **Murray *v* UK** [1996] 22 EHRR 29 that the abolition of the right to silence did not breach the European Convention on Human Rights, the courts will not always permit adverse inferences to be drawn from a defendant's silence. For example, a defendant's failure to answer questions cannot lead to adverse inferences being drawn when he explained his conduct and defence at the time in a written statement to the police (**R *v* McGarry** [1998] 3 All ER 805). It was also held in **R *v* N** [1998] *The Times* 13 February, that adverse inferences could only be drawn from a defendant's failure to answer questions on a matter, not from his failure to mention something that he had not been asked about. Such cases show the courts adopting some caution when interpreting the 1994 provisions in order to ensure that suspects retain some reasonable safeguards.

The question of whether adverse inferences can be drawn where a defendant fails to answer questions as a result of a solicitor's advice has also been considered by the courts.[6] In **Condron *v* UK** [2000] Crim LR 679, it was held that remaining silent upon a solicitor's advice in itself does not prevent adverse inferences being drawn by a jury, but that good reasons must be provided as to why this legal advice was given. Subsequently, the Court of Appeal has ruled that a defendant remaining silent on a solicitor's advice must have both a genuine and reasonable reliance upon that advice (**R *v* Beckles** [2004] All ER (D) 226 (Nov)). There is, thus, a certain threshold for a defendant to satisfy in order to prevent any adverse inferences being drawn. However, where a suspect is denied the opportunity to consult a solicitor at the police station, the 1994 Act was amended by section 58 of the Youth Justice and Criminal Evidence Act 1999

[4]This is an important point to emphasise. It can be used to support either side of the debate on the merits of the right to silence, as on one hand it suggests that the right was not subject to heavy abuse and in no real need of reform, yet on the other hand by showing the limited extent to which the right was exercised, it can be argued that its abolition will have little impact upon the safeguards currently enjoyed by most suspects in practice.

[5]You can consider further the impact of the 1994 provisions by exploring case law upon the Act in order to assess the manner in which these have been applied by the courts. The cases cited here all evidence a reluctance on the part of the courts to allow adverse inferences to be drawn too easily.

[6]This is an issue worth exploring as the case law evidences the extent to which a court's ability to draw adverse inferences is based upon a number of factors, as the cases in this area demonstrate.

to the effect that no adverse inferences may be drawn from the suspect's silence. This is arguably an important safeguard for suspects who may be especially vulnerable as a consequence of the absence of any legal advice of which they can avail themselves.

In conclusion, there is arguably a difference between the theoretical and practical impact of sections 34–37 of the 1994 Act.[7] While theoretically a long established safeguard is removed from suspects, the reality is that very few of them ever actually availed themselves of it. Furthermore, in some of the case law on the application of the statutory provisions the courts have shown a willingness to ensure that certain safeguards remain for defendants where adverse inferences cannot be drawn from their silence in certain circumstances.

[7]This conclusion flows logically from the discussion contained in the answer. A strong case can be made from the outset for distinguishing between the theoretical and practical impact of the 1994 Act upon the right to silence, and this is reinforced to some extent by consideration of some of the case law.

✓ Make your answer stand out

- Consider both the merits of the abolition of the so-called 'right to silence' and the extent to which any negative consequences have been increased or ameliorated by subsequent legal developments.
- Draw upon relevant case law to illustrate the application of the 1994 Act provisions in practice, particularly in a human rights context, upon which you can refer to Jackson, J., 'Re-conceptualizing the Right to Silence as an Effective Fair Trial Standard', *International and Comparative Law Quarterly*, 2009, v. 58, n. 4, pp. 835–61.

! Don't be tempted to . . .

- Simply outline the arguments for and against the removal of the 'right to silence'.

Question 6

Discuss the ability of the courts to exclude evidence in a criminal trial, with particular reference to evidence obtained by the police.

Answer plan

- ➜ Briefly explain the importance of relevance and reliability as key criteria governing the admissibility of evidence, and the central role of the police in the collection of evidence.
- ➜ Briefly refer to some of the general rules which govern the admissibility of evidence, such as the rule against hearsay evidence and restrictions upon the admission of character evidence.
- ➜ Explain the scope of section 76 of the Police and Criminal Evidence Act 1984 and discuss the extent to which it has been utilised by the courts to exclude evidence of confessions.
- ➜ Explain the scope of section 78 of the Police and Criminal Evidence Act 1984 and discuss the extent to which it has been utilised by the courts to exclude evidence on grounds of its unreliability.
- ➜ Conclude by commenting upon the extent to which the courts appear to be willing to exclude evidence obtained by the police.

Diagram plan

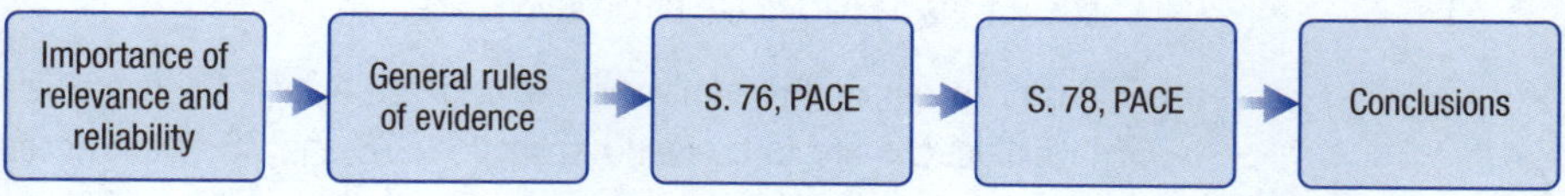

A printable version of this diagram plan is available from www.pearsoned.co.uk/lawexpressqa

Answer

A significant body of law governs the admission of evidence in criminal trials. The oral tradition of the English criminal trial places great emphasis upon the provision of testimony by witnesses present in court, and the suspicion attached to other forms of evidence is reflected in the law's careful regulation of its admissibility. The core principles upon which the law of evidence is based are, arguably, both the relevance and reliability of evidence that is admitted in court.[1] It must be relevant to the case being proven or rebutted,

[1]You can provide some useful context to your answer by explaining the centrality of the criteria of relevance and reliability to the rules which govern the admission of evidence. The importance of reliability in particular will be built upon later when you explore the law's regulation of police obtained evidence.

and its reliability should not be in question because it is tainted in some way. These principles are central to the guarantee of a fair trial, enshrined in Article 6 of the European Convention on Human Rights, now incorporated into domestic law by the Human Rights Act 1998. In the overwhelming majority of criminal trials, the primary body responsible for collecting evidence against the accused will be the police. In order to balance their need to conduct their legitimate investigations effectively with the protection of the rights of suspects, a statutory framework – found primarily in the provisions of the Police and Criminal Evidence Act 1984 – applies to the police's exercise of its powers of investigation which extend to the admissibility of police obtained evidence. Ultimately, whether a particular piece of evidence is admissible in a trial will be a matter for the judge who is the ultimate arbiter on such matters.

[2]Although the focus of your answer should be upon evidence obtained by the police, you can demonstrate wider knowledge by making brief reference to some of the key planks of the law of evidence and relate these back to the point made about the importance of reliability and relevance.

The law of evidence contains certain general rules applicable to the admission of evidence.[2] For example, to safeguard against the admission of unreliable evidence, as a general principle hearsay evidence may not be produced in court subject to a number of well established exceptions. Similarly, to avoid juries being influenced by irrelevant considerations, it is not ordinarily permissible to adduce evidence of the accused's bad character, such as any previous criminal convictions, although the effect of section 101 of the Criminal Justice Act 2003 was to make it easier to refer to previous convictions as part of the prosecution case.

[3]You should illustrate the extent to which the courts have made use of section 76(2) to exclude confession evidence by reference to a range of examples from the case law.

Restrictions upon the admissibility of evidence obtained during police investigations are to be found in sections 76 and 78 of the Police and Criminal Evidence Act. Section 76(2) applies to confession evidence and provides that evidence of a confession will be inadmissible where that confession has been obtained by oppression or in circumstances likely to render it unreliable.[3] Oppression is defined in section 76(8) as including 'torture, inhuman or degrading treatment, and the use or threat of violence'. The courts have taken a relatively narrow approach to the question of what will amount to oppression in practice. In **R *v* Fulling** [1987] QB 426, that the police extracted a confession from a woman after informing her that her partner had been unfaithful to her was held not to amount to an instance of oppression, the court ruling that the term should be given its ordinary dictionary meaning which entailed unjust treatment, cruelty or the wrongful use of power. In practice, the courts have seldom found oppression present in police interrogation procedures. For example, in **R v Miller** [1986] 1 WLR 1191, the existence of medical evidence that questioning of the suspect, a paranoid schizophrenic, produced voluntary insanity on his part was deemed by the Court of Appeal not to amount to evidence of oppression. By contrast, in **R v Paris, Abdullahi and Miller** [1993] 97 Cr App R 99, shouting at a suspect what the police wanted him to say after he had denied his involvement in the crime 300 times was held to amount to oppression. The value of section 76(2) is diluted by section 76(4) which states that even where confession evidence is excluded, any facts discovered from it may still be admissible. This effectively condones oppressive police questioning adopted for the purpose of soliciting further evidence.[4] The ability of the courts to exclude confession evidence unreliable for other reasons is limited by the fact that its unreliability must arise from anything said or done by a person other than the defendant, a point confirmed in **R v Goldenberg** [1988] 152 JP 557. This means that circumstances pertaining solely to the suspect's mindset will not be grounds for contesting the reliability of his confession.

[4]It is important that you explain the limited nature of section 76 as a safeguard against the use of oppressive police techniques to obtain evidence.

Section 78 (1) applies to evidence generally and provides that a court may refuse to admit evidence if it appears that, having regard to all the circumstances, it would have such an adverse effect on the fairness of the proceedings that it ought not to be admitted.[5] Section 78(1) particularly comes into play where there have been breaches of PACE provisions. For example, in **R v Samuel** [1988] QB 615, the denial of access to a solicitor, and in **R v Absalom** [1988] Crim LR 748, the failure to advise a suspect of his right to legal representation, were sufficient grounds for making use of section 78(1). Similarly, a failure to maintain a proper record of an interview with the suspect has been used as sufficient reason for excluding police evidence (**R v Keenan** [1990] 2 QB 54). There is no detailed list of the circumstances in which section 78(1) will be relevant, it having been applied in a wide range of situations. For example, in **R v Mason** [1988] 1 WLR 139, the police's lie to the suspect and his solicitor in an arson case that his fingerprints had been found on a bottle of inflammable liquid led to the exclusion of the resulting confession. The House of Lords has also ruled that evidence obtained by torture abroad should be excluded (**A v Secretary of State for the Home Department** [2004] UKHL 56).

[5]You are best able to illustrate the use of section 78(1) by the courts to exclude unreliable evidence by drawing upon case law examples to show the broad range of instances to which the provision can potentially be applied.

Notwithstanding the broad ambit of section 78(1), the courts appear prepared to tolerate a certain amount of deception on the part of the police as part of their investigative procedures.[6] For example, they refused to exclude evidence in **R v Latif and Shahzad** [1996] 1 WLR 104 where the defendant was tricked into entering the UK so that he could be prosecuted. Similarly, where police officers ran a 'mock' jewellers shop in order to intercept persons involved in handling stolen goods, this was regarded as a legitimate enterprise (**R v Christou and Wright** [1992] QB 979).

[6]You must demonstrate also that whereas section 78(1) has a potentially broad scope, the courts are not adverse to the admission of evidence obtained by deception on the part of the police *per se*. Again, you can make use of relevant case law examples to illustrate this point.

While it is possible to point to clear examples of the courts using sections 76 and 78 to exclude evidence where its reliability might be called into question, an examination of the case law demonstrates that the courts have set a relatively high threshold which must be satisfied if evidence is to be excluded,[7] with the admission of evidence being permitted in some instances where the police have either engaged in deceptive practices or otherwise failed to adhere to the standards ordinarily expected of them.

[7]Your conclusion reflects the balance of the case law considered. It is certainly not an overstatement to say that a stricter approach, whether desirable or not, could have been taken by the courts to the admission of evidence.

✓ Make your answer stand out

- Use a wide range of case law to illustrate the courts' approach to the exclusion of evidence under sections 76(2) and 78(1) of the Police and Criminal Evidence Act 1984.
- Make connections between the courts' powers to exclude evidence and provisions designed to protect suspects against inappropriate police behaviour.
- In an extended essay you might consider the courts' exclusion of evidence obtained from actions amounting to breaches of individuals' rights under the ECHR, for example, where the police adopts covert tactics which may infringe the Article 8 guarantee of the right to privacy. A good discussion of such issues is provided in Ormerod, D., 'ECHR and the Exclusion of Evidence: Trial Remedies for Article 8 Breaches?', *Criminal Law Review*, 2002, p. 61.

! Don't be tempted to . . .

- Provide a detailed account of the many rules of evidence which the law contains as the question does not ask for this;
- Provide discussion of only one of the two main provisions of the Police and Criminal Evidence Act 1984 that are relevant to the exclusion of evidence.

Question 7

PC Pea and PC Bean are patrolling an area which has a high incidence of burglaries. They encounter Lentil, known to them as he has previously been convicted of several burglaries in the area during the last four years. Lentil is wearing a large rucksack, out of which appears to be sticking two silver candlesticks. PC Pea stops Lentil, saying, 'been up to your old tricks, have we?' PC Bean adds that, 'there have been a lot of break-ins around here recently and candlesticks aren't something you normally carry around. Let's take a look in there please.' Lentil opens his bag and allows the two police officers to search it. All they find are two plastic candlesticks, evidently designed for children to play with. They are labelled 'KID'S TOY KITCHENWARE' and a price label reading £1.99 is attached to them. Lentil claims that they are a gift for his nieces and produces a receipt for them. 'We don't care', responds PC Pea, 'you're trouble anyway. You're nicked.' Lentil is then taken to the nearest police station without further explanation.

Advise Lentil as to the legality of the stop and search and his subsequent arrest.

Answer plan

- Explain the police power to stop and search suspects contained in Article 1 PACE and whether it justified stopping and searching Lentil.
- Explain the safeguards contained in section 1, PACE and whether they were satisfied in this situation.
- Briefly explain the requirement to inform a person of his arrest and the grounds for it, and whether the police complied with this requirement.
- Explain the need for an arrest to be based upon reasonable suspicion of involvement in an offence and whether this requirement was satisfied in respect of Lentil's arrest.
- Briefly explain the grounds upon which an arrest may be reasonably felt necessary and the ease with which they can be applied if reasonable suspicion of involvement in an offence can be demonstrated.

Diagram plan

A printable version of this diagram plan is available from www.pearsoned.co.uk/lawexpressqa

Answer

Police powers of stop and search are governed primarily by sections 1 and 2 of the Police and Criminal Evidence Act 1984 (PACE). Section 1 empowers the police to search persons in public places for stolen or prohibited articles, and to detain them for this purpose. In this case, PC Pea and PC Bean clearly search Lentil's bag for stolen articles. PC Bean's comments to Lentil that there have been 'a lot of break-ins around here recently' and that candlesticks are not an item normally carried around serves to reinforce this. Lentil should be made aware, however, that the police may only carry out a search if they have reasonable grounds for suspecting that they may find stolen or prohibited articles.[1] Guidance to assist in considering whether PC Pea and PC Bean could legitimately claim to have held reasonable grounds for suspecting that they would find stolen articles in Lentil's bag can be found in Code of Practice A. Paragraph 2.2 states that there must be an objective basis for a police officer's suspicion which is based upon facts, information or intelligence relevant to the likelihood of him finding the articles being searched for. However, reasonable grounds cannot be based upon purely personal factors, such as a suspect's age, race or the fact that he has previous criminal convictions. Thus, the fact that Lentil is known to the police as a former offender in itself would not be likely to constitute a reasonable ground to search him in the absence of any other objectively relevant information available to the police. However, in this situation, what appear to be candlesticks are sticking out of Lentil's bag – an unusual item to see being carried around – and he is apprehended in an area which has experienced a high incidence of burglaries. These facts may give an objective basis for the suspicion shown towards Lentil by the police officers concerned, something which may be reinforced by the fact that Lentil has a track record of having committed a number of burglaries. We do not have any further information upon the circumstances in which Lentil was apprehended[2], but the existence of certain factors – for example, if it was late at night – may strengthen further the prospects of establishing reasonable grounds for the police officers' suspicion.

[1]The first issue to address is whether the police officers had reasonable grounds for suspecting they would find stolen or prohibited articles in searching Lentil. You must relate the requirements imposed by section 1 of PACE directly to the scenario which you are presented with.

[2]It is common in a problem question to find that further information is required to adequately advise on a particular issue and you should not feel uncomfortable in saying so wherever this is the case.

Further requirements are imposed upon police officers by section 2 of PACE, which requires that before conducting a search, a police officer must identify himself, the police station at which he is based and the grounds for the search. A police officer not in uniform must provide documentary evidence of his identity. In this scenario, we are not provided with enough information to know whether section 2 has been satisfactorily complied with.[3] PC Bean does, possibly, allude to the grounds for the search when commenting to Lentil that there have been a lot of break-ins in the area and that candlesticks are not an item normally carried around. However, we do not know whether the two police officers have identified themselves and their stations appropriately. Furthermore, police are required to make a written record of any search. Again, we do not know if this has taken place. Lentil should be advised that if the requirements imposed by section 2 have not been satisfied, then this omission on the part of the police officers may render the stop and search unlawful, as was established in the Court of Appeal's decision in **R *v* Bristol** [2007] EWCA Crim 3214.

[3]Even where you lack enough information to definitively advise on a particular issue you should refer to the relevant legal provisions in order to establish what information is required and how this would affect the advice given.

When arresting Lentil, the police are obliged under section 28 of PACE to inform him of his arrest and the reasons for it.[4] There is no set form of words for arresting a person, so PC Pea's telling Lentil that he is 'nicked' is sufficient to inform Lentil of his arrest if this is clearly understood by him to be PC Pea's meaning. However, it is questionable whether the reasons for his arrest have been adequately explained.

[4]This is not a point which requires much detail, but it is important that you mention it for the sake of providing a thorough answer to the question.

A police officer may arrest any person where there exists a warrant for that person's arrest under section 1 of the Magistrates' Courts Act 1980. It is highly unlikely that there exists a warrant for Lentil's arrest as he has merely been encountered by police in a chance meeting in public. Police powers to arrest without warrant are contained in section 24 of PACE. These have been widened as a result of changes made to PACE by section 110 of the Serious Organised Crime and Police Act 2005. A police officer may arrest a person wherever he has reasonable grounds for suspecting that person to have committed any offence, or be about to, or in the process of committing an offence. It is doubtful whether PC Pea and PC Bean would be able to argue that there were reasonable grounds for suspecting Lentil to have committed an offence, given that the only items found during the search of his bag were two inexpensive toy items for which he possessed a receipt.[5] A two stage test for reasonable suspicion was established in **O'Hara *v* Chief Constable of the RUC** [1996] UKHL 6: there must be actual suspicion on the

[5]This is a critical point as there are strong grounds for doubting that Lentil's arrest is compatible with the relevant legal provisions.

part of the arresting police officer (the subjective part of the test) and there must exist reasonable grounds for that suspicion (the objective part of the test). Even if the police officers personally suspected Lentil of an offence, it is highly questionable whether there can be said to have existed reasonable grounds for this suspicion given their failure to find any incriminating articles during their search of Lentil's bag. This may render Lentil's arrest unlawful.

[6]While arguably not a major issue in relation to Lentil given the above point, this ought to be considered for the sake of comprehensivity.

If reasonable grounds for suspicion of Lentil's guilt of an offence were established, the police officers would still need to demonstrate that they reasonably believed his arrest to be necessary for one or more of several specified reasons.[6] These are very broadly phrased, however, and are likely to mean that wherever a police officer can demonstrate reasonable grounds for suspecting that a person has committed an offence, they can be invoked to justify arrest. For example, a police officer can arrest a suspect where he believes it necessary to ascertain or confirm that person's name and address, prevent physical injury to any person or damage to property, to protect a child or vulnerable person, to allow the prompt and effective investigation of the offence, or to prevent the disappearance of the suspect. Of these, the need for prompt and effective investigation of the offence will justify arrest in most instances. Thus, Lentil's best prospect of challenging the legality of his arrest is to demonstrate that there were no reasonable grounds for suspecting that he had committed any offence.

✓ Make your answer stand out

- Explain what further information you may require in order to be able to properly advise Lentil in respect of this incident.

! Don't be tempted to . . .

- Simply explain the applicable legal provisions without directly relating them to the scenario which you have been presented with.

Question 8

Tommy is seen by PC Plum running away from the scene of an armed robbery carrying what he believes to be a weapon used in association with the crime. PC Plum chases Tommy and manages to overpower him. He then tells Tommy he is under arrest on suspicion of having committed armed robbery and cautions him. Tommy is taken to the police station once back up has arrived. At the police station, Sergeant Strawberry decides that as part of the investigation into Tommy's involvement in the armed robbery he would like to take Tommy's fingerprints as well as a sample of his saliva, which he feels will be useful for DNA purposes. Tommy is adamant that Sergeant Strawberry is not entitled to take these samples.

Advise (a) PC Plum as to whether his arrest of Tommy was lawful, and (b) Sergeant Strawberry as to whether Tommy's fingerprints and a sample of his saliva may be taken, indicating what further information, if any, you would need to advise on these issues.

Answer plan

- Explain when a police officer may lawfully arrest a suspect and whether PC Plum has complied with the relevant provisions when arresting Tommy.
- Explain that PC Plum may use reasonable force in order to arrest Tommy and inform him of the fact of, and reasons for, his arrest and consider whether these requirements have been complied with.
- Briefly raise the question of the status of Sergeant Strawberry in the investigative process and explain why this is important.
- Explain the provisions applicable to the taking of samples without consent and whether these permit the taking of a sample of Tommy's saliva.
- Explain the provisions applicable to the taking of fingerprints without consent and whether these permit the taking of Tommy's fingerprints.

Diagram plan

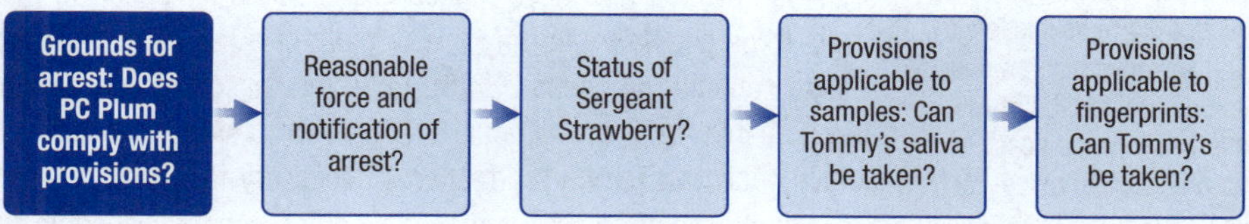

A printable version of this diagram plan is available from www.pearsoned.co.uk/lawexpressqa

Answer

Beginning with PC Plum's arrest of Tommy, a police officer may arrest any person for whom an arrest warrant has been issued under section 1 of the Magistrates' Courts Act 1980, or without a warrant if the requirements of section 24 of the Police and Criminal Evidence Act 1984 can be satisfied. Given that Tommy is apprehended immediately following an armed robbery, there is not going to exist a warrant for this arrest. Section 24 of PACE permits a police officer to arrest a person who has, or he has reasonable grounds for suspecting has, committed any offence, is in the process of committing or about to commit an offence.[1] In this situation, the offence which Tommy would be suspected of having committed is armed robbery. As there is no evidence that PC Plum has actually witnessed Tommy committing this offence, it is important that PC Plum can demonstrate that he had reasonable grounds for suspecting Tommy's involvement in the commission of this offence. A two-stage test for reasonable suspicion is applied following the decision in **O'Hara *v* Chief Constable of the RUC** [1996] UKHL 6. There must be actual suspicion on the part of the arresting police officer, and there must exist reasonable grounds for this suspicion. PC Plum sees Tommy running away from the scene of an armed robbery, carrying what he believes to be a weapon used in association with the offence. It would be helpful to know what weapon PC Plum believes he has seen in Tommy's possession[2], but assuming that it is an article of the kind ordinarily associated with armed robberies, then it would arguably seem reasonable for PC Plum to suspect Tommy's involvement in the offence.

[1] It is important to explain the grounds upon which a police officer can make an arrest and consider whether these can be applied to the scenario under discussion. The key point is that the arresting officer has reasonable grounds for suspecting involvement in an offence.

[2] You are not provided with this information and it is legitimate to raise this issue as it could be highly relevant to the likelihood of Tommy having been involved in the relevant offence.

Even where a police officer reasonably suspects a person has committed an offence, for an arrest to be legitimate under section 24(4) of PACE he must also have reasonable grounds for believing the arrest to be necessary for any one or more of a series of specified reasons outlined in section 24(5). However, these are very broad and it should not prove difficult for PC Plum to show that he reasonably believed Tommy's arrest was necessary for one of them.[3] For example, an arrest will be regarded as necessary to ascertain or confirm the name and address of the suspect, to allow the prompt and effective investigation of the offence, or to prevent the disappearance of the suspect. Any of these could, arguably, be applicable in this case.

[3] It is not necessary to list all of the reasons given in section 24(5) as it is lengthy. The key point is to emphasise its breadth and that it will nearly always be possible for an arresting officer to justify an arrest by reference to one of these reasons, the examples referred to being good cases in point.

Although we know that PC Plum 'overpowered' Tommy in order to facilitate his arrest, we do not know how much force was used.[4] Section 117 of PACE permits a police officer to use 'reasonable' force in order to perform his functions, including the power of arrest. As Tommy was running away from a crime scene, it can be envisaged that some force may have been necessary to prevent his escape and this will be lawful so long as reasonable in the circumstances. There is no evidence that PC Plum used excessive force, but the availability of more information could clarify this point. PC Plum must also comply with section 28 of PACE when arresting Tommy[5], which requires that he inform Tommy that he is under arrest and the grounds upon which he is being arrested. It would appear that PC Plum has complied with these requirements, as the available information tells us that he tells Tommy he is under arrest on suspicion of armed robbery. Thus, based upon the available information, it would appear that PC Plum has acted in accordance with the law in arresting Tommy.

[4]Again, it is legitimate to indicate that further information would have been useful in order to give fuller consideration to this issue.

[5]This point does not require a great amount of detail but should be covered for the sake of comprehensively considering the relevant issues.

Before considering Sergeant Strawberry's wish to take samples from Tommy, it is worthwhile noting that we are not informed of the role being played by Sergeant Strawberry in the investigation of offences committed by Tommy.[6] For example, we do not know if he is the custody officer assigned to Tommy upon his arrival at the station. This could be relevant as the custody officer is responsible for maintaining a record of the treatment of the suspect while in police custody which will include details of any searches made and items seized or samples taken from his person.

[6]Credit should be given for raising this issue. You are not told who Sergeant Strawberry is and his status may be relevant, for example if he is the custody officer who will have a series of specific obligations in respect of Tommy's detention and treatment. By raising the issue you evidence a wider understanding of the area of police powers.

In relation to the taking of samples from suspects in custody, a distinction must be made between intimate and non-intimate samples[7] as different rules apply to each of these. Sergeant Strawberry wishes to take a sample of Tommy's saliva. Intimate samples are defined by section 65 of PACE, as amended by section 119 of the Serious Organised Crime and Police Act 2005, as swabs 'taken from any part of a person's genitals or from a person's body orifice other than the mouth'. As saliva is taken from the mouth, it is only regarded as a non-intimate sample. Non-intimate samples can be taken from suspects notwithstanding their failure to consent. Under section 63 of PACE, the taking of non-intimate samples can be authorised in writing by someone of the rank of inspector or above where he has reasonable grounds for suspecting the

[7]You must not make the mistake of assuming all samples taken from suspects are subject to the same rules. You need to identify the rules applicable to non-intimate samples and apply them to the scenario.

person concerned to have been involved in a recordable offence and believes that the sample will prove or disprove this. Sergeant Strawberry would thus need the appropriate authorisation from an inspector in order to take a saliva sample from Tommy. However, an inspector would arguably be able to demonstrate that he had reasonable grounds for suspecting Tommy's involvement in a recordable offence given the circumstances of his arrest. We do not have any further information from which we can assess the likelihood of such a sample serving to prove or disprove Tommy's involvement in the offence, but if likely to do so there would be strong grounds to justify the taking of a saliva sample.

[8]The issue of taking fingerprints is fairly straightforward and it is likely to require only brief discussion in relation to the scenario.

Section 61 of PACE governs the fingerprinting of suspects without their consent.[8] These are rather broad, having been extended by section 9 of the Criminal Justice Act 2003. They include where a person has been arrested and detained for a recordable offence, as indeed Tommy has. There is no requirement for authorisation to be obtained from a senior officer. Thus, so there should be no difficulty in Sergeant Strawberry deciding to take fingerprints from Tommy.

✓ Make your answer stand out

- Indicate where the provision of further information would better enable you to advise on the issues raised by this situation.
- Raise the issue of the unknown status of Sergeant Strawberry and the possible implications of this.

! Don't be tempted to . . .

- Simply explain the applicable legal provisions without directly relating them to the scenario which you have been presented with;
- Confuse intimate and non-intimate samples;
- Overlook changes made to PACE by more recent legislative provisions.

Question 9

DC Lock and DS Key are questioning Poppy, who has been arrested on suspicion of drug-dealing. they have been questioning her for three hours consecutively, during which time she has not been provided with an opportunity to inform anyone of her arrest or to receive any legal advice, and have been unable to extract from her the information they feel is necessary to secure a conviction against her. In frustration at their 'lack of progress', DS Key whispers in Poppy's ear that unless she confesses to the offence with which she is being charged he will ask DC Lock to go and 'see that your children spend a night in casualty'. In fear for her children's safety, Poppy confesses to the offence.

Advise Poppy as to whether DC Lock and DS Key acted lawfully when interrogating her, and how her treatment might be used as part of her case at her trial.

Answer plan

- → Explain the provisions applicable to the detention of suspects for questioning and the time limitations applicable.
- → Explain the standards required for the treatment of detainees by Code of Practice C and that interviews must be tape-recorded.
- → Explain that Poppy is entitled to have someone informed of her arrest and when the police would be entitled to deny her this right.
- → Explain that Poppy is entitled to consult with a legal adviser and the possible consequences of the denial of this right upon proceedings under section 78(1) of PACE.
- → Explain that DS Key's threat to Poppy is likely to constitute oppression which will make her confession inadmissible evidence under section 76(2).

Diagram plan

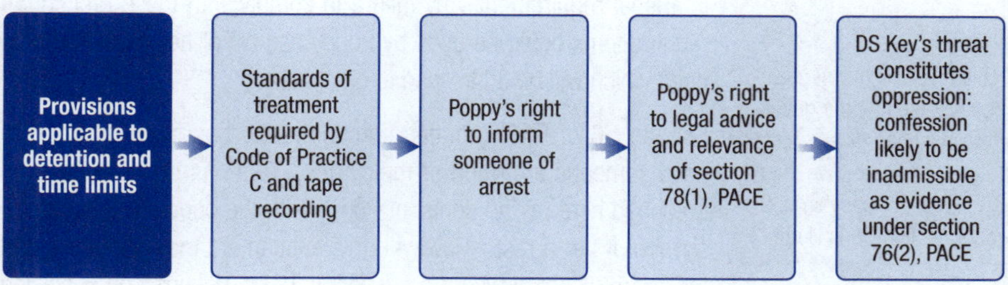

A printable version of this diagram plan is available from www.pearsoned.co.uk/lawexpressqa

Answer

Several issues arise from Poppy's detention and questioning. Under section 37(2) of the Police and Criminal Evidence Act 1984 (PACE), an arrested person may be detained where the custody officer has reasonable grounds for believing it necessary 'to secure or preserve evidence relating to an offence for which he is under arrest or to obtain such evidence by questioning him'.[1] We do not know what information has been used in this instance as the basis for Poppy's detention, but given that she has been arrested upon suspicion of drug-dealing, it would not be unreasonable for the police to want to question her in order to solicit further evidence. Although time limitations apply to the detention of suspects, these are not in issue here.[2] Poppy has only been questioned for three hours. Following arrest, a suspect may be detained for six hours before a review needs to take place and further authorisation for detention be granted (section 40(3) PACE).

Although it may appear that Poppy's detention for questioning is prima facie lawful, it must be noted that further safeguards are applicable to her treatment while in custody. PACE Code of Practice C sets out a series of standards which must be complied with in relation to the detention of suspects, which include the provision of regular meals, rest and breaks from questioning. We are not provided with enough information to ascertain whether such standards have been satisfied,[3] although that Poppy has been interrogated for three hours without a break may be considered a breach of these guidelines. We are not told whether Poppy's interview with the police has been tape-recorded, but under section 60 of PACE this is a legal requirement. Any failure to comply with these procedural requirements could be used by Poppy as part of her case at trial, a point which will be addressed in detail later.

Section 56 of PACE entitles someone who has been arrested to have someone informed of their arrest. This has prima facie been breached here by the denial of Poppy with the opportunity to inform anyone of her arrest.[4] However, this entitlement may be suspended for up to 36 hours where a suspect is being detained on suspicion of involvement in an indictable offence, and the relevant police officer reasonably believes that to permit the suspect to inform someone of his or her arrest would lead to interference with, or

[1]Although this may appear obvious, it is appropriate to begin your consideration of the situation involving Poppy as this is the first legal requirement which the police would need to be able to satisfy before Poppy could be detained for questioning in the first place.

[2]Although there is no problem in relation to the time for which Poppy has been detained, by mentioning it you show that you are aware of the application of time limitations to the detention of suspects.

[3]It is common within problem questions to be given insufficient information to provide definitive answers to all points raised. Where you would benefit from the provision of further information you should indicate this.

[4]This is an important issue clearly raised by the details you have been given. You are not able to assess whether the denial of Poppy's right under section 56 is likely to be deemed unlawful unless you are given further information upon which you can base your assessment and must say so.

harm to, evidence connected to the offence or other persons, or will lead to the alerting of other suspects, or hinder the recovery of any property obtained as a result of the offence. Again, we are not party to the information upon which Poppy has been denied the opportunity to inform someone of her arrest although it is conceivable that given the nature of the offence being investigated there may exist reasonable grounds to believe that allowing Poppy to inform someone of her arrest may alert other potential suspects involved in the same offence and lead to the removal or destruction of evidence. Drugs offences are often of an ongoing kind involving a chain of several offenders, so there may be legitimate grounds for denying Poppy the right to have someone informed of her arrest.

Access to legal advice is guaranteed by section 58 of PACE and is widely regarded as a key requirement of a fair trial. Although section 58 does permit the police to deny access to legal advice for up to 36 hours for the same reasons for which suspects may be prevented from informing a person of their arrest, the right to consult with a legal adviser can only be denied in very exceptional circumstances and a higher threshold must be satisfied for it to be justified. We do not have sufficient information to judge whether the police could legitimately deny Poppy the opportunity to consult with a legal adviser. However, at her trial the court could conclude that her non-access to legal advice constitutes sufficient reason to exclude any evidence obtained through DC Lock's and DS Key's interrogation of her.[5]

[5]This is an important point as it could be highly relevant to Poppy's case at trial, something which the question asks you to consider. You should refer to some of the relevant case law in order to show the likelihood of interview evidence being excluded where access to legal advice has been denied.

Section 78(1) of PACE allows a court to exclude any prosecution evidence where it appears, having regard to all circumstances, including those in which the evidence was obtained, that its admission would have such an adverse effect on the proceedings that it should not be admitted. This provision is essentially designed to enable the courts to exclude any evidence which has been obtained in such circumstances that its reliability can be called into question. In **R *v* Samuel** [1988] QB 615, the admission of evidence of a police interview was not permitted where the suspect had been denied the right to consult with a legal advisor under section 78(1). Notably the court stated that a belief on the part of a police officer that one of the grounds for denying access to legal advice contained in section 58 existed could only rarely be genuinely held. However, a court may decline to exclude evidence of an interview conducted in the absence of legal representation if it felt that this would have made no difference to the course and outcome of the interrogation, as occurred in **R v Alladice** (1988) 87 Crim App R 380. Section 78(1) could potentially be used by the court at Poppy's trial to exclude any evidence obtained in circumstances where the police had not complied with PACE requirements in relation to her treatment during questioning.[6] As noted above, we have insufficient information to draw any firm conclusions upon whether the police acted unlawfully in relation to some of the issues raised.

DS Key's threat to Poppy, which results in her confession, is highly relevant to her defence. It undoubtedly constitutes an unlawful means of seeking to extract a confession from a suspect, involving a threat to use unlawful force against her children. Her confession is consequently made under a form of duress. Section 76(2) of PACE provides that evidence of a confession will be inadmissible in court where it has been obtained by oppression.[7] Although the case law has given rise to varying interpretations of 'oppression', DS Key's threat will almost certainly constitute an instance of oppression. Section 76(8) provides a definition of oppression which includes the use or threat of violence, which is clearly what has emanated from DS Key, and has been a common theme in several cases of miscarriages of justice. Evidence of Poppy's confession is highly unlikely to be admissible at her trial, irrespective of whether other evidence obtained during her interrogation is excluded due to the failure of the police to conform to procedural requirements imposed by PACE.[8]

[6]You should make this general point in relation to any failings to comply with relevant procedural requirements on the part of the police.

[7]You should enter into as full a discussion of section 76(2) and its utility to Poppy as time will allow you and draw upon any relevant case law to demonstrate its relevance. This is the strongest tool which Poppy will have as part of her case at trial, as it is likely to render evidence of her confession inadmissible.

[8]This is a logical conclusion, as you show that the manner in which Poppy was coerced into making a confession is likely to be used to exclude this as evidence, while indicating still that other procedural failings may also have an impact upon the admissibility of evidence at trial.

✓ Make your answer stand out

- Make comparisons where appropriate with the police's treatment of Poppy and that of suspects in similar relevant cases, particularly where miscarriages of justice have resulted from police oppression to induce confessions.
- Indicate where appropriate what further information you may need in order to be able to provide a more definitive answer to certain questions.
- Be prepared to raise issues which are not expressly mentioned by the scenario, but may nonetheless be relevant, for example in this case the issue of tape recording of Poppy's interview or the standards applicable to her detention under Code of Practice C.

! Don't be tempted to . . .

- Omit to discuss any issue which you consider to be so straightforward as to not merit any attention, as you still have an opportunity to demonstrate your understanding of the applicable law;
- Make assumptions on factual matters where you are not provided with the relevant information.

Question 10

Stan and Stella voluntarily came to the police station in the early evening to assist the police with a criminal inquiry. After an hour the police stumble upon evidence that strongly suggests Stan is guilty of several criminal offences. He is arrested while still at the station and advised that he is entitled to consult with a legal adviser, although he declines to receive any legal assistance. Questioning of him continues for a further nine hours, during which time he is provided with regular snacks and breaks from questioning. When questioned, Stan refuses to answer a substantial number of the questions put to him by the police. Although the police initially tape-record their questioning of Stan, halfway through questioning there is a problem with the equipment and they opt to continue to question Stan without recording it. At the end of this nine-hour period Stan is charged with several serious criminal offences. Stella has willingly remained at the police station throughout this time, but now says that she wishes to go home unless the police are going to arrest her. She is told that there is no evidence to arrest her, but that she cannot leave as they hope to 'find some dirt' so that they can arrest her.

Advise Stan and Stella as to the lawfulness of their detention and whether the police have complied with relevant provisions in their treatment of Stan while in custody, indicating what further information, if any, you require. Stan is also concerned that his refusal to answer police questions may be held against him in court.

Answer plan

- Explain that following arrest the police can detain Stan for questioning, but that after six hours his detention ought to have been reviewed and re-authorised for a further period.
- Explain that Stan has not been deprived of his entitlement to legal advice under section 58 of PACE.
- Indicate the need for further information in order to be able to assess whether the police have satisfied the standards required for detainees, but explain that they have failed to comply with the obligation to tape-record all interviews with suspects.
- Explain the possible consequences of procedural failings on the admissibility of prosecution evidence under section 78(1) of PACE.
- Explain the impact of Stan's failure to answer a substantial number of police questions under section 34 of the Criminal Justice and Public Order Act 1994.
- Explain that Stella's detention is unlawful as she has not been arrested.

Diagram plan

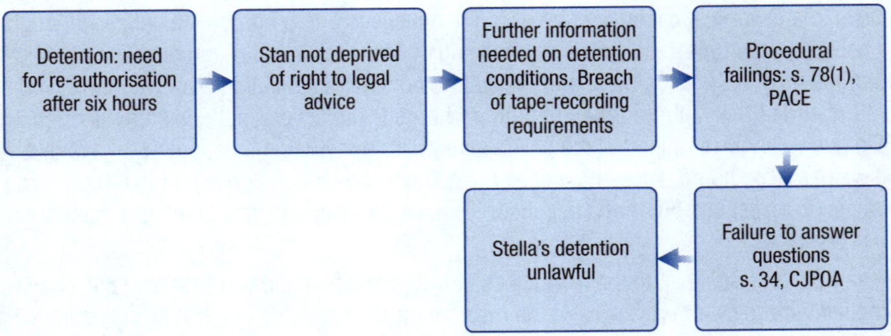

A printable version of this diagram plan is available from www.pearsoned.co.uk/lawexpressqa

Answer

Although Stan has attended the police station voluntarily, meaning that initially he would have been free to leave at any time, the fact of his arrest entitles the police to detain him in custody for questioning under section 37 of the Police and Criminal Evidence Act 1984 (PACE),[1] which provides that an arrested person may be detained where the custody officer has reasonable grounds for believing this to be 'necessary to secure or preserve evidence relating to

[1]This point is fairly straightforward but it is important to mention that it is only following Stan's arrest that the police are able to detain him for the purpose of questioning.

an offence...or to obtain such evidence by questioning him'. This requirement would appear to be satisfied here as we are told that the police have stumbled upon evidence strongly suggesting that he is guilty of several criminal offences.

We are told that Stan is questioned for nine hours before he is charged with an offence. While it is possible for the police to detain a suspect for this amount of time for purposes of questioning, strict rules govern detention procedures. Upon arrest, a suspect may be detained for an initial period of six hours, at the end of which a review of his detention must take place. Detention may be authorised for a further nine-hour period at this point by the reviewing officer under section 40 of PACE. We are not informed whether Stan's detention was reviewed after six hours and further detention authorised.[2] If this has not occurred, then there has been a breach of the procedural requirements imposed by PACE to govern the treatment of detainees and this may be relevant to the admission of prosecution evidence at Stan's subsequent trial, a point which will be re-visited later.

[2]This is an issue which requires further information and you should indicate so. That the scenario tells you of the length of Stan's detention is relevant, implying that it is an issue to be considered.

Section 58 of PACE entitles a detainee undergoing questioning access to legal advice. This is regarded as a fundamental right within the criminal justice process and its denial by the police is treated as a very serious matter with the potential to undermine the perceived reliability of any evidence obtained from questioning in the absence of a legal adviser for the suspect. However, although Stan is questioned in the absence of a legal adviser there is no evidence to suggest that he has been denied his entitlement under section 58.[3] To the contrary, he has been informed of his right to legal advice and has declined to avail himself of it.

[3]This issue is relatively straightforward here, but should be mentioned as it gives you an opportunity to illustrate your understanding of the potential application of section 58 to this kind of situation.

Code of Practice C governs the treatment of detainees in police custody and imposes certain standards to be satisfied, including the provision of regular breaks from questioning, regular meals and snacks, and adequate sleep. There is insufficient information to enable us to know whether the standards required by the code have been satisfied in relation to the treatment of Stan. We are told that he has been provided with regular breaks and snacks, which may be taken as a positive indication of the police's compliance with the code's requirements. However, we are also told that Stan's questioning continued for a period of nine hours after his arrest. Given that Stan and Stella came to the police station in the early evening, this would seem to imply that Stan was questioned well into the early hours of the morning and may not have been given the opportunity to sleep at an appropriate time.[4] Although we know he received breaks from questioning, we do not know whether these included any periods of sleep. Sleep deprivation would be likely to constitute a serious breach of the code of practice and may have some bearing upon the reliability of evidence to be submitted at trial.

[4]Again, you require further information in order to be able to fully advise on this issue. However, you are able to demonstrate the ability to make logical deductions from the information with which you have been provided, in this instance that Stan may have been questioned throughout the night and the possible relevance of Code C.

Tape-recording of police interviews with suspects is made mandatory by section 60 of PACE.[5] Due to technical difficulties the latter half of Stan's interrogation has not been tape-recorded. This constitutes a major breach of the safeguards provided for suspects, and as will be seen below may render the evidence of the interview inadmissible in court.

[5]This is a simple issue to deal with as the information provided makes it quite apparent that there has been a breach of this requirement.

Prima facie there appear to be at least some procedural failings on the part of the police. Their failure to record half of their interrogation of Stan is undoubtedly a breach of section 60 of PACE, whereas although we would need further information to clarify these issues, it seems possible that there has been a failure to comply with provisions relating to the need for a review of Stan's detention after the first six hours and with the requirements of code of practice C in relation to the possible deprivation of sleep. Such failings can be invoked by the defence to exclude any prosecution evidence under section 78(1) of PACE[6] on the ground that 'having regard to all the circumstances, including the circumstances in which the evidence was obtained', its admission 'would have such an adverse effect on the fairness of the proceedings that the court ought not to admit it'. This is a 'catch-all' provision which enables the court to exclude any evidence obtained in an unfair manner if it is likely to adversely affect proceedings. A breach of PACE safeguards when questioning suspects has been used on many cases by the courts to exclude evidence obtained during that process. For example, non-compliance with relevant recording requirements has led to the exclusion of evidence taken from police interviews in cases such as **R *v* Canale** [1990] 2 All ER 187.

[6]You can summarise the possible effects of any procedural failings on the part of the police by invoking section 78(1) and the ability which it gives to courts to exclude evidence. You might usefully cite relevant case law examples to illustrate the likelihood of its invocation in relation to some of the failings highlighted in this scenario.

Under section 34 of the Criminal Justice and Public Order Act 1994, when a suspect questioned by the police fails to mention facts later relied upon as part of his defence, the court is entitled to draw such inferences from his silence as appear proper. Thus, Stan's refusal to answer a substantial number of the questions put to him by the police may provide grounds upon which a court could draw adverse inferences.[7] If the evidence of the police interview with Stan is admissible in evidence, which is questionable given some of the procedural failings on the part of the police, Stan would have cause to be concerned that his refusal to answer police questions could adversely affect his subsequent defence in court.

The position relating to Stella is relatively straightforward.[8] She has remained at the police station voluntarily for ten hours, and as she has not been arrested by the police she is free to leave at any point of her choosing. This is reinforced by code of practice C, paragraph 3.21. Stella cannot be detained against her will unless the police arrest her. If she is prevented from leaving the police station she is likely to have an action against the police for false imprisonment or a similar offence.

[7] If you have time you might explore the application of section 34 further by referring to some of the case law upon the extent to which the courts have permitted inferences to be drawn from suspects' refusal to answer questions while in custody and how this may affect the likelihood of adverse inferences against Stan being made.

[8] Stella's position does not require much consideration and it will suffice to address it briefly at the end.

✓ Make your answer stand out

- Indicate where appropriate what further information you may need in order to be able to provide a more definitive answer to certain questions.
- Draw upon relevant case law in order to assess how certain aspects of the law may be applied to the situation at hand.

! Don't be tempted to . . .

- Assume that you need to spend equal time addressing the position of both detained suspects;
- Make assumptions on factual matters where you are not provided with the relevant information.

8 The civil law process

How this topic may come up in exams

Examination questions on the civil law process may require you to demonstrate an understanding of the civil jurisdiction possessed by different courts, particularly the County Court and High Court, as well as remedies available in civil law proceedings. You could be asked to explain and evaluate civil procedure rules, including awareness of the main reforms to the management of civil cases introduced in 1999. Questions which test your understanding of the funding of civil legal services are also possible within this topic, and you may specifically be asked to consider the merits of initiatives such as conditional fee agreements.

Attack the question

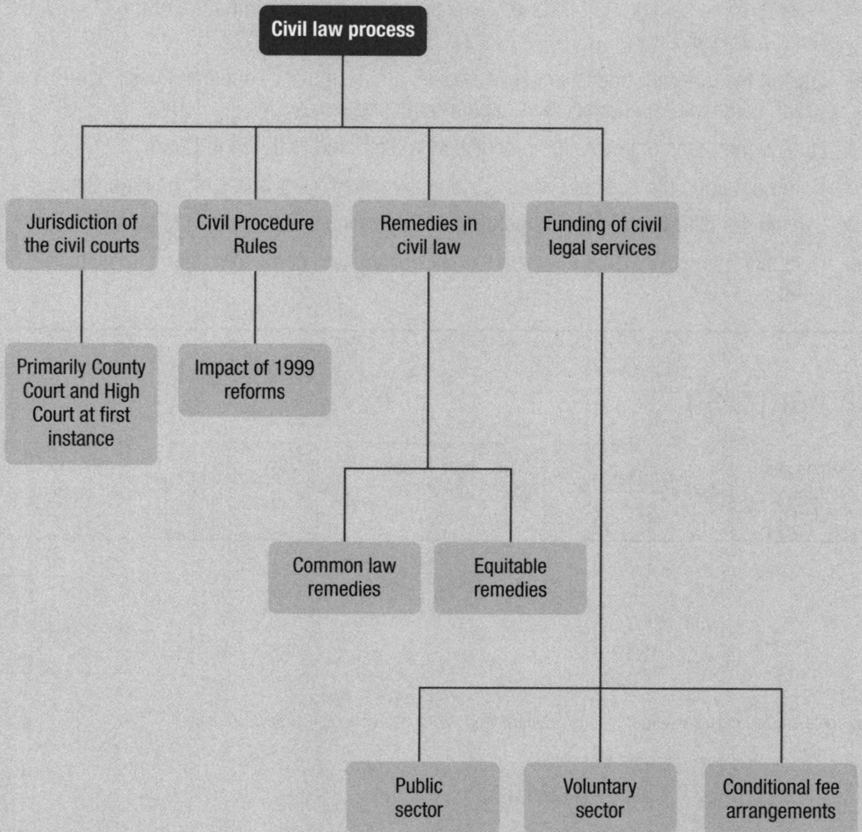

A printable version of this diagram plan is available from www.pearsoned.co.uk/lawexpressqa

Question 1

Evaluate the main differences and similarities in the civil jurisidiction of the County Court and High Court.

Answer plan

- → Provide some background by briefly explaining the origins and nature of the County Court and High Court.
- → Explain the different tracks which civil cases are assigned to and how these determine which court will have jurisdiction to hear particular cases.
- → Outline the areas of law where jurisdiction is restricted to the High Court.
- → Comment upon the specialised jurisdiction exercised by divisions of the High Court.
- → Explain the difference in the range of remedies which may be awarded by each court.
- → Conclude upon the extent to which the civil jurisdiction of the two courts is radically different.

Diagram plan

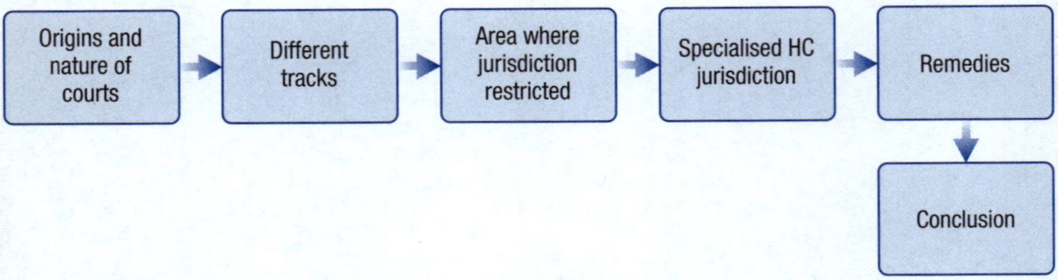

A printable version of this diagram plan is available from www.pearsoned.co.uk/lawexpressqa

Answer

The significance of civil litigation is often overlooked, but the frequency with which individuals have resort to the civil courts is underlined by the fact that in the year 2008 over two million civil cases were initiated. The County Court and High Court serve as the two courts of first instance for civil cases.[1] County Courts were established by the County Courts Act 1846, with the intention of providing litigants with a forum within which small-scale litigation could be dispensed that was local and accessible to them. Today,

[1] You can provide some context to your answer at the outset by briefly referring to the origins of the respective courts and the much greater geographic spread of the County Courts.

according to Her Majesty's Courts Service, there are 216 County Courts spread throughout England and Wales, meaning that there will be a court located relatively conveniently for everyone. Cases in the County Court are ordinarily heard by a circuit or district judge, although High Court judges are competent to sit in the County Court. The High Court was established in 1873 under the Supreme Court of Judicature Act, and while centrally based in London it sits additionally in a number of regional centres and is presided over by High Court judges. Prior to 1999, separate procedural rules governed the workings of the High Court and County Court respectively, although as a consequence of the Woolf reforms both courts are now subject to a unified set of civil procedure rules.

In comparing and contrasting the civil jurisdiction of the County Court and High Court, there are, arguably, four key considerations.[2] These are the financial limits upon the jurisdiction of the respective courts; the exclusion of certain categories of cases from the County Court's jurisdiction; the specialised jurisdiction possessed by the High Court; and the restrictions upon the remedies obtainable from the County Court.

[2]This is helpful to the marker as it identifies the key points to be addressed, providing a clear structure to the answer by breaking it down into four key parts.

In order to improve the efficiency with which the civil courts manage litigation, Part 26 of the Civil Procedure Rules introduced in 1999 established three different tracks to which cases could be allocated. These tracks are based largely upon the value of the civil action in question and will in turn determine which court is assigned jurisdiction to hear the case.[3] The three tracks are the small claims track, the fast-track and the multi-track. Small claims cases are those where the value of the claim is under £5,000, or £1,000 where the action is one for personal injury. Small claims are to be handled by the County Court. Most civil actions are likely to fall within this bracket and small claims actions are well suited for relatively minor consumer disputes, accident claims and disputes between landlords and tenants. The high proportion of civil actions which these cases represent is probably evidenced by the fact that whereas 1.6 million proceedings were commenced in the County Court during 2002, only 54,500 were commenced in the Queen's Bench and Chancery divisions of the High Court combined. Claims for amounts exceeding £5,000 and below £15,000 (£50,000 where the action is for personal injury) are assigned to the fast-track and also commence in the County Court. Actions for higher amounts will be assigned to

[3]It is very important that you explain the different kinds of tracks to which cases can be assigned and the bearing which this has upon where jurisdiction is likely to lie, the value of claims being of the utmost importance in this respect.

the multi-track, and while these are more likely to commence in the High Court they may begin in the County Court at the choice of the parties depending upon the nature of the claim.

The value of a claim is not the sole determinant of the court which will be assigned jurisdiction to hear it. Certain types of case may not be heard by the County Court. A Practice Direction [1991] provided that a number of specified actions were too important to be transferred to a County Court, underlining the higher status of the High Court within the court hierarchy.[4] These include actions for professional negligence, fatal accidents, allegations of fraud or undue influence, defamation, malicious prosecution or false imprisonment. However, such actions account for a relatively small proportion of litigation and the vast majority of civil actions are amenable to County Court jurisdiction.

[4]Although this is an important point to note, you should stress that these cases account for a small proportion of civil litigation, thus overstating the significance of the County Court's lack of jurisdiction to entertain them.

The superior status of the High Court is exemplified further by its division into three branches each having its own specialism in particular types of civil law,[5] and within these branches there are even narrower specialist courts for particular matters. The Queen's Bench Division has the highest workload of any of the branches, as a result of the fact that it deals predominantly with contractual and tortious actions. Of the actions began in the Queen's Bench Division during 2008/9, 23% were for personal injury and 21% for debt. There are specialist commercial and admiralty courts within the division. The Chancery Division deals with a range of specific matters, including land, mortgages, trusts, bankruptcy, contentious probate, company and revenue law. It also has specialist courts, these dealing with patents and company matters respectively, and has appellate jurisdiction to hear some appeals from the County Court. Perhaps reflecting economic shifts, the Chancery Division saw a 14% increase in proceedings during 2008. The Family Division forms the final branch of the High Court. That the County Court deals with less serious actions for modest amounts of money is perhaps reflected in its lack of a specialist division of labour along the lines apparent in the High Court.

[5]This can be overlooked, but the various specialisms accommodated within the High Court structure does demonstrate that there is a somewhat different emphasis in its jurisdiction to that of the County Court.

[6]Don't overlook the issue of remedies. While the significance of this difference between the courts is unlikely to be of relevance in the majority of cases, it is nonetheless a difference in jurisdiction.

Whereas most remedies can be obtained equally from the High Court and the County Court, including the common law remedy of damages, there are some restrictions placed upon the range of remedies which the County Court is entitled to award.[6] It may not grant the prerogative remedies, which are reserved to the jurisdiction of the High Court, and freezing orders are also ordinarily outside of its jurisdiction.

[7]The conclusion reflects the content of the answer. You show a number of differences in the jurisdiction of the two courts, yet throughout have demonstrated the extent to which these can be over-stated.

In certain respects, the civil jurisdiction of the County Court does not differ radically from that of the High Court. Both abide by the same procedural rules and the most common types of civil action which form the subject of litigation can proceed in either court subject to the value of the claim. Theoretically, there are substantial differences between the jurisdiction of the two courts, but these can be over-stated.[7] While certain matters are reserved to the High Court, these only represent a relatively small proportion of civil actions. That the High Court consists of a number of specialised branches may reflect the more distinguished nature of the court, but it does not detract from the fact that the vast majority of cases will be amenable to the jurisdiction of the County Court and will be resolved within that forum. Although the High Court enjoys a broader range of remedies to award, in the vast majority of cases the ordinary remedies available in either court will be sufficient.

✓ Make your answer stand out

- Provide context to your answer through the citation of evidence of the nature of modern civil legal action.

! Don't be tempted to . . .

- Provide a detailed point by point description of the jurisdiction enjoyed by the relevant courts.

Question 2

'The reforms introduced by the Access to Justice Act 1999 to state funding for civil cases, while effective in cost-cutting, significantly restrict access to civil justice.' Discuss.

Answer plan

- ➜ Explain the nature of civil legal aid prior to 1999 and the problems which served as the impetus for reform.
- ➜ Discuss the main features of the system of legal aid introduced by the Access to Justice Act 1999.
- ➜ Evaluate the impact of the reforms on the cost of civil legal aid.
- ➜ Evaluate whether the 1999 reforms have led to a shortfall in the availability of affordable civil legal services.
- ➜ Conclude by directly addressing the statement contained in the question.

Diagram plan

A printable version of this diagram plan is available from www.pearsoned.co.uk/lawexpressqa

Answer

The importance of affordable access to legal assistance with civil disputes is often under-estimated, with research for the Legal Service Commission in 2004 finding that over a period of three and a half years, a third of the population experienced a civil problem of some description. Legal aid, whereby the state meets certain legal costs incurred by parties to legal action, formed an important part of the post-war welfare state. By the 1980s, six different state funded legal assistance schemes were in operation covering most types of legal action and administered by the Legal Aid Board. Growing concern at the costs of civil legal aid led to major reforms enshrined in the Access to Justice Act 1999. While the major objective of the reforms was to bring the cost of legal aid under control, there have been numerous charges that they have restricted access to affordable legal assistance to such an extent that they cause injustice in many cases.[1]

[1]Your introduction should provide some background to the issues addressed by the question. It is important that you briefly explain the rationale for the 1999 reforms, thus setting the scene for the discussion to follow.

Part 1 of the 1999 Act replaced the Legal Aid Board with a new Legal Service Commission (LSC), which is entrusted with a fixed budget for maintaining the Community Legal Service (CLS) (essentially civil legal aid) and the Criminal Defence Service (CDS) (essentially criminal legal aid). The LSC manages the CLS fund, which is capped by section 5 of the Act. Under the old civil legal aid system, there was no cap upon available funding, which was available to all applicants satisfying the relevant means and merits tests. Entitlement to aid under the current system is dependent upon a financial eligibility test, to be set by the Lord Chancellor under section 7, and criteria laid down in a funding code that is drawn up by the LSC and approved by the Lord Chancellor.[2] Financial eligibility for CLS funds is governed by 2007 regulations, which are rather restrictive in prescribing who is entitled to assistance. According to Elliott and Quinn, whereas 52% of the population would satisfy the eligibility test in 1998, today only 29% would qualify for CLS funds. This demonstrates the extent to which assistance is largely restricted to those on very low incomes. Many who receive CLS funds are only likely to receive a modest contribution towards their overall legal costs and section 10 of the Act extends the financial conditions which can be imposed upon the recipients of CLS funds. The funding code is designed to establish priorities which will govern the allocation of funds, and which are set out following regional assessments of particular areas of need.

[2]You should discuss the main features of the 1999 Act, in particular drawing out their impact upon the availability of state funding for civil legal services. This relates back directly to the question and reinforces some of the arguments to follow later in the answer.

Legal work funded by the CLS can only be undertaken by solicitors firms or agencies which have contracts with the LSC to perform that kind of work. The LSC is obliged to obtain the best value for money in awarding franchises to undertake funded work and minimum standards taking the form of quality marks must be demonstrable by bidding firms or agencies. Theoretically, this enhances the economic efficiency of state funded legal services.[3] While a wider range of services are covered under the CLS, certain cases are ineligible from state funding. These are those involving actions for personal injury, defamation, disputes arising in the course of business and matters concerning company or partnership law.

[3]This point can easily be overlooked, but reinforces the alleged economic benefits of the reforms.

Arguably, the 1999 reforms have been relatively successful in tackling the growing costs of civil legal aid. A 2003 report for the National Audit Office identified improvements in bringing costs accruing from civil legal aid under control.[4] The cap on the CLS budget, strict financial eligibility tests and the requirement that the LSC obtain best value for money have all helped in this respect. In addition, the introduction of contracting, it is argued, encourages higher standards of work as firms will want to ensure that they do not lose their contracts. Controlled costs also facilitate the better allocation of public resources as the money saved on civil legal aid can be spent elsewhere.

[4]The question requires you to consider the impact of the reforms upon legal aid costs. Making reference to official reports or statistical evidence is useful in detailing their impact.

While the economic benefits of the 1999 reforms are clear, there is good reason to believe that they have resulted in a shortfall in the availability of affordable legal assistance leading to an increase in cases of injustice.[5] As a result of the contracting system introduced by the 1999 Act, the number of firms offering CLS funded work has declined considerably. Whereas prior to the reforms, approximately 11,000 firms provided services funded by civil legal aid, this number has more than halved with only about 5,000 firms doing so today. The shortfall in CLS funded work has been particularly noticeable in some specialist areas of law, such as housing and debt, where the number of firms holding contracts with the LSC to provide such services declined respectively from 743 to 489 and from 462 to 206 in the period 2000–3. Gaps in the provision of state funded services were identified in reports issued by the National Audit Office and Citizens Advice Bureau in 2003 and 2004. The risk is that in a substantial number of cases, citizens requiring legal assistance will not be able to find a solicitor authorised to provide state funded assistance, especially if the legal problem in question is specialist in nature. This danger is exacerbated by the strict financial eligibility tests in place and the disparity in the geographical spread of solicitors across the country.

[5]It is very useful if you are able to cite evidence to support the contention that the availability of state funded civil legal services has been reduced.

Access to civil justice is potentially further restricted by other features of the 1999 reforms. For example, the exclusion of cases concerning disputes arising in the course of a business from state funding ignores certain economic realities.[6] Low-paid individuals

[6]This point is easy to overlook, but is a very valid one to make.

operating small businesses such as taxi drivers and other self-employed people will fall under this exclusion, while often lacking the means to pursue legitimate civil action.

The statement would appear to accurately describe the effects of the 1999 reforms to state funding of civil legal assistance.[7] The benefits of the reforms in terms of reducing the cost of the civil legal aid budget are apparent, yet as has been noted there are grounds for believing that the reforms increase shortfalls in the provision of legal assistance. Undoubtedly, as with any area of state expenditure there is a very difficult balance to be struck between meeting what are perceived to be legitimate priorities within society and keeping the costs to the taxpayer under control. While the 1999 reforms strive to strike such a balance, it is easy to see why some may feel that cost-cutting has been the driving force behind them.

[7]The conclusion should relate back directly to the statement contained in the question. The conclusion is consistent with the arguments advanced throughout the answer. If answering this question for a longer piece of coursework, there is some scope to consider how current shortfalls in state-funded civil legal assistance might be remedied through fresh reforms or the provision of alternatives.

✓ Make your answer stand out

- Assess current shortfalls in the availability of legal aid by reading Hynes, S. and Robins, J., *The Justice Gap: Whatever Happened to Legal Aid?* (London: Legal Action Group, 2009) and make reference to some of the arguments advanced therein.
- Consider possible future reforms to civil legal aid which might improve access to legal services.
- Consider the extent to which the current shortfall in the provision of state funded civil legal assistance can be provided by alternative sources of legal assistance.

! Don't be tempted to . . .

- Simply discuss the various advantages and disadvantages of the 1999 reforms: your focus must be on the issues referred to in the question;
- Simply provide a detailed descriptive overview of the many provisions of the Access to Justice Act 1999.

Question 3

'Greater use of conditional fee agreements should be encouraged.' Critically assess this statement.

Answer plan

- → Explain what conditional fee agreements are and the circumstances which have led to their greater use in recent years.
- → Discuss the main benefits of the use of conditional fee agreements.
- → Discuss the main problems which are associated with conditional fee agreements.
- → Conclude by explaining whether you agree with the statement or not.

Diagram plan

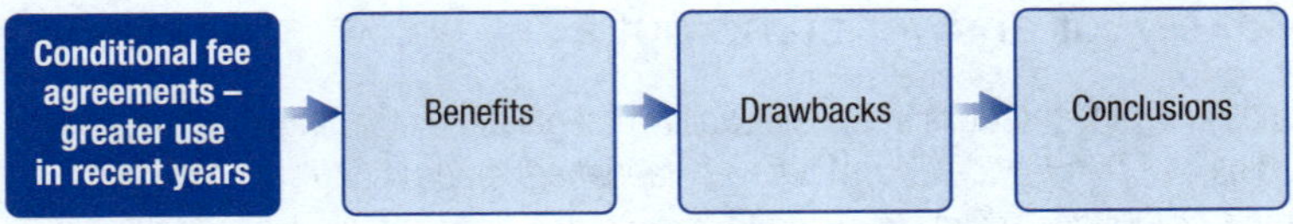

A printable version of this diagram plan is available plan from www.pearsoned.co.uk/lawexpressqa

Answer

[1]You should begin your answer by briefly explaining what conditional fee agreements are and their recent emergence within the UK. This provides relevant context to your discussion to follow of their relative merits.

Conditional fee agreements have become an increasingly popular way of funding civil actions,[1] especially personal injury litigation. Under the terms of a conditional fee agreement, a solicitor takes on a client's case on the understanding that payment of the solicitor's fees will be conditional upon a successful outcome. Although common in the US, conditional fee agreements were not permitted in the UK until section 58 of the Courts and Legal Services Act 1990 provided for their use in a limited range of cases. The Access to Justice Act 1999 promoted greater use, making them available in all civil cases bar medical negligence. When entering into conditional fee agreements, solicitors are now entitled to raise their fees by up to double the normal fee, and courts can order losing parties to pay this 'success fee' in addition to ordinary legal costs. Although increasingly used by litigants, conditional fee agreements have generated some controversy, which warrants greater exploration of their merits.

Arguably, the most compelling argument for the encouragement of conditional fee agreements is that they reduce the financial burden placed upon the state.[2] Money which might previously have been spent funding certain civil actions can now be spent elsewhere. There is little doubt that conditional fee agreements have been hugely popular. Within two years of their introduction, 30,000 had been entered into, and have been used for several hundred thousand personal injury actions since. It should be noted, however, that while perhaps a convenient method for financing personal injury litigation, conditional fee agreements are not as likely to constitute a practical option in other forms of legal action. It is arguable that there are performance incentives for lawyers where their payment is dependent upon success. As they will not be paid unless successful, they should have all the encouragement which they need to 'be at their best'. Although the logic of this argument cannot be dismissed, it is somewhat overstated given that under conditional fee agreements lawyers will only ordinarily take cases where they are reasonably confident of success anyway. That said, it could be said that a virtue of conditional fee agreements is that they reduce the number of weak claims, as solicitors are unlikely to take them on.

[2]It makes sense to begin your discussion of the advantages of conditional fee agreements with consideration of the less controversial arguments, as these can be dealt with quickly and build up to the more debatable issues to follow.

It has been argued that conditional fee agreements facilitate greater access to justice. They provide a means of taking legal action for individuals who might not have the financial means to enter litigation otherwise, and may be used for types of legal action ineligible for state funding, for example defamation. The sustainability of the 'greater access to justice' argument is questionable.[3] Firstly, conditional fee agreements are only going to be a viable option for litigants with a sufficiently reasonable chance of success to encourage solicitors to take on their case. Secondly, as the discussion to follow of some of the problems associated with conditional fee agreements will reveal, the consequences of their greater use for insurance costs, hardship faced by losing parties and the general promotion of a 'compensation culture' may warrant the assertion that whereas conditional fee agreements promote 'individual justice' they produce unjust results within society more generally.

[3]It is essential that you probe this argument as there are obvious flaws to it as alluded to here. You can relate the criticisms of this argument to some of the criticisms of conditional fee agreements to be considered later.

Although some merits of conditional fee agreements are evident, a number of their alleged advantages are open to challenge, suggesting that greater encouragement of their use may not be desirable.[4] The experience of conditional fee agreements to date

[4]This comment serves as both an accurate summary of the consideration of the perceived advantages of conditional fee agreements, and an introduction to an overview of the problems associated with their use.

has highlighted a number of problems associated with their use. A major criticism of conditional fee agreements is that they have given rise to a 'compensation culture', encouraging speculative claims fuelled by solicitors advertising 'no win no fee' deals with such vigour that they have become commonly dubbed as 'ambulance chasers'. This perception led the former Secretary of State for Justice, Jack Straw, to express concern over soaring legal costs arising from a significant increase in (particularly personal injury) litigation. There is evidence that the promotion of conditional fee agreements has proceeded to a stage whereby their aggressive marketing has led to many claimants being misled in relation to the nature of the undertakings which they thought they were entering into.[5] This problem was highlighted in a 2005 report by the Citizens' Advice Bureau, which investigated the tactics adopted by claims management companies, organisations which effectively canvass business which can be passed on to solicitors for a fee. The report found that some claimants actually stood to lose more than they would gain from litigation as a result of being incorrectly advised by the claims management companies who sometimes artificially escalated costs. An example of such a case is **Bowne and ten others *v* Bridgend County Borough Council** (2004) Unreported 25 March, where the compensation awarded to a group of claimants was less than the legal costs sought by their solicitors.

[5]This is a very important issue upon which you might be able to cite practical examples from your studies to receive greater credit.

Litigation proceeding on the basis of conditional fee agreements may give rise to unfair trials,[6] whereby the defendant is unrepresented. This is illustrated by the case of **Steel *v* UK** (2005) 41 EHRR 22, the well publicised case of the 'McLibel two'. The defendants had distributed material which made a series of allegations against McDonalds. This resulted in McDonalds bringing a libel action. As legal aid is not available for defamation proceedings and they could not afford legal assistance, the defendants were not legally represented in court whilst McDonalds were represented by a prolific team of eminent lawyers. The unfairness of the case was pronounced upon by the European Court of Human Rights when determining that there had been a breach of both the right to fair trial and the right to freedom of expression, under Articles 6 and 10 of the European Convention on Human Rights.

[6]More could be made of this point, perhaps, by relating it to the later point about the need for defendants to be adequately insured in anticipation of litigation.

Finally, it must be noted that the greater use of conditional fee agreements, and the increase in litigation which it has given rise to, has hugely escalated insurance costs.[7] This has consequences for all of society. Increased insurance costs for public-sector bodies drains public resources, diverting funds from other uses, whereas private-sector bodies must raise operating costs to finance higher and more comprehensive insurance premiums. Individual defendants facing litigation may need to take out 'after-the-event insurance' at the cost of great personal and financial hardship.

[7]This point could be reinforced in a coursework essay by reference to statistical evidence illustrating the increased cost of insurance.

In conclusion, it is difficult to accept that a compelling case exists for the greater encouragement of conditional fee agreements. Whilst they have their benefits, the various concerns which have been highlighted in relation to their operation suggests that rather than promote their even more extensive use, a detailed review of the problems which they give rise to would be worthwhile.[8]

[8]The conclusion reflects the discussion provided in the answer, which emphasised a number of problems with conditional fee agreements without questioning their merits completely.

✓ Make your answer stand out

- Provide context to your answer by illustrating the extent to which the law has facilitated the greater use of conditional fee agreements since they became permitted.
- Cite statistical evidence to reinforce some of the problems associated with the use of conditional fee agreements, such as increased insurance costs and aggressive marketing by claims management companies.
- Refer to the Citizens Advice Bureau report, No Win, No Fee, No Chance (CAB, 2005) in considering the argument that contrary to their objectives conditional fee agreements have resulted in reduced access to justice for many in the area of personal injury litigation.
- In a lengthy coursework essay, you could draw comparisons between the operation of conditional fee agreements in the UK with their use in other jurisdictions.

! Don't be tempted to . . .

- Simply summarise the main arguments for and against conditional fee agreements.

Question 4

Evaluate the major changes introduced to the management of civil cases by the 1998 Civil Procedure Rules.

Answer plan

- ➜ Explain the perceived problems which led to the Woolf reforms.
- ➜ Briefly explain the major objectives of the reforms.
- ➜ Discuss the major changes to case management brought about by the reforms.
- ➜ Conclude by evaluating the consequences of the reforms.

Diagram plan

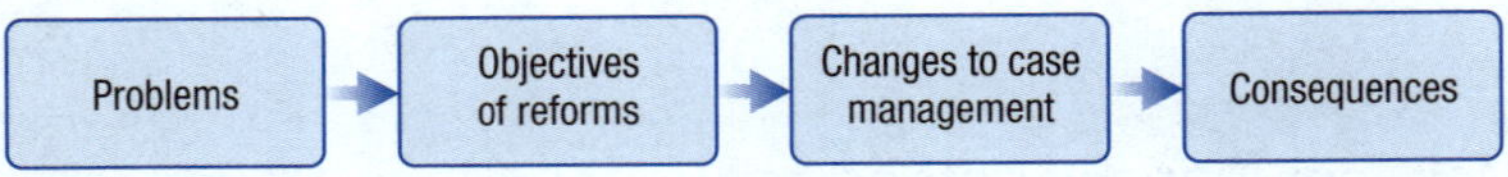

A printable version of this diagram plan is available from www.pearsoned.co.uk/lawexpressqa

Answer

Prior to 1999 there were separate rules of civil procedure for the County Court and the High Court respectively, the former being governed by County Court rules and the latter the rules of the Supreme Court. Whereas High Court actions began with a writ, County Court actions were commenced by a summons. In addition, there was a series of specialised and complicated procedures applicable to certain actions. The pre-1999 civil justice system was perceived to suffer from a number of problems.[1] Firstly, the system was regarded as being too expensive for many parties to civil actions. For example, the Woolf Review found that for claims lower than £12,500, in 40% of cases the amount at stake was exceeded by one side's costs alone. The old system was notorious for experiencing delays in the conclusion of court proceedings, which could typically amount to three years in the County Court and five years in the High Court. The adversarial process, which effectively emphasises a 'contest' between two sides, was felt to discourage

[1] Before proceeding to discuss the changes introduced by the 1999 rules, you should explain what problems created the need for reform. This also provides standards against which you can later measure the success of the reforms.

co-operation between the parties, and the emphasis on oral evidence which is a key feature of the English trial also served to slow down progress in proceedings as well as often being unnecessary. Injustice was also threatened in the huge number of cases where settlement was reached out of court, as a result of the unequal bargaining powers of the parties.

To address these problems, the Lord Chancellor in the government of John Major, Lord Mackay, requested Lord Woolf to undertake a review of the civil justice system and make recommendations for reform, which he did in his 1996 report. Most of these recommendations were implemented in the new civil procedure rules issued in 1999. The new rules constituted a unified procedural code containing simplified procedures and documentary requirements which replaced the previous separate sets of rules used by the County Court and High Court. The new rules aimed to address the perceived problems of the old system. While there is much emphasis upon avoiding litigation and encouraging early settlement, the overriding objective of the reforms was to ensure that the civil courts deal 'justly' with the cases they receive.[2]

[2]This summarises well the driving objective of the reforms, against which you can assess their outcomes.

[3]This is a key feature of the reforms and will be further illustrated as you discuss some of the specific changes which they introduced.

In order to improve the efficiency of civil proceedings, the 1999 rules place great emphasis upon the role to be played by the courts in case management.[3] Courts were required to become 'active' managers of litigation by taking on a much more direct role in handling the progression of actions. Case management is governed by Part 3 of the rules, which make provision for the use of case management conferences and pre-trial reviews in facilitating more efficient progression of cases through the courts. Active case management by the courts theoretically makes it harder for litigants to delay proceedings and a 2000 poll found that 76% of solicitors felt that the new rules increased the prospects of early settlement.

Part 26 of the rules concerns the allocation of cases to particular tracks and courts. Small-claims cases will be heard in the County Court, as will fast-track cases ordinarily, whereas multi-track cases will usually be reserved for the High Court. This relatively smooth division of labour is another step designed to enhance the efficiency with which civil litigation progresses through the courts. Both time and cost efficiency are also theoretically enhanced by the duty imposed upon courts to restrict the admission of expert evidence to where this is absolutely necessary. To ensure that the Civil

Procedure Rules (CPR) are strictly complied with, the courts now enjoy the ability to impose tough sanctions to enforce them including an adverse award of costs against a defaulting party or striking out part or all of that party's claim.[4]

[4]In this paragraph you demonstrate effectively some of the potential benefits of the reforms in terms of enhancing efficiency.

In pursuit of the objective of avoiding litigation, a number of mechanisms are promoted by the 1999 rules which should make early settlement of disputes easier to achieve.[5] A number of pre-action protocols have been introduced under the CPR for specific types of action. These establish timetables according to which proceedings should progress which are designed to encourage early settlement. Under Part 36 of the CPR, when deciding upon the award of costs courts are required to take into account any pre-trial offers to settle which have been made, thus providing incentives to settle out of court and avoid litigation. Courts are also to encourage the use of alternative dispute resolution at various stages during proceedings, another initiative that is likely to lead some potential litigants to attempt to settle their disputes out of court.

[5]As this was a driving objective of the reforms, it is imperative that you consider ways in which the reforms have sought to achieve this.

The main changes introduced to civil procedure by the 1999 civil procedure rules have not met with universal satisfaction. That the main objective of the reforms was to discourage litigation and encourage early settlement of disputes becomes very apparent when consideration is given to some of the major features of the reforms discussed above. In this respect, it is arguable that the reforms have achieved their objective.[6] There has been a huge increase in the number of cases now being settled out of court. 70% of disputes are in fact settled much earlier than the trial stage. There is evidence that commercial proceedings within the High Court have more than halved since the introduction of the new CPR. This considerable reduction in litigation and increase in out of court settlements should theoretically yield benefits in time and cost savings for individual litigants and the civil justice system as a whole. However, there remain charges that despite the 1999 reforms, there remain problems within the civil justice process which have yet to be adequately tackled.

[6]After having considered the main features of the reforms, you should evaluate their main benefits and cite evidence in support of these.

Notwithstanding the reduction in litigation, there is evidence that civil legal costs have continued to increase.[7] These have been complicated by the growth in conditional fee agreements under which losing parties are required to pay the other side's costs. Court fees have also increased significantly, and while this forms part of a drive

[7]Continuing problems associated with civil procedure should also be emphasised. In a longer coursework essay there may be scope for you to consider how continuing problems might be addressed through further possible reforms which you are able to suggest.

to make courts self-funding, unaffordable costs undoubtedly have a disproportionate effect upon the ability of the less well off to attain successful resolution of legitimate civil problems. Enforcement of judgments has also given rise to some problems. For example, difficulty has been experienced by parties seeking to enforce small claims awards in 25% of cases. New provisions, however, have been introduced by the Tribunals, Courts and Enforcement Act 2007 to improve enforcement.

[8]This is a logical, balanced conclusion which reflects the discussion contained in the answer. As noted in the previous comment, you might elaborate here to consider further possible reforms if time constraints permit.

In conclusion, the 1999 reforms have clearly brought about some benefits. However, they have not been a panacea for rectifying all of the problems of the civil justice process which continues to evidence a number of shortcomings which may benefit from additional reforms.[8]

✓ Make your answer stand out

- Suggest further possible reforms to civil procedure rules and their potential benefits.
- Reinforce your arguments with documentary evidence where appropriate.
- Assess the long-term consequences of the reforms to civil procedure by considering the arguments made in the 2008 Hamlyn lectures by Hazel Genn, *Judging Civil Justice* (Cambridge: Cambridge University Press, 2009).

! Don't be tempted to . . .

- Provide a detailed account of the various provisions contained in the Civil Procedure Rules;
- Confuse the 1999 changes to civil procedure with reforms to civil legal aid contained in the Access to Justice Act 1999.

9 Alternative dispute resolution

How this topic may come up in exams

Questions on this topic are likely to assess your understanding of methods of dispute resolution other than the courts, and may require you to consider their relative strengths and weaknesses when contrasted to other forms of dispute resolution. You may specifically be asked to explain and evaluate the role performed by tribunals and ombudsmen as systems of dispute resolution, either individually or in comparison to one another or the courts. You could also be asked to explain and comment upon the increased prominence of mediation, conciliation and arbitration as forms of ADR.

Attack the question

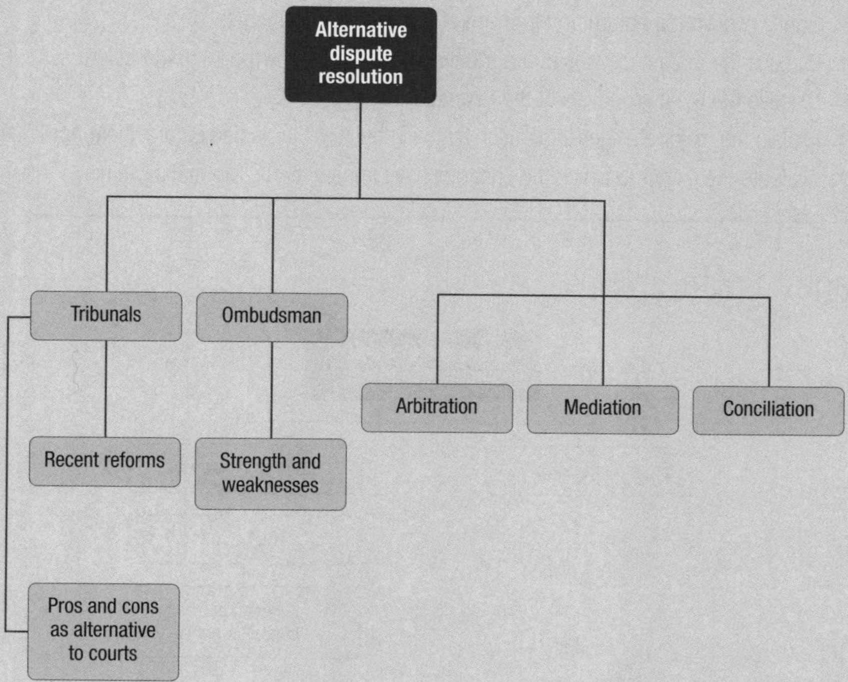

A printable version of this diagram plan is available from www.pearsoned.co.uk/lawexpressqa

Question 1

'The administrative tribunal system has been greatly improved by changes introduced by the Tribunals, Courts and Enforcement Act 2007.' Discuss, with reference to the requirement that tribunals be characterised by openness, fairness and impartiality.

Answer plan

- → Briefly explain the nature and function of administrative tribunals.
- → Discuss the main criticisms of the tribunal system made by the Leggatt Review.
- → Discuss the main proposals of the Leggatt Review.
- → Explain the major changes introduced by the Tribunals, Courts and Enforcement Act 2007.
- → Evaluate the extent to which the changes have improved the Tribunal system.

Diagram plan

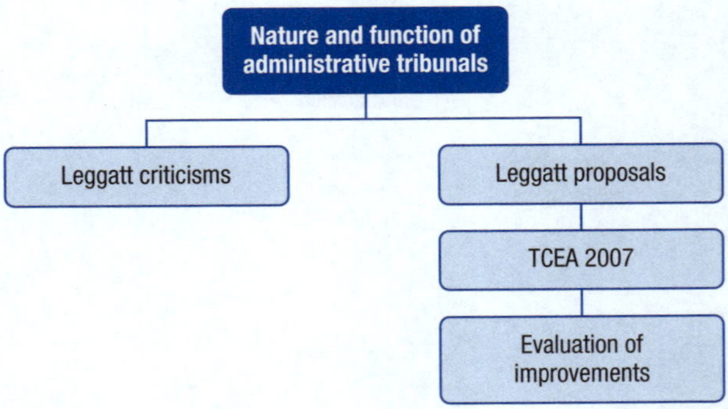

A printable version of this diagram plan is available from www.pearsoned.co.uk/lawexpressqa

Answer

Although dating back over two centuries, modern tribunals are a product of the expansion of the welfare state. In response to the subsequent growth in the number of disputes between individuals and state bodies, a substantial number of tribunals have been created which now hear over one million cases annually. Unlike courts, tribunals enjoy specialist jurisdiction and traditionally operate on a more informal basis free of the procedural rules associated with court hearings. Other main strengths usually associated with tribunals include the expertise they afford, the relative speed with which cases are heard and the low costs associated with their utilisation.[1] However, concerns over the operation of tribunals led the Lord Chancellor to task Sir Andrew Leggatt in 2000 with conducting a review of tribunals and making proposals for any necessary reforms, which he did the following year.

[1]You can provide useful context to your answer by briefly referring to the main features and perceived advantages of tribunals.

The Franks Committee which investigated the operation of tribunals back in 1957 recommended that tribunals should operate in accordance with principles of 'openness, fairness and impartiality'. Leggatt reiterated the importance of these standards, but felt that they were not adequately satisfied by tribunals as they currently functioned.[2] He found that the quality of administrative tribunals varied 'from excellent to inadequate' and directed a number of specific criticisms at tribunals. These related to their openness or accessibility, relationship with government departments, and the incoherence of the tribunal system as a whole. Tribunals were not sufficiently open or accessible as in order to be so required that citizens knew of their existence and the circumstances in which they could make use of their procedures to resolve a dispute against a government department or agency. It is easy to assume that tribunals are accessible because of citizens' entitlement to use them, but of course unless the aggrieved citizen is aware of their relevance in any given situation, their theoretical accessibility becomes meaningless because he is not in a position to make practical use of their procedures. The perceived fairness and impartiality of tribunals was compromised by their dependence upon the government departments whom they would hear disputes concerning. Each tribunal's administrative support would be provided by the department whose decisions and actions it was concerned with, and that department's minister would also appoint the tribunal's members. Not only do such arrangements threaten to breach Article 6 of the European Convention on Human Rights' guarantee of a fair trial, they run counter to one of the core principles of natural justice, the rule against bias,[3] which has been invoked in judicial review proceedings to render decisions invalid where judgment has been given by a person with an interest at stake in the matter in contention. Leggatt also concluded that there was no coherent tribunal system. Individual tribunals were created in a haphazard manner, in response to needs in a particular area. As a result, they were all

[2]This focus is important as it relates back to the question's concern with 'openness, fairness and impartiality'. This paragraph effectively considers ways in which tribunals workings pre-2007 could be seen as falling short of adequately satisfying these requirements, usefully leading into the later consideration of the merits of the changes introduced in 2007.

[3]This is a good argument which not only highlights problems with the dependence of tribunals on government departments, but also evidences awareness of other areas of law which have relevant application to the operation of tribunals.

subject to their own different procedures and provided various routes of appeal. There was no uniformity across the tribunal system, and it could rightfully be asserted that the resulting confusion impacted negatively upon their user-friendliness and, thus, accessibility.

[4]This leads into consideration of the 2007 reforms. You need to explain how this seemingly rather straightforward proposal, which was largely acted upon in the 2007 Act, could enhance the 'openness, fairness and impartiality' of tribunal proceedings.

The main proposal of the Leggatt Review was to create a single unified tribunal to be responsible for administering all administrative tribunals.[4] Existing tribunals could be brought within one tribunal system, where they would operate by the same procedures. Citizens would submit cases to the tribunal service which would decide which tribunal to allocate them to. Although clearly aimed at improving the coherence of the tribunal system, and consequently its user-friendliness, it was intended also to address the other perceived problems of tribunals. The creation of a tribunal service responsible for the administration of tribunals which was independent of individual government departments would go a long way towards answering criticisms that tribunals were too reliant upon the departments against which they heard disputes. It would also be hoped that the creation of a specialist tribunal service would be able to generate greater public awareness of the existence of tribunal procedures, thus enhancing their accessibility to citizens who could benefit from their use.

[5]You do not need to attempt to outline in great detail the provisions of the 2007 Act. The question is concerned with the extent to which they improve the 'openness, fairness and impartiality' of tribunals. You only need to ensure that you mention the main changes introduced insofar as they impact upon these requirements.

The Leggatt Review's recommendations were largely endorsed in a 2004 white paper, the main proposals becoming part of the Tribunals Courts and Enforcement Act 2007.[5] In accordance with the proposal that there be a single tribunal service, the Act created two generic tribunals to which the jurisdiction of most existing administrative tribunals would be transferred; the new generic tribunals are divided into a number of chambers each with their own specialist area of jurisdiction. Whereas previously tribunals were subject to their own individual procedures, the 2007 Act created a Tribunal Procedure Committee charged with establishing rules of procedure for the new tribunals, which it has now produced; the common procedural rules created for tribunals bear the influences of the rules of civil procedure established for the courts following the Woolf reforms in 1999. The 2007 Act also created a unified appeal structure for tribunals and legally qualified tribunal members are now conferred with the title of 'judge', meaning that their independence is guaranteed by the Constitutional Reform Act 2005.

Prima facie, the reforms made by the 2007 Act appear designed to enhance the 'openness, fairness and impartiality' of administrative tribunals.[6] It is to be hoped that the creation of a unified, coherent tribunal system will ultimately improve the publicity afforded to the workings of tribunals to the extent that citizens aggrieved by administrative decisions will be sufficiently well informed of their availability as a forum for airing their disputes. The accessibility or openness of tribunals will thus be improved. The creation of a tribunal service responsible for the administration of all tribunals should also enhance their perceived fairness and impartiality by severing their dependence upon the government departments against which they subsequently hear disputes brought to them. As noted, the independence of legally qualified members will be reinforced by their elevation to the status of 'judge'. However, while the 2007 changes are welcome for these reasons, a couple of caveats are necessary.[7] Firstly, it is too soon to know what impact the changes will have upon the functioning of tribunals in the longer term as the new tribunal system has only been in place since 2008. Secondly, it is possible that some of the changes will have negative effects upon some of the traditional features of tribunals. For example, the creation of unified procedural rules for all tribunals and the conferment of 'judge' status upon some tribunal members have been seen by some commentators as evidence of increasing formalisation of tribunals at the expense of their traditional perception as an informal alternative to the courts.

[6] This conclusion reinforces the arguments advanced earlier in respect of the merits of the reforms proposed by the Leggatt Review. At this stage you can briefly summarise the main likely benefits of the changes to build upon the earlier discussion.

[7] These are useful points to make. In an extended essay on this question you could explore further the extent to which the 2007 reforms have, or may, affect some of the traditionally perceived virtues of tribunals.

✓ Make your answer stand out

- Refer to documentary evidence in order to reinforce your arguments.
- Read and make reference to Carnwath, R., 'Tribunal Justice: A New Start', *Public Law*, 2009, pp. 48–69 in considering the likely benefits of the recent reforms to the tribunal system.
- Suggest possible further reforms which may address any weaknesses of the tribunal system not adequately tackled by the 2007 changes.

! Don't be tempted to . . .

- Provide a descriptive account of the content of the Leggatt Review and the 2007 Act.

Question 2

'Administrative tribunals are much better suited to the resolution of disputes between individuals and the state than ordinary law courts.' Discuss.

Answer plan

- → Briefly explain the origins of the modern tribunal system, and comment upon their nature and function.
- → Discuss the main benefits of tribunals as an alternative to litigation in the courts.
- → Discuss the main shortcomings of tribunals as an alternative to litigation in the courts and briefly comment upon the extent to which any shortcomings have been addressed by changes introduced by the Tribunals, Courts and Enforcement Act 2007.
- → Conclude by directly addressing the statement contained in the question.

Diagram plan

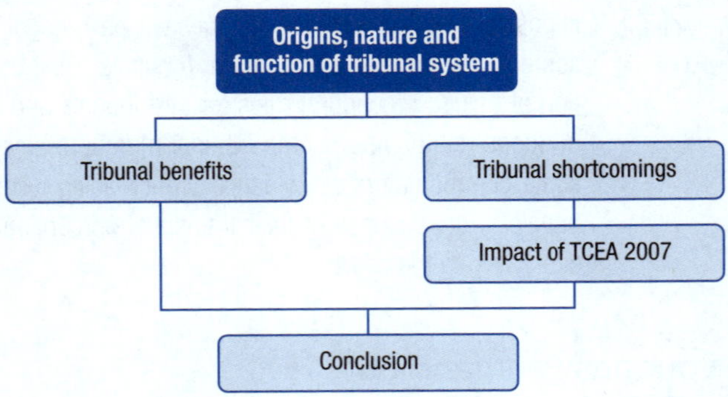

A printable version of this diagram plan is available from www.pearsoned.co.uk/lawexpressqa

Answer

Tribunals are not a new phenomenon, having their origins over two centuries ago, although the modern system of administrative tribunals stems from the growth of the welfare state since 1945. As the state became engaged in a greater number of disputes with citizens many specialist tribunals have been established over the past few decades to hear a wide range of disputes. Over a million cases are heard by tribunals annually. Tribunals differ from courts in a number of important respects.[1] They enjoy specialist jurisdiction and are not traditionally bound by all of the formal procedures applicable to court hearings. While chaired by a legally qualified person, lay members also sit upon tribunals. Until recently each tribunal was subject to its own rules and procedures, but the Tribunals, Courts and Enforcement Act 2007 has created a new unified tribunal system.

[1]As the question asks you to consider the benefits of tribunals vis-à-vis the courts, it is helpful if you briefly explain how they differ in nature from the courts.

Administrative tribunals are regarded as having a number of distinct advantages over ordinary courts.[2] For example, the specialisation they offer is often cited as one of their foremost virtues. As specialist bodies, they are able to develop expertise in the subject matter of their jurisdiction. For example, a tribunal handling social security disputes is likely to have a much greater appreciation of the issues involved where this is the sole focus of the tribunal's work in contrast to a court which will only deal with such matters as a small proportion of a larger, varied caseload. Furthermore, as a result of their specialisation tribunals should be able to draw upon a greater awareness of policy matters. Tribunal hearings are also held in private, which may be particularly appealing to parties who for various reasons may not want to air their business in public as would happen in court proceedings. This feature of the tribunal system may be particularly important for individuals with especially sensitive disputes, although the closed nature of tribunal proceedings does appear to fly in the face of the recommendation of the Franks Committee that tribunals exhibit the characteristics of 'openness, fairness and impartiality', a requirement more recently reiterated by the Leggatt Review of the tribunal system.

[2]The main focus of the question is the purported benefits of tribunals over courts and this should form the bulk of your discussion. It is logical to begin with the strongest arguments for the use of tribunals.

While a number of supposed strengths of the tribunal system can be highlighted, the extent to which these constitute undisputed benefits of taking cases to a tribunal rather than the courts in some cases is questionable.[3] It is commonly asserted that tribunals provide a much quicker resolution of disputes than the courts with many hearings being concluded within a day and tribunals being able to specify precise hearing times unfettered by the kinds of procedural backlog which can clog up the courts. This is good for individuals and more generally relieves the burden placed upon ordinary courts. However, while it is not unreasonable to expect a tribunal to resolve a dispute with greater speed than the courts, this strength can be overstated. As far back as 1993, the Vice Chairman

[3]Having considered the stronger arguments in favour of the use of tribunals, you can move on to consider those arguments which are more questionable. These arguments are related and can be effectively considered in the same paragraph.

of the Employment Lawyers Association commented that hearings which had previously taken three to five months to be concluded by tribunals had come to take over 18 months. Furthermore, the greater formalisation of the tribunal system introduced by the 2007 Act may run the risk of eventually dragging out tribunal proceedings longer. Traditionally, the informality of tribunal proceedings has been held up as one of their key virtues. The inapplicability of strict rules of evidence employed by the courts and the absence of many of the hallmarks of an ordinary court case help to put individuals at ease, as well as speeding up proceedings. However, while tribunals remain less formal forums than the ordinary courts, the degree of this informality is certainly being challenged by the 2007 reforms.[4] For example, tribunals are now presided over by judges. Greater formalisation of the tribunal system may impact upon another of its commonly cited strengths, namely its relative inexpensive cost for users when compared to the far greater costs associated with litigation in the courts. Tribunals do not usually charge fees, the infrastructure used by tribunals being small-scale. Parties usually pay their own costs and are often able to dispense with the need for legal representation. The 2007 reforms may come to have some bearing upon the costs associated with tribunal hearings if they do result in greater formalisation of procedures and, for example, increase the need for parties to be legally represented.

[4]In considering the relative merits of tribunals it is worthwhile considering any possible impact upon these by the reforms introduced by the Tribunals Courts and Enforcement Act 2007. This is very relevant to the question and evidences awareness of recent developments in the area.

Although the advantages of using tribunals over courts will hold good in many circumstances, the point being made is that they should not be overstated, particularly in light of what may in the long term come to be the consequences of the reforms introduced to the tribunal system by the 2007 Act. There are, however, some drawbacks of the tribunal system which have received the attention of commentators. Traditionally, there was no uniformity to tribunals with each tribunal enjoying its own procedures and routes of appeal. This was a source of confusion to some individuals. This has, however, been remedied as a result of the creation of one unified tribunal system by the 2007 reforms.[5] All tribunals now share a common procedural code and appeals mechanisms. One ongoing issue of concern is the unavailability of state funding for actions brought in tribunals in most instances. Although less costly than

[5]Again, you are showing the impact of the 2007 Act, in this case highlighting one of the ways in which it has addressed one of the perceived weaknesses of tribunals.

court proceedings, on some occasions the lack of funding will put individuals at a disadvantage when bringing a dispute against a government department which will have a wealth of resources to draw upon, as research by Hazel Genn has highlighted. Although specialist help will sometimes be available from sources such as community law centres or the Citizens' Advice Bureau, this cannot be guaranteed. The lack of state funding, however should not be seen as a reason for pursuing litigation in court instead, as state funding for civil legal disputes is also heavily restricted.[6]

There are certainly various reasons why tribunals are likely to be better suited to resolving disputes between individuals and the state than ordinary law courts in many cases. However, the purported benefits of tribunals cannot be assumed to universally apply to every instance where an individual is in dispute with a government department. Although too early to draw any conclusions, the possible effects of the 2007 reforms upon the nature and functioning of tribunals also need to be borne in mind. The drawbacks of using tribunals are not numerous or overly exceptional, and so it would thus seem reasonable to accept the assertion that very often tribunals will provide a better forum for the resolution of disputes between individuals and the state than the courts.[7]

[6]This is a good point to make as you demonstrate that a weakness of this form of dispute resolution does not imply a strength of the alternative.

[7]Based upon the discussion provided in the answer, this is a reasonable conclusion. The answer has demonstrated a number of strengths of the tribunal system, and while you have shown that these have their limitations you have not given any cause to presume the courts to be a better alternative for resolving individual-state disputes where this availability of recourse to a tribunal is present. At the same time, your conclusion acknowledges that tribunals are not always the preferable method of dispute resolution.

✓ Make your answer stand out

- Cite documentary evidence to reinforce your arguments where appropriate.
- Consider the impact of the 2007 Act on the relative benefits of the tribunal system.

! Don't be tempted to . . .

- Present your answer as just a briefly explained series of pros and cons of the tribunal system.

Question 3

Discuss the extent to which the Parliamentary Commissioner for Administration provides a meaningful mechanism for the redress of citizens' grievances.

Answer plan

- ➜ Briefly explain the origins of the ombudsman system within the UK.
- ➜ Comment upon the main features of the ombudsman's jurisdiction.
- ➜ Discuss the vague concept of 'maladministration' and the extent to which it restricts the range of cases which the ombudsman may investigate.
- ➜ Discuss the restrictions placed upon the utility of the ombudsman system by the MP filter and his lack of enforcement powers.
- ➜ Conclude upon the extent to which the ombudsman system provides a meaningful mechanism for the redress of citizens' grievances.

Diagram plan

A printable version of this diagram plan is available from www.pearsoned.co.uk/lawexpressqa

Answer

The ombudsman concept is Scandinavian in origin and is intended to provide citizens with an additional mechanism through which grievances against state bodies can be investigated and remedied. The 1961 Wyatt Report noted a number of shortcomings in the existing mechanisms through which individuals could pursue grievances against state bodies and recommended that an ombudsman system be established within the UK.[1] This eventually happened with the passage of the Parliamentary Commissioner Act 1967, which created the post of Parliamentary Commissioner for Administration, commonly referred to as the ombudsman. The

[1] The first paragraph provides useful contextual background to your answer. In a longer coursework essay on this question you could devote more attention to the problems with other mechanisms for grievance redress identified by Wyatt and consider how the ombudsman system addresses these.

ombudsman was created to investigate complaints of maladministration made against central government departments, although the ombudsman concept was extended with the creation of an ombudsman system for local government, the NHS and legal services. There are now also some ombudsmen systems within the private sector, present in such areas as banking and insurance.

[2]Before considering the main problems associated with the ombudsman system, you should demonstrate an understanding of its main features, ensuring that you note any strengths – for example, robust powers of investigation – as well as flagging up problems for further scrutiny.

Section 5(1) of the 1967 Act summarises the ombudsman's principal function,[2] which is to investigate complaints emanating from members of the public who claim to have suffered injustice as a consequence of maladministration on the part of a government department or body arising from the performance of its functions. Importantly, the ombudsman is not concerned with the merits of decisions or actions of government bodies, but simply the process by which they are taken. This limits the range of grievances for which recourse to the ombudsman is likely to be appropriate. However, the ombudsman has determined maladministration to have occurred in some well publicised cases. For example, in the Sachsenhausen case he found there had been defects in the administration of compensation payments to victims of Nazi persecution, and in the Barlow Clowes case found maladministration on the part of the Department of Trade and Industry to have contributed to huge losses on the stock exchange. An individual may not submit a complaint directly to the ombudsman. Instead it must be submitted to an MP, who can then forward it on to the ombudsman. The 'MP filter' system thus means that there is no guaranteed access to the ombudsman in any given situation. In order to investigate complaints of maladministration leading to injustice, the ombudsman does enjoy relatively robust powers. The powers conferred upon the ombudsman to collect evidence and call witnesses under section 8 are akin to those of a High Court judge, and obstruction of his investigations can amount to contempt of court (section 9). In this sense, the ombudsman is provided with the means to conduct his investigations thoroughly. However, upon conclusion of an investigation he is limited by section 10 to only being able to issue a report detailing his findings. He has no power to impose any sanctions in the case of an adverse finding against a government department.

[3]Here the essay is given clear focus as three main issues worth particular consideration are flagged up.

The utility of the ombudsman as a grievance redress mechanism is, arguably, restricted in three main ways.[3] Firstly, the need to establish the presence of maladministration in the decision-making process of a government body means that the ombudsman cannot be used as a vehicle through which the merits of a decision itself can be challenged. Even accepting the restriction of the ombudsman to procedural matters, the term 'maladministration' gives rise to difficulties.[4] No statutory definition has been given to the term. The cabinet minister Richard Crossman provided an indicative list of examples of maladministration in the early years of the Ombudsman's operation. A detailed list of examples of maladministration was provided by then Ombudsman William Reid in his 1993 Annual Report to Parliament, which included rudeness, giving misleading advice, and showing bias among a substantial number of varied instances of maladministration. The courts have contributed to the definition of maladministration in some cases, such as **R *v* Commissioners for Local Administration, *ex parte* Bradford MBC** [1979] QB 287, where it was held to constitute 'faulty' or 'bad' administration. Nonetheless, there is still no definitive agreed definition of maladministration. That said, it is a difficult concept to define and in most cases it is arguably relatively straightforward to identify occurrences of maladministration.

[4]Several attempts have been made to give greater clarity to this term and you should illustrate your awareness of these, while acknowledging the difficulty of providing a definitive definition.

A major criticism of the ombudsman system has been the retention of the MP filter, preventing individuals from being able to submit complaints directly to the ombudsman.[5] While the filter system can be used to weed out frivolous complaints, one danger is that whether complaints are referred to the ombudsman or not will depend upon the political views of the MP to whom it is initially submitted. The filter also slows down the progress of complaints through the addition of an extra layer of bureaucracy within the process and is not common within ombudsman systems in other jurisdictions. For reasons such as these there have been growing calls for the abolition of the MP filter. However, many MPs remain committed to the view that they serve an important constitutional role as the primary defenders of constituents' rights, and as an instrument of Parliament, it is their function to handle complaints en route to the ombudsman. In 2000, a bill to abolish the MP filter was rejected by Parliament.

[5]This is arguably the biggest criticism of the ombudsman system and must be addressed.

The final main restriction placed upon the utility of the ombudsman lies in his inability to enforce his findings. While he must produce a report detailing the findings of any investigation, which is provided to the body investigated and MP who referred the complaint, he cannot impose any sanctions.[6] Despite this, the power of the ombudsman should not be underestimated. He has the important power of publicity in issuing his reports and can make recommendations for compensation where appropriate, or changes to administrative procedures, which are often acted upon. For example, his reports upon the Sachsenhausen and Barlow Clowes cases discussed above led to compensation being paid to those affected by the maladministration found to have occurred.

[6]While an important point, you should also emphasise the extent to which the ombudsman's reports can produce positive outcomes in individual cases.

While there are clearly limits to the role which the ombudsman can play in redressing citizens' grievances, it is possible to over-state some of these.[7] Although restricted to considering claims of maladministration and lacking any real sanctions, it should be remembered that the ombudsman is one of several mechanisms for the redress of grievances, and is designed to serve as an additional mechanism to the courts and tribunals, not as a replacement. The removal of the MP filter would, arguably, improve access to the ombudsman, but generally speaking there is a high level of satisfaction with the function performed by the mechanism provided by the ombudsman system for the redress of grievances.

[7]This summarises well the balance of the arguments considered in the answer. While problems are identified within the ombudsman system, it is important to remember that it was created to supplement, not replace existing mechanisms for the redress of grievances, and in light of this the perceived drawbacks of the ombudsman system can easily be overstated.

✓ Make your answer stand out

- Reinforce your arguments by referring to practical examples from the work of the ombudsman.
- Make comparisons with other mechanisms for resolving disputes between citizens and the state, such as tribunals or the courts.
- Make suggestions for possible reform to the ombudsman system.

! Don't be tempted to . . .

- Provide a detailed account of each feature of the Ombudsman system as set out in the Parliamentary Commissioner Act 1967;
- Confuse the different ombudsmen systems in operation: your answer should relate primarily to the Parliamentary Commissioner for Administration.

Question 4

Explain the difference between mediation, conciliation and arbitration and assess the merits of alternative dispute resolution over litigation in the courts.

Answer plan

- → Explain the increased emphasis that has been placed upon the use of ADR in recent years.
- → Explain the concepts of mediation, conciliation and arbitration, and provide examples of their use in practice.
- → Assess the main benefits of these methods of dispute resolution.
- → Assess the main problems associated with these methods of dispute resolution.
- → Conclude upon the extent to which these methods of ADR provide appropriate alternatives to litigation in the courts.

Diagram plan

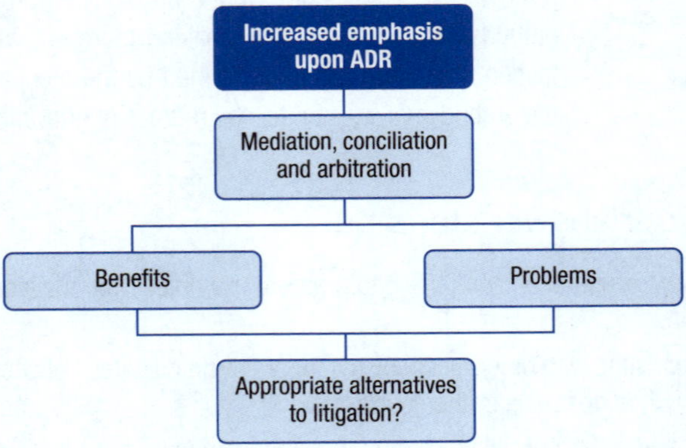

A printable version of this diagram plan is available from www.pearsoned.co.uk/lawexpressqa

Answer

[1]This provides important context to your answer, which is improved further by the provision of examples of how greater emphasis has been placed upon the use of ADR.

In recent years, an increased emphasis has been placed upon the use of alternative dispute resolution mechanisms as an alternative to litigating disputes in the courts.[1] Governments have sought to encourage greater use of ADR and the civil procedure rules introduced as a consequence of the Woolf reforms require courts to actively promote the use of ADR by parties before having recourse to court proceedings. Indeed, the courts may punish parties who refuse to make use of ADR mechanisms by depriving them of the award of costs, a principle established by the Court of Appeal in **Dennett *v* Railtrack plc** [2002] 2 All ER 850. The Court of Appeal and Commercial Court within the High Court have established mediation and ADR schemes respectively.

[2]The question asks you to explain these three terms. You can illustrate their utility and significance by citing practical examples.

The three established forms of ADR are mediation, conciliation and arbitration.[2] Mediation is the least intrusive mode of dispute settlement and involves the parties in dispute appointing a third party as a mediator tasked with helping them to attempt to reach an agreement acceptable to both of them. Any resulting agreement can then be put into writing and form a legally binding contract. Mediation does not necessarily require the parties to actually meet with one another. The non-adversarial nature of mediation makes it well suited for handling sensitive disputes where personal relationships are involved, and the Family Law Act 1996 placed great emphasis upon its suitability for dealing with divorce cases. Unfortunately, a 2007 National Audit Office report identified a low take-up rate for mediation. Although in many respects a form of mediation, conciliation does have some distinct features of its own with the third party appointed by the disputing parties taking on a more interventionist role by attempting to bring the parties together and proposing possible solutions to the dispute. A good example of conciliation can be found with the use of ACAS procedures to attempt to resolve unfair dismissal disputes before they can proceed to a tribunal hearing. Two thirds of such cases are either withdrawn or successfully settled by conciliation.[3]

[3]This is a good example, and you evidence its value well by reference to statistical evidence.

Arbitration constitutes a more formalised method of ADR and involves the parties in dispute conferring upon a third party the power to make a legally binding decision which they will accept. A number of trade associations provide arbitration schemes, for example, ABTA for the travel industry. Arbitration is especially popular as a means of resolving commercial disputes and the Arbitration Act 1996 provides a clear framework for commercial arbitration.

[4]The question asks you to consider the merits of ADR over litigation, so you need to consider its main benefits. You can do this effectively by drawing upon examples to reinforce your arguments.

There are several reasons why parties in dispute may find it preferable to opt to attempt to resolve their disputes through a form of ADR rather than resorting to litigation in the courts.[4] ADR can provide parties with a mediator or arbitrator better equipped to handle a dispute because he has expertise of the particular matter in issue. For example, ACAS has built up a well regarded expertise for tackling employment related disputes. Mediators in family disputes tend to specialise in that area. By contrast, courts are presided over by judges who are very much generalists adjudicating upon the full range of legal issues resulting in litigation. The privacy and informality of ADR mechanisms also provide powerful incentives for disputants to prefer them to court proceedings.[5] Parties to commercial disputes may prefer arbitration to litigation because its private nature prevents potentially sensitive commercial information being publicised or any general resulting damaging publicity from legal action, which would be a more likely outcome of resort to court proceedings which generally take place in public. The informality and privacy of ADR are potentially of great advantage where the parties concerned have a longstanding mutual relationship likely to be jeopardised by adversarial court proceedings. Any desire to achieve conciliation of the parties is likely to be better served by recourse to ADR, hence the popularity of arbitration among commercial parties with longstanding relationships and the drive to increase the use of mediation in family disputes.

[5]This is a particularly strong benefit of ADR which you can discuss in some detail and reinforce by reference to practical examples.

[6]This is a very effective use of research evidence in order to reinforce the arguments which you are considering.

It has been suggested that ADR mechanisms tend to be quicker and cheaper than litigation, although research conducted by Hazel Genn in 1998 suggests that this may not necessarily be the case.[6] While she found that 62% of cases subjected to mediation settled at the time of appointment, where a successful outcome cannot be reached there is a danger that action through the courts will remain necessary. Genn found no evidence that resort to ADR saved costs particularly, with the failure to resolve cases continuing to produce expensive litigation in such situations. It, therefore, cannot be assumed that ADR is a panacea for all of the drawbacks of litigation, although as later research conducted by Genn in 2002 found, there is a relatively high level of customer satisfaction among those who have had recourse to ADR.

[7]Ensure that you consider also some of the possible drawbacks of ADR. A good point alluded to here is that ADR can be both particularly worthwhile and problematic depending upon the circumstances in which it is used.

ADR is not without its critics.[7] It has been argued that ADR procedures are endowed with an imbalance of power between the parties in the absence of available legal representation as a matter of course. This has been noted particularly in the context of disputes between employers and employees where the former are generally better represented. However, such imbalances are not standard to ADR procedures, and would be less likely to arise in commercial arbitration or family mediation for example. A drawback of mediation in particular is that any decisions reached through it may be difficult to enforce and could require a party to initiate court proceedings in order to enforce them, thus defeating the very objective of using ADR in the first instance. On the other hand, the desire to avoid litigation would be a strong reason for parties to stick firmly with the mediation process. Regardless of one's views of the strengths of ADR, it is unfortunately the case that it has suffered from a relatively low take-up rate among parties in dispute.

[8]This is a very valid point and reflects your discussion of the merits of ADR. The conclusion is very logical and balanced, flowing naturally from the earlier content of the answer.

In conclusion, in appropriate circumstances there are clearly benefits to making use of ADR mechanisms as opposed to having recourse to court proceedings. However, it should not be suggested that one mechanism for dispute resolution is necessarily superior to the other.[8] ADR mechanisms are not without their potential drawbacks and much will depend upon the nature of an individual dispute. Where there is a strong chance of quick resolution, ADR mechanisms may be the more suitable route to pursue, and where close longstanding relationships or sensitive issues are involved this may militate in favour of the use of ADR. However, as noted above, any failure to resolve a dispute through ADR may add to the time and costs involved in ultimately resolving the dispute through the courts. These are all considerations to be borne in mind by disputants when choosing which route to utilise.

✓ Make your answer stand out

- Provide context to your answer by illustrating how ADR has been increasingly encouraged by government and the courts.
- Critically consider the main challenges to greater use of ADR by making reference to the discussion provided in Partington, M., 'Alternative Dispute Resolution: Recent Challenges, Future Developments', *Civil Justice Quarterly*, 2004, p. 99.
- Draw comparisons between methods of ADR and court proceedings as means of resolving disputes.

! Don't be tempted to . . .

- Simply describe the different forms of ADR.

Bibliography

Abel, R.L., (1987) 'The Decline of Professionalism', *Arbitration*, v. 53, n. 3, pp. 187–208.
Allan, T.R.S. (1985) 'The Limits of Parliamentary Sovereignty', *Public Law*, p. 614.

Baldwin, J. and McConville, M (1979) *Jury Trials*. Oxford: Clarendon.
Benion, F.A.R. (1978) 'Statute Law: Obscurity and Drafting Parameters', *British Journal of Law and Society*, v. 5, n. 2, p. 235.
Bingham, T.H. (1993) 'The European Convention on Human Rights: Time to Incorporate', *Law Quarterly Review*, v.109, p. 390.
Bradley, A. (2007) 'The Sovereignty of Parliament', in Jowel, J. and Oliver, D. (eds) (2007) *The Changing Constitution* (6th edn). Oxford: Oxford University Press.
Burns, S. (2006) 'Tipping in the Balance', *New Law Journal*, v. 156, p. 787.
Burrows, A. (2002) 'We Do this at Common Law but that in Equity', *Oxford Journal of Legal Studies*, v. 22, n. 1, pp.1–16.

Carnwath, R. (2009) 'Tribunal Justice: A New Start', *Public Law*, pp. 48–69.
Citizens' Advice Bureaux (2005) *No Win, No Fee, No Chance*. www.citizensadvice.org.uk/microsoft_word_-_no_win-_no_fee-_no_chance_report_final.pdf
Craig, P. (2007) 'Britain in the European Union', in Jowel, J. and Oliver, D. (eds) (2007) *The Changing Constitution* (6th edition). Oxford: Oxford University Press.

Derbyshire, P. (1991) 'The Lamp that Shows that Feedom Lives – Is It Worth the Candle?' *Criminal Law Review*, p. 740.
Duxbury, N. (2008) *The Nature and Authority of Precedent*. Cambridge: Cambridge University Press.

Genn, H. (2009) *Judging Civil Justice*. Cambridge: Cambridge University Press.
Griffiths, J.A.G. (1997) *The Politics of the Judiciary*. London: Fontana.

Hale, B., Dame (2002) 'Equality and the Judiciary: Why Should We Want More Women Judges?', *Public Law*, p. 489.
Hynes, S. and Robins, J. (2009) The Justice Gap: Whatever Happened to Legal Aid?. London: Legal Action Group.

Jackson, J. (2009) 'Reconceptualizing the Right to Silence as an Effective Fair Trial Standard', *International and Comparative Law Quarterly*, v. 58, n. 4, pp. 835–61.

Kavanagh, A. (2009) 'Judging the Judges under the Human RIghts Act: Defence Disillusionment and the "War on Terror"', *Public Law*, pp. 287–304.

Leigh, I. and Lustgarten, L. (1999) 'Making Rights Real: the Courts, Remedies and the Human Rights Act', *Cambridge Law Journal*, v. 58, n. 3, pp. 509–45.

Ligere, E. (2005) '*Locus Standi* and the Public Interest: a Hotchpotch of Legal Principles', *Journal of Planning and Environment Law*, p. 292.

Miller, J. (2010) 'Stop and Search in England: a Reformed Tactic or Business as Usual?', *British Journal of Criminology*, v. 50, n. 5, pp. 954–74.

Sander, A. *et al.* (1989) *Advice and Assistance at Police Stations and the 24-Hour Duty Solicitor Scheme*. London: Lord Chancellor's Department.

Slapper, G. and Kelly, D. (2010) *The English Legal System*, 11th edn. Oxford: Routledge.

Spencer, J.R. (2006) 'Does Our Present Criminal Appeal System Makes Sense?', Criminal Law Review, p.677.

Steyn, J. (2001) 'Pepper v Hart: A Re-examination', *Oxford Journal of Legal Studies*, v. 21, n. 1, p. 59.

Ormerod, D. (2002) 'ECHR and the Exclusion of Evidence: Trial Remedies for Article 8 Breaches?', *Criminal Law Review*, p. 61.

Partington, M. (2004) 'Alternative Dispute Resoultion: Recent Challenges, Future Developments', *Civil Justice Quarterly*, p.99.

Wasik, M. (2008) 'Sentencing Guidelines in England and Wales – State of the Art?' *Criminal Law Review*, p. 253.

Windlesham, D.J.G.H., Lord (2005) 'The Constitutional Reform Act 2005: Ministers, Judges and Constitutional Change, *Criminal Law Review*, p. 211.

Zander, M. (1979) 'Investigation of Crime', *Criminal Law Review*, p. 211.

Index